ooooooooooooooooooooooooooooooooooooooooooooooooooooo

CONFESSIONS OF A MOVIE ADDICT

ooooooooooooooooooooooooooooooooooooooooooooooooooooo

by

Betty Jo Tucker

HATS
OFF™

Published by Hats Off Books™
610 East Delano Street, Suite 104
Tucson, Arizona 85705
www.HatsOffBooks.com
ISBN: 1-58736-085-3
LCCN: 2001119701
Book design by Summer Mullins.
Photographs by Larry Tucker.
Cover design by Mike Berry.
Printed in the United States of America.

P R E V U E

Film Stars! Dancing! Popcorn!

At last, a life story with everything

but the movie stuff edited out.

CONFESSIONS OF A MOVIE ADDICT

reveals the shocking secrets of a woman

obsessed with films for over 60 years.

Incredible? Yes.

Still, you **will** believe.

DEDICATION

*To the next generation of movie fans, especially
Elizabeth, Jennifer, Lauren, Leslie, Marie, Sam, and Taylor—
my dear grandchildren.*

"I would say life is pretty pointless,
wouldn't you, without the movies?"

—Christopher Walken
in *The Funeral* (1996)

TABLE OF CONTENTS

CHECKLIST FOR MOVIE ADDICTION

1.   When you haven't seen a movie for over a week, do your eyes twitch and your hands shake?

2.   Do you have periods of "blackouts" when all you can remember is what happened in the last film you saw?

3.   Do you avoid anyone who doesn't like movies?

4.   If you can't buy a ticket to a movie, do you try to talk someone into buying one for you?

5.   Do you get defensive when someone accuses you of seeing too many movies?

6.   Do you find globs of old ticket stubs stuck together with Mason Dots in the bottom of your purse or pockets?

7.   Have you ever taken money from a child's piggy bank to pay for admission to the movies?

8.   Do you sometimes tell co-workers you have an important meeting to attend-but go to a matinee instead?

9.   Have you actually paid money to see an Adam Sandler film?

10. Would you rather eat stale popcorn for lunch than a juicy hamburger?

11. Is your conversation filled with comments like "Show me the money," "May the Force be with you," and "You can't handle the truth"?

If you answered "Yes" to over half the questions above, you're probably a movie addict. Welcome to the club.

EPISODE ONE: FADE IN

The Reel Early Years

My problem began with *Frankenstein*. I remember being a frightened six-year-old hiding under the seat at Clyne's Theater in Pueblo, Colorado, hoping for protection from that scary monster on the big screen. Despite my terror, I couldn't stop peeking. Both horrified and amazed, I became hooked on movies then and there. This addiction continued throughout my childhood and adult life. I even fell in love with my husband because he resembled a certain handsome actor, and we named both our children after movie stars. As I enter my seventies, I'm still a practicing movieholic. Luckily, because I write film reviews now, I see more movies than ever.

During grade school, my cousins and I spent most of our weekends at the Clyne and the Avalon, two movie houses located across the street from each other in a working class neighborhood called Bessemer. Both theaters always scheduled a double feature plus "added attractions" which included one cartoon, a serial, film previews, and a newsreel. Wide-eyed, we enjoyed every offering while gorging ourselves on popcorn, Milk Duds, and ice cream bars. Sometimes we went from one "picture show,"which is what we called the theatres then, directly to the other. We were insatiable when it came to movies and goodies.

When we were a bit older, we hopped on a streetcar for a bumpy ride to one of the downtown cinemas. We loved the Chief because of its lavish red and gold interior-but preferred the Main's more buttery popcorn. The Colorado usually offered a double feature which was hard to resist. And sometimes we stopped off at the Mesa Junction to take in another flick at the Uptown, famous for its "bank night" giveaways.

Reacting to my obsession with film, my mother actually tried to land me a part in a movie. After hearing about MGM's search for a young girl to star in *National Velvet*, she sent the studio a picture of me on a horse. Unfortunately, that role went to Elizabeth Taylor, who sells perfume now. I recall she appeared earlier in *Lassie Come Home*, a film I didn't get to see all the way through. Because Ruella, my sensitive little sister, made too much noise sobbing over the collie's misfortunes, we had to take her home in the middle of the movie. I forgave her—a few years later.

It's not surprising my first work experience came about as a result of movie mania. Here's a glimpse into the mind of that naïve 14-year-old as she pondered employment possibilities:

I've just gotta earn some money this summer. Those movie magazines cost an arm and a leg, but I can't live without them. Photoplay is running a story about Rita Hayworth this month, and I think Modern Screen has an interview with Glenn Ford. I'm not sure what's in the others, but I know it'll be great stuff. Guess I better get a job. Grandma wants me to try babysitting or housework. But why should I ruin my last summer before high school doing things I hate? What else do I know how to do? Cooking is definitely out. I better stay away from the kitchen after that last goof. I still think Mother should've explained what she really meant when she asked me to check the baked potatoes by putting a fork in them. Wow, did she let out a yell when she opened the oven and found a fork in all eight spuds!

Too bad there's no movie studio in Pueblo. I'm not old enough to be an usher down at the Uptown Cinema. I'll just have to think of something else. What about teaching tap dancing to the neighborhood kids? Tapping is great fun and I've taken lessons ever since I could walk. Hmm, how much should I charge? I'm not very good at math, but I need about $5 a month for my magazines. If I can talk even three parents into letting me give their kids one lesson a week, I'll ask for one dollar a lesson. That will be enough for a few movies as well as all the magazines I can read. What a neat plan!

I'm proud to say three precocious toddlers made their Pueblo show business debuts at the end of that summer with a "shuffle step, shuffle step, shuffle step, ball change" routine-to the tune of "On the Good Ship Lollipop." According to six smiling parents, the first dance recital of these Shirley Temple wannabes was a huge success. As for me, I was just happy to earn enough money for my precious movie magazines.

Tappin' through Teens

During my teens, next to the movies I loved tap dancing best. Put the two together and I was in seventh heaven. While watching MGM musicals, I always knew something special was in store every time Mickey Rooney said to Judy Garland, "Let's put on a show!" Never mind about strikingly similar plots and characters in such films as *Babes in Arms, Babes on Broadway, Girl Crazy* and so on. That didn't faze me. I could hardly wait for the dancing and singing to begin.

I was also enchanted by glorious musicals from other studios. I couldn't get enough of stars like Ginger Rogers, Fred Astaire, Betty Grable, Alice Faye, Gene Kelly, and Rita Hayworth. My cousin JoAnne and I wrote fan letters to all our favorites, amassing quite a collection of autographed photos. JoAnne claims I later gave her my signed glossies with the announcement, "I've outgrown all this." My husband believes that's impossible. He insists I still haven't outgrown my passion.

Because my ambition was to become a dancer in the movies, I decided to write for advice from someone who knew all about it. I picked Vera-Ellen, the wonderfully athletic dancer who co-starred with Danny Kaye in *Wonder Man* and Fred Astaire in *Three Little Words*. She actually answered me. I still have her personal letter.

January 26, 1946

Dear Betty:

I am sure you must think I have forgotten all about you but Dear I have been so busy I just couldn't find time to write. Thanks for your nice letter and I hope you received the autographed photo I sent you. I was so pleased to know that you enjoyed Wonder Man as it was my first screen picture. My next picture to be released will be Kid from Brooklyn also with Danny Kaye and I understand this will probably open in New York within the next six or eight weeks. At the present time, I am working on my new picture Three Little Girls in Blue but this will not be finished until about March. I hope you will enjoy all of our pictures.

I see you are also interested in dancing, well Dear if you should make it your profession, I wish you all the luck in the world. Of course, you know it means a lot of hard work, but if you love it, you won't mind the work. I started dancing at nine years old back in my home town Cincinnati, Ohio, but later went to New York to study professionally. After that I went on the stage in New York and this was where Mr. Goldwyn saw me and signed me up immediately for pictures. I had been in five Broadway shows before I came out here to Hollywood. So if you like dancing enough to make it your profession, then keep up the good work and I am sure you will be successful.

I hope you had a nice Christmas and that the New Year will bring you lots of good luck, health, and happiness. I am sorry to have kept you waiting so long for an answer to your nice letter but it just couldn't be helped.

With all good wishes to you and the family.

Sincerely,

Vera-Ellen

Excited as I was about this letter, I realized my chances for success as a dancer were slim. Unlike Vera-Ellen, I couldn't go to New York for professional training. Also, what about all that "hard work" she emphasized? I didn't want anything to interfere with going to the movies as often as I wanted to. Continuing dance lessons in Pueblo seemed my best option. Every week, my cousin Josephine and I had a private session from Daisy Hedges, a well-known local teacher. Josephine, whose beautiful voice always amazed me, received 15 minutes of singing instruction. Then, for another 15 minutes, Mrs. Hedges helped me work on dance technique. Hollywood stardom would have to wait. Although not in any Broadway shows, we were happy performing for various groups in our own community and for holiday programs at Undercliff, a country school supervised by my Grandma Mayer. Grandma wasn't related to movie mogul Louis B. Mayer, but show biz blood flowed through her veins too. Her brother, Charlie Brown, substituted for George M. Cohan in road show productions of his famous musical comedies.

EPISODE TWO: ACTION!

Central Casting

In the forties, students at Central High School were expected to demonstrate school spirit every day—which meant showing an interest in sports, especially football. Although that required an Oscar-caliber performance from me, I didn't have to fake my enthusiasm for pep assemblies. I quickly became involved in writing skits and choreographing dance numbers for these almost weekly events. One of my favorites featured imitations of Al Jolson, Rita Hayworth, Mae West, Mickey Rooney, and Judy Garland. I'm sure Margie (my debate partner) and I had more fun performing this act than the students had watching it. Except for my "Put the Blame on Mame" rendition, that is. Evoking so many laughs for impersonating Rita Hayworth didn't sit well with me. I was going for Gilda's sexy persona. Maybe that's why my friends started calling me "Torchy" while giggling behind my back.

At one of the pep assemblies put on by a different class, I sat in the audience enjoying four girls singing and dancing to "Ramblin' Rose." Suddenly, I was shocked when a boy came onstage to join the routine. It was Larry, my cousin Sanford's best friend. I didn't know he could dance! This talent, plus his Glenn Ford-type good looks and offbeat sense of humor which I admired since our first meeting, made him irresistible. "If he likes movies, he's the one for me," I thought to myself that day.

On our first date, Larry took me to—surprise—a movie! *Romance on the High Seas* featured Doris Day and Jack Carson in a rather predictable love story. After the film, the evening became more interesting. Larry drove to City Park and turned on the car radio. We danced in the silvery moonlight, using the vacant tennis court as our private ballroom. Both of us laughed when we recognized one of the selections being played as "It's Magic," a tune from the movie we had just seen. What a perfect song for such a magical night!

Larry and I dated all during our senior year. We saw as many movies as possible and loved talking about them. I began to worry about leaving for college after graduation. Although I had a scholarship to Barnard in New York City, I feared I would miss Larry terribly. I was right.

New York, New York

Grandma Donahue, longtime-owner of Pueblo's Cosmopolitan Club, where I entertained as a toddler for pennies thrown on the dance floor, escorted me to New York City by train. She wanted to see me settled in at Barnard with her own eyes. Shortly after arriving in the Big Apple, I persuaded her to take us to Radio City Music Hall. We marveled at the splendor of that grand movie palace with its gigantic sweeping staircase and plush décor. The Rockettes and their famed precision dancing held me spellbound, but I was also enthralled by Ingrid Bergman's performance in Alfred Hitchcock's *Under Capricorn*, the movie showing that night. Bergman's portrayal of an Irish noblewoman suffering from manic-depression was so real it made me cry—or maybe I was crying because Larry wasn't with me.

While at Barnard, I began to suffer a bit of depression myself, especially as Thanksgiving approached. This would be the first holiday I spent away from my family and friends. Homesick and lonely, I looked forward to a trip to Brooklyn to visit some distant relatives I had never met. With visions of sparkling conversation and a delicious turkey dinner dancing in my head, I took my first ride on the subway from New York to Brooklyn—which turned out to be my *second* favorite trip of all time. My *first* involved going to the doctor's office for a tonsillectomy. Still, I felt optimistic about meeting new relatives.

Standing at the doorway with snow swirling around me, I rang the bell eagerly. No one answered, but I could hear voices inside. I rang the bell three or four more times. Then I knocked rather loudly on the door. Finally a smiling cousin who was three, four, or five times removed opened the door and apologized matter-of-factly for the delay by explaining, "We were watching Uncle Miltie."

Thinking Miltie might be an ailing relative, I replied, "I hope he's feeling better now." How was I to know he was referring to the Milton Berle show? After all, television remained untapped as family entertainment back in Pueblo. We were still "movie people."

Walking into the cozy living room, I made my way through a group of people huddled around a small box with a screen showing figures moving around in what looked like the same kind of snow falling outside. "Hi!" I called out in my most cheerful voice. They all nodded and kept watching their fascinating new toy.

Needless to say, I didn't get well acquainted with my distant relatives that Thanksgiving Day. But what an introduction to television! We watched every program scheduled that day and on into the evening. Much later, a cold turkey dinner was served—on TV trays, of course.

Buying tickets for *South Pacific*, the hottest show on Broadway during my New York adventure, proved quite a challenge. I heard "standing room only" admissions were available if one arrived at the box office before it opened. That's why, on a chilly fall morning, I mustered enough courage to sneak out of my dorm at 3 a.m., line up at the theatre, and manage to be one of those lucky people who made the cut. That evening, Mary Martin's legendary voice delighted me as it projected all the way to the back row where I stood in awe of her performance. I can imagine Martin's disappointment when the Nellie Forbush movie role went to Mitzi Gaynor, but Gaynor did a great job too. Still, neither of these actresses put as much pep and vitality into the bouncy "Honey Bun" number as my sister Ruella, who surprised me with her musical talent in a school production later.

Dorothy Gale clicked her ruby slippers three times to return to Kansas in *The Wizard of Oz*. I, on the other hand, used the last of my New York allowance for a train ticket back to Colorado in the winter of 1949. After completing almost an entire semester at Barnard, I knew it wasn't working out for me. I arrived home just in time to celebrate Christmas.

No Place Like Home

Love, marriage, and children became the most important things in my life for the next 20 years. Lucky for me, my husband, son, and daughter enjoyed movies almost as much as I did. Captivated by Gene Kelly's dynamic work in *Singin' in the Rain*, Larry and I named our son John "Kelly" in his honor. Because of our admiration for Susan Hayward's performance in *My Foolish Heart,* we christened our daughter "Susan" Claire.

Convinced the drive-in theater represented one of the greatest inventions of the 20th century, we prepared for an outdoor movie adventure at least once each week by packing up nursing bottles, diapers, and enough snacks to last through a double feature at the Mesa or Lake Drive-In.

Thanks to Larry's terrific help with all the family chores, I finished educational degrees at Pueblo Junior College, Colorado College, and the University of Northern Colorado. Larry always joked about my degrees when introducing us at parties by saying, "This is my wife, Betty Jo—A.A., B.A., M.A., Ed.D., and I'm Larry—L.A.R.R.Y."

While serving as a teacher and administrator at various schools in Pueblo, I usually found ways to arrange lessons and activities relating to movies. Teaching second grade in Bessemer, I put on frequent music programs with the children performing songs from their favorite films. When my South High social studies classes were studying brainwashing, I took the students to see *The Manchurian Candidate*, starring Frank Sinatra, Angela Lansbury, and Laurence Harvey. After watching this thriller about an assassination plot involving post-hypnotic suggestion, students seemed highly motivated to learn more about brainwashing. I realized then what a powerful teaching tool movies could be.

As a Student Council advisor, I worked with counselor Martha Gorder in writing and directing a variety show about Hollywood. Our production, *A Date with Oscar*, showcased students in acts saluting various stars and films. We even composed an original title song. Although our musical efforts fell short of Hit Parade caliber, South High patrons applauded them enthusiastically, thereby proving their unwavering loyalty and school spirit.

My next position, Dean of Women at Pueblo Junior College, required high moral standards. Counseling female students with their problems and supervising discipline were among the various duties assigned to me. One fateful night at the movies, my chances of being effective in such a capacity almost faded into oblivion. Every weekend, Larry and I always sat in the sixth row from the screen while watching movies at the Uptown Theatre. On the night in question, we tried to sneak into Pueblo's first X-rated film, one with a title I've repressed. We arrived a little late, so the movie had already started. Eager to get to our regular seats, I went ahead of Larry.

Gazing up at the opening scene, I walked briskly down the aisle of the darkened theater. That's the last thing I remember before waking up to see paramedics standing over me, giving me oxygen. I had fallen over a picket fence placed in the aisle to keep people from going into the first few rows because they were being repaired. As the paramedics carried me from the theatre, I heard someone standing in the ticket line shout, "Look, there's our Dean of Women. She probably fainted. Wow, this must be a *really* hot flick!"

Later, bringing peace activists Jane Fonda and Dan Berrigan to the University of Southern Colorado campus, where I was serving as Associate Dean of Students and Upward Bound Director, caused me serious problems with my supervisors. Father Berrigan gained notoriety as one of the protestors who poured blood on draft records during the Vietnam war. (After moving to San Diego, I was surprised to see Berrigan on the big screen as a Jesuit priest in *The Mission*, a film he served as consultant on.) If I hadn't received support from people like Dr. Sallie Watkins of the Physics Department, a respected nun who kicked the habit (well, only her uniform) when she moved to Colorado, and the town's beloved Catholic Bishop, Charles Buswell, my tenure might have been short-lived indeed. Instead, I remained at USC for several years, and the voters of Pueblo elected me to the local School Board. Go figure.

EPISODE THREE: SCENE CHANGES

Scenes from San Diego

After Larry and I divorced —which had nothing to do with the movies (that's another story entirely), he stayed in Pueblo and I moved to San Diego. While working as Dean of Humanities at San Diego Mesa College, I supervised departments closely related to my area of addiction. Both Drama and English included classes in film studies. I'm VERY grateful to President Allen Brooks and Executive Dean Robert Arnold for moving me into that position after a short stint as Dean of Technologies, a job I couldn't put my heart into. As a Humanities dean, I quickly became involved in activities more suited to my interests.

When Cliff Robertson came to Mesa to accept a special award for his Oscar-winning performance in *Charly*, I served as emcee of the program. Because Robertson went over his allotted time explaining why he wanted to make a sequel, I asked him to sum up in one sentence the movie's most important message. "Well, that's the nicest way I've ever been kicked off stage," he announced to the audience.

Because Annette Bening attended Mesa right after high school, I asked her to return and conduct an acting workshop for our current drama students. Her enthusiasm for acting delighted everyone. "My goal is to become a very old woman playing all sorts of character parts," she told the students. She also expressed a desire to play Hamlet, reminding the group about Dame Judith Anderson's success in that leading role. Bening had just completed filming *Bugsy* with Warren Beatty and appeared very careful when answering questions about him. *Those two must be up to*

23

something, I thought to myself. When they married each other within the next few months, it failed to surprise me. Also attending Bening's presentation at Mesa were Shirley and Grant, her mom and dad, who still lived in San Diego. To this day, Shirley remains one of my dearest friends.

Steve Allen and Jayne Meadows made quite an impression on everyone at Mesa when they participated in the campus "Reel to Real" Film Forum. I found their playful attitude with each other amusing both on-stage and off. Allen made no attempt to hide his adoration of Meadows, and she never missed a chance to praise her husband, although sometimes with tongue-in-cheek. Grabbing the microphone in the Apolliad Theatre after accepting his Humanities Appreciation Award for *Meeting of the Minds*, Allen informed the audience, "I've seen better lighting at the Nuremburg Trials."

Meadows, who brightened the occasion with her vibrant red hair and exquisite floral gown, let everyone know Allen was joking. She simply shrugged her shoulders and said, "Here we go again!"

This charming couple refused to accept their honorarium when I handed them the check. "Return it to the Exchequer for student scholarships," Allen said, and Meadows nodded in agreement.

Along with several Mesa College instructors, I attended the famous Hotel del Coronado's 100th Birthday Celebration in 1988. We partied with a galaxy of movie stars including Robert Loggia, Jane Withers, the Gabor sisters, Lloyd Bridges, and Cesar Romero. At one point in the evening's festivities, I noticed a lonely little woman sitting in a corner and went over to keep her company. As I came closer, I realized she looked familiar. When I sat down beside her, I recognized the legendary Ruby Keeler. "What a coincidence," I said. "I'm taking a tap dancing class, and the instructor showed *42nd Street* last week. She wanted us to see the best."

Keeler, suffering from crippling arthritis, smiled and replied, "That's good news. I didn't know people watched my films anymore." After assuring her she was wrong about that, I enjoyed an intimate conversation with one of filmdom's great hoofers.

For one Mesa College Humanities Variety Show, counselor Rich Pearson and I, billed as Ginger Dodgers and Fred Upstairs, shocked our colleagues with a short dance routine to "Puttin' on the Ritz." Because I had so much fun doing that number, I joined the Mesa Musical Comedy Touring Troupe, directed by Evonne and Art Noll. We performed for nursing homes, rehab centers, and various other groups throughout San Diego. It was great to be tapping again! Every time we sang and danced to "Just Go to the Movies" (from *A Day in Hollywood/A Night in the Ukraine*), my spirits were lifted by Jerry Herman's wonderful lyrics advising everyone to "let some shadows appear on the screen" whenever "your life seems a bit lean." Wonder if Mr. Herman realizes he's given movie addicts such a perfect anthem?

Music professor Liz Hamilton and I wanted to share our "joy of tap" with others, so we organized "tappercize" sessions for faculty, staff, and students during lunch periods. Right before I left the School of Humanities, speech professor Pat Olafson, assisted by my clever secretary Desiree VanSaanen, recited a funny story to well-wishers about how she discovered I had been Fred Astaire's first dancing partner, and she had the doctored photos to prove it!. Along with English instructor Pat Reming, Professor Olafson served refreshments at my retirement party from a table arranged to resemble the concession stand at a movie theater. But the biggest surprise of all was when Professor Juan Castro and the drama department announced the creation of a special "Scholarship of Drama Excellence" in my name.

I realized then how difficult leaving these wonderful people was going to be.

A Film Critic Is Born

After retirement, I threw myself into a moviegoing frenzy. My movie buddy, Karen Kaye, showed courage beyond the call of duty by accompanying me to some dreadful films. I'm surprised she didn't disown me as a friend because of my raucous laughter at Chris Elliott in *Cabin Boy*, one of the worst movies of that year.

Karen was probably embarrassed to walk out of the theater with me.

With nothing to stand in my way now, I thought about becoming a film critic. David Elliott (no relation to Chris), one of San Diego's most prominent critics, taught a class on this very subject for the Learning Annex, so I signed up. For homework, Elliott asked students to do a review of *Atlantic City*. Here's what I wrote:

On the Boardwalk in Atlantic City, so the old song goes, "life can be peaches and cream." Not so for Sally Matthews (Susan Sarandon), a wannabe croupier with a philandering husband, and Lou Pascoe (Burt Lancaster), an old-time hood now reduced to taking care of an elderly Betty Grable look-alike (Kate Reid in a gem of a performance).

When Sally and Lou meet after a dope deal set up by Sally's husband goes bad, each has something the other needs. Longing to be the important Atlantic City crime figure he was in the past (or was he?), Lou sees Sally and the money from the drug deal as his way back to glory. Sally, much younger than Lou but not immune to his considerable charm, wants him to "teach her stuff" so she can deal her way to Monte Carlo. Lancaster and Sarandon make us really care about Lou and Sally. We want their dreams to come true. We share their pain when attacked by vicious hoods and forced to leave Atlantic City.

We especially feel for Lou who hasn't been out of Atlantic City for 20 years.

Atlantic City itself plays a key role in this critically acclaimed Louis Malle film—from an early-on building demolition shot to scenes inside the casinos and on the Boardwalk. Like Sally and Lou, the City is going through changes; the old is giving way to the new. Robert Goulet's cameo scene serves as a not-so-subtle reminder of how our senses can be dulled during periods of transition.

John Guare's intelligent script contains humorous surprises. After Lou makes all the funeral arrangements for Sally's husband, Sally asks, "Why are you doing this for me?" Lou answers pretentiously, "Sinatra gives wings to hospitals. We all do what we can do." In another scene, Lou tries to impress Sally concerning his criminal past by telling her that "casinos are too wholesome for me."

Although Susan Sarandon gives him a run for his money, *Atlantic City* belongs to Burt Lancaster. His remarkable interpretation of the sometimes pathetic, mostly elegant Lou Pasco is pure Lancaster movie magic and earned him his last Oscar nomination.

Fairly primitive stuff, but that review earned Elliott's encouragement. Deciding to continue with my new goal, I sent several reviews to local newspapers, hoping for the best. Within a few months, my articles appeared regularly in the La Mesa News and all six East County Forum publications. Thankfully, radio film critic and Mesa English professor Andrew Makarushka vouched for me with studio publicists operating in the San Diego area. I was on my way! Being a bona fide film critic meant attending free screenings and receiving press kits as well as having the opportunity to interview movie stars, directors, and screenwriters on personal appearance tours.

Many former colleagues began to contact me for movie advice. I joked with one of my neighbors by asking her "What do an African Art expert, a ceramics genius, a poet, two secretaries, and a Humanities professor all have in common?" When she admitted she had no idea, I explained, "They all want to know what movie to see this weekend." That was the week Barbara Blackmun, John Conrad, César González, Susan Schwartz, Dianne Lamb, and Candy Waltz all wanted the same information. I believe everyone is entitled to my opinion, so I willingly obliged. In Cesar's case, I usually tell him about movies receiving my "FB" rating, which means they are suitable for his wife Bette, who avoids films with excessive violence, sex, and obscene language. Too bad the trend in movies today makes it harder and harder to come up with "FB" recommendations.

Like all the founding members of our San Diego Film Critics Society, I considered annual voting for Best Performances, Best Picture, and so forth a matter of utmost importance. But sometimes my opinions conflicted with the rest of the group as well as with the Academy of Motion Picture Arts and Sciences. For example, I panned *American Beauty*, the film SDFCS picked as Best Movie in 1999. That film also went on to win an Oscar for Best Picture. Nevertheless, I stand by my review and continue to to speak out against films I dislike, no matter how popular they are. Three of my teenage granddaughters—Marie, Elizabeth, and Jennifer—couldn't believe I trashed *Titanic*, a movie they saw thirteen times.

One of my early critiques took on a bizarre tone and probably alienated Oprah Winfrey fans. As the only critic in America who saw *Beloved* and *Bride of Chucky* on the same day, I became fascinated by the similarities in these two movies. How could I ignore such an incredible discovery? I revealed my findings in the following review:

Neither *Beloved*, the film version of Toni Morrison's acclaimed anti-slavery novel, nor *Bride of Chucky*, another campy sequel to 1988's *Child's Play* should be viewed by the faint of heart. Moviegoers brave enough to see these two films will be surprised at the gruesome plot points they share, in spite of their very different subject matter.

Both films deal with the supernatural. *Beloved*, from Touchstone Pictures, features the adult ghost of a dead child come back to life to haunt its killer. Universal's new *Chucky* presents the further misadventures of a psychopathic doll that comes to life after a dying serial killer transfers his soul into the doll's body. Blood and gore fill the screen in both movies. Beatings, lynchings, and baby killing make up most of the violence in *Beloved*, while *Chucky* concentrates on explosions, severed body parts, and deaths by shattered mirror glass.

An eyeball figures prominently in each film. In *Beloved*, former slave Sethe (Oprah Winfrey) puts her dog's eyeball back into its socket after the animal is slammed into a wall by a ghost. In *Bride of Chucky*, the woman who was once Chucky's girlfriend (Jennifer Tilley) places a toy eyeball into his doll face before bringing him back to life while performing a kind of "Voodoo for Dummies."

I know it's hard to believe, but both Sethe and Chucky's girl-friends purchase dolls for their loved ones. Sethe spends the last of her meager funds on a doll for the ghost child. Chucky gets (you guessed it) a bride doll. A strange pregnancy occurs in each film also. The ghost becomes pregnant by Sethe's boyfriend (Danny Glover), and Chucky impregnates his re-vamped bride doll. (I smell sequels.)

Bride of Chucky mixes weird humor with its scare tactics, including Tilley's wickedly amusing bubble bath while watching the classic *Bride of Frankenstein* on TV. But there is nothing funny about Beloved. Instead, it reveals the intense pain and suf-fering of a woman who will do anything to keep her children from becoming slaves. Clearly, imaginary evils like those on the latest *Chucky* flick are no match for the real horrors of slavery depicted so graphically in *Beloved*.

It Had To Be Larry—Again

Twenty years had passed since Larry and I divorced. Then, during one of my holiday visits to Pueblo, we saw each other again at our daughter Sue's house on Christmas morning. Although nervous in each other's company, we found ourselves laughing together and eager to spend some time "catching up." Because both of us love movies, our second "first date" was spent watching Jim Carrey in *Dumb and Dumber*. We had fun dis-cussing how the movie title related to us.

After returning to San Diego, I couldn't stop thinking about Larry. I even sent him a Valentine. On April Fool's Day, we met in Las Vegas. Larry accompanied me to the opening of the Debbie Reynolds Hollywood Museum. As the first ones into the museum the moment it opened to the public, we were escorted into a small theatre similar to a Hollywood screening room and then dazzled by a multimedia extravaganza lasting about 35 minutes. Film clips from classic movies filled the screen while costumes were displayed on revolving stages. We watched scenes from *Ben Hur,* *How the West Was Won, Cleopatra, There's No Business Like Show Business*, and many other marvelous old films. Debbie Reynolds popped in and out of scenes, through the wizardry of virtual reality, and tied everything together like a magical cinematic guru.

Next, we enjoyed a guided tour of Hollywood's most memorable costumes. Presented elegantly in glass compartments were such classic items as Marilyn Monroe's famous white dress from *The Seven Year Itch*, Judy Garland's ruby slippers from *The Wizard of Oz* (oh, how I wanted them for my very own!), and Barbra Streisand's beaded gown from *Hello, Dolly*. Afterwards, Todd Fisher, Debbie's son, invited us backstage for a look at the technology involved in this multimedia experience. As the genius behind the technical aspects of the museum, Todd made no effort to hide his sense of accomplishment.

Because I needed additional information about the costumes for one of my articles, I went back for another tour the next day. Debbie herself participated in this one. When I asked her what musical number the *Singin' in the Rain* display depicted, she belted out a few bars of "Fit as a Fiddle and Ready for Love"—which reminded me about my feelings for Larry. I thought about the bittersweet nature of our rendezvous. Sadness overwhelmed me at the thought of parting again so soon. Larry's responsibilities in Pueblo included coordinating a senior golf league. And I had to return to San Diego to review movies for East County publications. We planned to meet again after Larry's golf league duties were completed, but that wouldn't be for another long six months.

Back at our respective homes, neither of us could eat or sleep. We spent most of the time telephoning each other. Three days later, he surprised me with an early morning call to announce he was quitting the golf league and would be moving to San Diego as soon as possible. When he arrived at my condo, *Romance on the High Seas*, the film we saw on our first date in high school, was playing on the American Movie Classics channel—with Doris Day singing "It's Magic" as romantically as ever. In the immortal words of Yogi Berra, "Déjà vu, all over again."

We re-married a few months later and honeymooned at the Hotel Del Coronado, the very place Billy Wilder filmed *Some Like It Hot*. I sometimes think Larry wanted to marry me again in order to attend all those press screenings with me. We see almost 200 movies a year—so, if my suspicions are correct, he must be as happy as I am. Still, he pays for the privilege by doing all the driving and by taking pictures at my interview sessions. What a guy! ("Larry's Gallery," a selection of his photos, can be viewed on pages 65 to70.)

Hooray for the Hollywood Musical

While active members of the San Diego Cinema Society, Larry and I worked with Andy Friedenberg, the group's director, to develop a special program saluting the Hollywood Musical. Dennis Howard, a former colleague at Mesa College, also loved this genre, so he agreed to participate in the planning too. Dennis and I already had survived a visit to the Institute of the American Musical in Los Angeles. After making it through horrendous LA traffic and past two overly friendly guard dogs, we met the legendary Miles Kreuger, founder of the Institute. Occupying an unassuming California bungalow, Kreuger has assembled the world's largest collection of materials and recordings of musical theatre and motion pictures. A walking encyclopedia on the subject, Kreuger glowed with enthusiasm while giving us the royal tour. Later, when I called him about our San Diego event, he graciously agreed to be a panelist, suggesting we contact Saul Chaplin to round out the program.

"Not THE Saul Chaplin?" I asked. "He wrote one of my favorite songs," I explained. After telling him Larry and I loved "You Wonderful You" from *Summer Stock*, Kreuger mentioned Chaplin's recent autobiography, *The Golden Age of Movie Musicals and Me* (University of Oklahoma Press, 1994). Reading his informative and entertaining book convinced me we had to recruit Chaplin as our second speaker. One of the great contributors to movie musicals, Chaplin served as a songwriter, vocal arranger, pianist, musical director, or producer for over sixty films. He won Academy Awards for *An American in Paris, Seven Brides for Seven Brothers*, and *West Side Story*. Among his published songs are such memorable hits as "The Anniversary Song," "All My Love," and "Dedicated to You."

In talking with Chaplin on the phone, I explained that Larry and I had re-married after so many years apart. I also mentioned how much "You Wonderful You" meant to us. Imagine our surprise when Chaplin and his wife appeared at our program bringing a gift of the original song sheet autographed especially for us! Larry helped the 83 year-old gentleman with a book signing before the program began, and the two got along famously. As Chaplin was leaving, he took me aside and said, "I don't blame you for marrying Larry again. If he asked me, that's what I'd do too."

Chaplin charmed the audience with his intelligence, wit, and candor. In his opinion, Gene Kelly ranked as the hardest working musical star. After naming Al Jolson and Judy Garland as the most talented performers, he added that Jolson was also the most egotistical. Asked to pick his favorite musical, Chaplin stated he couldn't because he loved so many of them.

Betty Chaplin chided her husband about his answer. She felt he should have mentioned *The Sound of Music*, especially since they met during its filming. She served as the script supervisor on that movie. With a twinkle in his eye, the white-haired, savvy music man quickly agreed.

Seeing Stars

Movie actors and filmmakers rarely miss coming to San Diego to promote their new films, probably because of the city's proximity to Hollywood. During my work as a film critic there, I met Angelina Jolie, Jonny Lee Miller, Ben Kingsley, Guy Pearce, Ian McKellen, Joey Lauren Adams, M. Night Shyamalan, Hope Davis, John Herzfeld, Mike Figgis, Gregory Nava, Michael Rapaport, Lorenzo Lamas, Douglas McGrath, Charlton Heston,

Masayuki Suo, Mickey Rooney, Tony Shalhoub, Jan Sverak, Emilio Estevez, and Matthew Broderick. I also obtained phone interviews with Lauren Holly, Aaron Eckhart, Bob Saget, and Randall Wallace. (Many of these interview articles appear on pages 79 to 116.)

Although I view having my picture taken with celebrities as unprofessional, Angelina Jolie and Jonny Lee Miller, co-stars of *Hackers*, insisted. I'm glad they did. My grandchildren ask to see that photo every time they come to visit. They are among Jolie's many fans now, so my status with the younger set seems secure— for a while, at least.

Visiting San Diego for a personal appearance in connection with *L.A. Confidential*, Guy Pearce looked nothing like the prim detective from that acclaimed film. With his spiked hair and leather jacket, the diminutive actor resembled a rock star instead. Larry whispered to me, "I think they've brought in a ringer." But I disagreed. Why? Looking closer at the Australian-born Pearce, I spotted those penetrating blue eyes and high cheekbones that make him so photogenic in such movies as *Priscilla, Queen of the Desert, Rules of Engagement,* and *Memento.*

Instead of the elitist Shakespearean actor I expected, Sir Ian McKellen was very easy to talk with. He described growing up in an area of England where he attended live theater productions three times a week, which probably explains his great love for the theater over film. However, by serving not only as the lead actor but also as executive producer for *Richard III*, McKellen claimed he gained a new respect for making movies. Recognizing the need to include American film stars to make his movie a more bankable production, he supported casting Annette Bening and Robert Downey Jr. in the roles of Queen Elizabeth and her brother. "Obtaining Bening was an example of virtue rewarded," he declared. "Our director, Richard Loncraine, had Warren Beatty's phone number from 10 years ago when Warren called to congratulate him on his direction of *The Missionary*. I warned Richard that the number was not current, but he called anyway, and Warren answered the phone. When Richard asked if he knew how we could get Annette for our project, Warren replied, 'Why don't you ask her yourself?' He put Annette on the phone, and the rest is history."

Before being interviewed at San Diego's Planet Hollywood, Emilio Estevez, who stunned me by his uncanny resemblance to my late cousin Sanford, added his hand prints to the celebrity collection there. Wanting to be known as something more than a "comedy guy" from those *Mighty Ducks* movies, he had recently directed, wrote, and co-starred in *The War at Home*. "My father (Martin Sheen) and my brother (Charlie Sheen) have each appeared in Vietnam War films, so some critics are calling me the last Sheen out of Saigon," Estevez said.

Insisting his new film, which featured his father in a starring role, emerges as more than a Vietnam War film, he explained it focuses on the tragedy in a dysfunctional family resulting from loss of love and communication. Admitting to feeling intimidated by his father while directing him, Estevez stated, "I held my ground anyway and wouldn't let him play the role exactly the way he wanted. I really believe this is the best work he's done in years." Having seen *The War at Home*, I agreed with him.

Although I didn't officially interview Matthew Broderick, I met the popular star of *Ferris Bueller's Day Off* at a holiday celebration in Horton Plaza. Broderick's musical comedy performance in the San Diego trial run of *How To Succeed in Business Without Really Trying* received unfair pans by local critics. While shaking his hand, I told him not to worry. "I saw your show and you were terrific," I exclaimed. I mentioned my background in musical comedy to make sure he understood my credentials. Broderick thanked me, smiled one of the widest grins I've ever seen, and wouldn't let go of my hand. Later, when he won the Tony for this same performance, he said nothing about my encouraging words. I was heartbroken.

New director Douglas McGrath entertained us with his witty responses during a spirited interview. Looking much too young to be the successful filmmaker who had just finished adapting for the screen and directing *Emma*, Jane Austen's most amusing literary masterpiece, McGrath confessed he hadn't even heard of *Emma* before joining the team of writers at *Saturday Night Live*. "All the SNL writers were surprisingly well-read," he said. "They could even put together complete sentences. One day they started talking about *Emma* and encouraged me to read the book."

Drawn to comedy because of his own humorous outlook on life, McGrath explained he knew right away that Austen's novel would make a wonderful movie. "I took my screenplay and recommended myself as the director," he admitted. He got the job, but only after explaining that he wanted to pace the movie like George Cukor's bubbling comedies of the 1930s and 40s and to give it a visual impact similar to Vincente Minelli's famous musicals (*Gigi* and *Meet Me in St. Louis*). When I asked him why he added an archery contest between Emma and Mr. Knightley that wasn't in the book, he laughed and said, "To tie into the summer Olympics. McDonald's may soon offer little Emma puppets complete with their tiny bows and arrows!"

Like most humorists, McGrath "always leaves them laughing." For my last question, I inquired what he wanted readers to know about him. "Where to send money!" he replied.

The more sedate Masayuki Suo, director of Japan's enchanting *Shall We Dance?* turned the tables on Larry and me. He videotaped our entire interview to include in a documentary about his trip to America. At the close of the interview, he persuaded us to pose in a ballroom dance position. Suo sends no word yet about our stardom in Japan.

Two other directors surprised us, but not quite in the same way. Darkly handsome and very serious M. Night Shyamalan, doing a press tour for his first movie *Wide Awake*, looked more like a film star than a director. Because *Wide Awake* went straight to video, we never dreamed Shyamalan would be one of Hollywood's most acclaimed filmmakers a few years later. I believe this director's experience working with a child actor in his debut movie prepared him for the challenge of *Sixth Sense*, his Oscar-nominated second flick about a young boy, played brilliantly by Haley Joel Osment, who sees dead people everywhere.

John Herzfeld also came across more like an actor than a filmmaker. In San Diego to promote *2 Days in the Valley*, the energetic director acted out his first movie job right in front of our eyes. He jumped to his feet to show how he stood as an extra in "some movie about graduation " that ended up being Dustin

Hoffman's *The Graduate*. I think he even expected applause as he sat down. Instead of clapping for Herzfeld, I gave his edgy ensemble crime drama a glowing review the following day.

I hesitate to write about my most embarrassing interview. However, it resulted in a great story for director Jan Sverak to tell his friends in the Czech Republic. Sverak and his father Zdenek came to San Diego in February of 1997 to arouse interest in their wonderful film, *Kolya*, winner of the Oscar for Best Foreign Language Film that year. The handsome Zdenek, who plays a middle-aged Czech cellist saddled with a six-year-old Russian refugee named Kolya, resembles Sean Connery both physically and in terms of his screen charisma. Naturally, I was eager to meet him in person. But the elder Sverak suffered jet lag and opted for a nap in his Hyatt Hotel room instead of doing interviews. Claiming his father doesn't travel well, the younger Sverak said, "Maybe you can take a peek at him before you leave." At the close of the interview, I reminded him of his offer by saying, "I'd like to peek at your father now. I'll be very quiet." Sverak just looked at me, stunned. "I was kidding, of course," he declared as he ushered me quickly to the door.

When Charlton Heston received his 1995 Lifetime Achievement Award in San Diego, one of the multiplexes honored him by showing a different one of his films on each of their 24 screens. But *Touch of Evil*, my favorite, was missing. I expressed my disappointment to Heston as he held court in the huge lobby. Not expecting to hear any more about my concern, I felt pleased when he later announced to the group during his acceptance speech that program officials had not been able to secure a proper print of *Touch of Evil*. Evidently, Heston was disappointed too, probably because he wanted fans to view this Orson Welles classic on the big screen. "People see most of their movies at home on television today instead of in movie theaters," he complained. "And the emotional impact is not the same." I couldn't agree more.

Meeting Mickey Rooney at the Palm Springs International Film Festival turned out to be the highlight of that 1995 event. Rooney expressed enthusiasm over playing Father Flannigan in *The Road Home* (shown on television as *The Brothers' Destiny*), a movie premiering there. At a question and answer session for the San Diego Cinema Society, Mickey recalled portraying a *Boys Town* orphan as a co-star with Spencer Tracy, who originated the role of Father Flannigan, in that much earlier movie. "I've come full circle," he said. He also reminisced about working with Judy Garland. "I loved her. She was the greatest performer who ever lived," he announced. Rooney then reminded us, "I was the biggest box-office star in the world for two decades."

How well I remember those popular *Andy Hardy* films—there were 15 of them—with their unsophisticated and amusing plots about a teenage boy and his family!

Talking to the Animals

My most unusual interview took place over the phone. Most people have never had a telephone conversation with a famous shellfish, let alone one who speaks from a Park Avenue apartment in New York City. But this amazing experience really happened to me. No need to call agents Scully and Mulder of *The X-Files*. Just read on. As part of the public relations campaign for re-release of Disney's *The Little Mermaid*, Samuel E. Wright, who provided the vocal antics for Sebastian, the Calypso crab, agreed to phone interviews while appearing on Broadway in *The Lion King*.

Wright, obviously excited about the re-release of Disney's popular film, explained to me how he kept Sebastian alive since the movie's 1989 debut through concerts showcasing his two big musical numbers, "Under the Sea" and "Kiss the Girl." Noticing the enthusiasm in his deep, friendly voice as he talked about Sebastian, I couldn't resist asking, "Would you be able to put Sebastian on the phone?"

"Well, he might be scurrying around here someplace," Wright replied. When I mentioned it might be difficult for Sebastian to talk on the phone, because of his claws and all, Wright declared, "Oh, no. I'll just hold the phone down to his ear."

And thus began the following conversation with Sebastian, a tiny Calypso crab with a very big ego (as reported in *Forum Publications*, November 20, 1997):

Sebastian: Hello. Who is dis person who wants ta talk with me?

Me: Hi, Sebastian. I'm one of your biggest fans.

Sebastian: Well, who isn't? Whadda ya wanna know?

Me: Well, for one thing, Sebastian, how did you like the job of watching over Ariel, the little mermaid, to keep her out of trouble?

Sebastian: Have ya ever held a greasy fish in *your* hand? Dat's what it's like. She's very slippery, dat Ariel. But she's flambunctious! Dat's one a' my two hundred dollah words.

Me: Do you have any advice for other crustaceans who might get offered a similar job?

Sebastian: Stay in your shell! Don't get outta da water. Cause da only one who can take care o' Ariel is me!

Me: Do you think Ariel and Prince Eric lived happily ever after?

Sebastian: I know dey did. I saw dem two days ago.

Me: What were dey, I mean they, doing?

Sebastian: Watchin' da *Lion King* on t.v.!

After Sebastian put his roommate back on the phone, I inquired about any new projects. Wright revealed he would be doing the voice of Kron, leader of the iguanadons, in *Dinosaur*, another Disney film. I asked if it might be possible to visit with him again when that movie was completed. He answered, "Maybe so. Perhaps you can talk with Kron then too." I'm disappointed that interview never happened.

Shortly after reading my interview with Sebastian, Penny Langford, of Pre-Vue Magazine, asked me to do a similar one with the star of *Mouse Hunt*. "That won't be easy," I replied. "After all, Sebastian is voiced by a real live human, whereas that little mouse happens to be a real mouse. And he doesn't talk in the movie."

"Don't worry," Penny said. "We'll call the article *If This Mouse Could Talk*, and you can have fun with it."

I did have fun. Here's how that article appeared in Pre-Vue's 1997 Holiday Issue:

Through the magic of imagination and wishful thinking, Pre-Vue brings you the following exclusive interview with the wily rodent star of *Mouse Hunt*, the first comedy from DreamWorks SKG.

PRE-VUE: Thanks for consenting to this interview, Mr. Mouse. How did you get into the movie business?

MOUSE: I had just moved to California—for the cheese—when a casting agent spotted me and said I was perfect for the lead in *Mouse Hunt*. They offered me all the fromage I could eat, but I never dreamed I'd get the chance to work with my favorite funny human, Nathan Lane. When I look into his bright little eyes, I swear he's part rodent!

PRE-VUE: Did you enjoy working at DreamWorks SKG?

MOUSE: I sure did. My buddy Sparky is a great guy—that's what we call Mr. Spielberg—he's a really big cheese, you know. He's the "S" in SKG and you have to be really important to get first billing. He did a great job keeping those vicious cats out of sight between takes and he never interfered with my artistic freedom.

PRE-VUE: What do the other letters in SKG stand for?

MOUSE: To me they mean Shoo, Kitty, Go! But that Geffen Fellow, he's the G. He offered me a record deal. Katzenberg, he's the K—there's something about his name that bothers me...

PRE-VUE: The Hollywood buzz is that you come across much smarter than the humans in *Mouse Hunt*. Is that right?

MOUSE: Absolutely! It's not the size of the brain that counts but what you do with it. Remember, it was Mighty Mouse who always saved the day.

PRE-VUE: Did you perform your own stunts?

MOUSE: And risk damaging these valuable whiskers? We recruited about 60 stunt mice and used special effects plus computer generated images. Thankfully, I came out unscathed.

PRE-VUE: And obviously fit to take on new challenges. What's next?

MOUSE: I'm gnawing on the script for an all-animal remake of *Silence of the Lambs* and sniffing at the villain's part this time. Hannibal Lecter was a deviously clever rat.

PRE-VUE: Almost perfect casting! One last question, sir. What did you like best about making *Mouse Hunt*?

MOUSE: I felt honored to be in a movie that squeaks out against stereotypes about mice. Humans need to learn what we mice are really like.

PRE-VUE: And what are you really like?

MOUSE: Go see *Mouse Hunt* and find out.

According to Penny, the folks at DreamWorks loved this piece. But they didn't tell me.

A Wild Premiere

Holding a traditional Hollywood premiere for *George of the Jungle* wasn't exciting enough for the adventurous execs at Walt Disney Pictures. They decided to take over San Diego's Wild Animal Park. Lucky for Larry and me, we were among the press invited to cover this event. Starting around 4:30 on that particular hot afternoon, we joined a large group of media representatives and eager fans assembled at the park's entrance. Celebrities began walking down the red—excuse me, leopard-spotted—carpet a little before 6 p.m.

As expected, the film's buffed-up star, Brendan Fraser, captured most of the media attention. Looking exactly like he does on screen, the popular actor appeared to have time for everyone. When I mentioned to him how much the youngsters wanted to see

George of the Jungle, he added, "And their parents, too, because they remember this character from the 1960s cartoon."

Veteran actor Richard Roundtree, who starred in the original *Shaft* movies, also hit it off with the press. As Kwame, the guide in *George of the Jungle*, Roundtree said the most difficult shoot for him involved a dangerous swinging bridge scene in the African sequence. Lovely leading lady Leslie Mann expressed delight over her role as George's love interest, but her long see-through dress rated two thumbs down as a costume choice for Wild Animal Park.

Other actors spotted among the many celebrities attending included Thomas Hayden Church, Holland Taylor, Penelope Ann Miller, Eric Idle, and Christine Lahti. Almost everyone brought their families.

After completing the obligatory press line, Sam Weisman, who directed *George of the Jungle*, needed an energy boost. "Where's the food?" he asked. Wondering the same thing, Larry and I followed him past assorted fierce creatures and their brave keepers, over the Congo Fishing Village Bridge, down the Kilimanjaro Backcountry Trail, and finally into the Heart of Africa.

A sumptuous buffet awaited all guests at our destination, making the long trek worthwhile. Adding to the festivities, live African music put the crowd in the right mood for the movie to follow. The lavish party ended with an outdoor showing of *George of the Jungle* on a newly installed giant screen in the Bird Show Amphitheater. An appreciative audience applauded and cheered with great enthusiasm—and that was just for the opening credits.

The film amused me with its combination of innocent slapstick comedy and sophisticated dialogue. My favorite character, the elephant who thinks he's a dog, almost stopped the show with his incredible canine-like movements, thanks to Jim Hensen's Creature Shop. No doubt about it, those Disney folks throw a great party. They also know how to make entertaining movies. Larry and I rank *George of the Jungle* as one of their best.

Fargo Fanatics

Imagine a pregnant police chief with a husband who paints ducks for postage stamps. Add a financially-troubled car salesman with plans to hire someone to kidnap his wife. Throw in some inept crooks and a deadly woodchipper. Are these the elements of a fascinating movie? You betcha, especially if it comes from film-makers Joel and Ethan Coen. In 1996, their *Fargo* took critics and moviegoers by storm. While watching the press screening of this film, I noticed the actor playing Frances McDormand's sensitive husband looked and sounded familiar. In checking through the press notes, I found his name was John Carroll Lynch. Larry and I both remembered a high school friend of ours, Dan Lynch, who once worked in a political campaign for Colorado senator John Carroll. Could this actor be related to Dan?

Hoping our friend still lived in Colorado, I called Information for his number. There were twelve "D. Lynch" or "Dan Lynch" listings in Denver, but the first one I called turned out to be the right one. After filling me in on his son's acting career, Dan gave me John's phone number. Obtaining a *Fargo*-related telephone interview proved quite a boon for me in more ways than one. First, I learned something about how the Coen brothers work with their actors. John expressed his admiration for the precision of their writing and direction. "There's no room for improvisation," he said. "The Coens know exactly what they want."

Even more significantly, talking personally with John Carroll Lynch opened the door to a welcome new friendship. Duncan Shepherd, one of San Diego's toughest critics, also fell under the *Fargo* spell. When Larry and I began telling him about our *Fargo* connection, it created a bond for us with Duncan and Merilyn, his lovely wife. Duncan liked to look for Lynch's name in the credits for other movies. We frequently sat near each other, so whenever that name appeared, I saw Duncan's head bob approvingly. I can't help wondering what he thinks now about Lynch's continuing role as the cross-dressing brother in Drew Carey's television sitcom.

EPISODE FOUR: CUT!

Return of the Natives

Thanks to the wonders of modern technology, film critics can work anywhere in the world today. When Larry and I moved back to Pueblo to be closer to our children and grandchildren, my editors knew I would continue to meet their deadlines by sending them articles via e-mail. Both Steven Saint of *Forum Publications* and Diana Saenger of *Uptown-Marquee* supported me in this decision. The publisher of *Uptown-Marquee*, Jim Colt Harrison, began referring to me as the magazine's "Rocky Mountain Cowgirl Reporter."

What follows is a scene from our first family Christmas after returning to Pueblo. Early that morning, Larry and I went to our daughter Sue's house. Our son Kelly, his wife Marcia, and their children joined us too. I felt happy to be with the entire family again, and watching the youngsters play with their holiday gifts boosted my spirits considerably.

As I followed Sue into the kitchen to help her make coffee, she said, "I'm so glad you guys moved back to Colorado."

"I am too, hon," I replied. "It wasn't difficult persuading your Dad."

Taking coffee and goodies into the living room, I overheard Larry talking about our experience at the Telluride Film Festival which I covered for *Uptown-Marquee, Colorado Senior Beacon*, and KOAA Online. "Your mom got in trouble with Roger Ebert," he reported to Kelly.

"But it was all your fault," I chimed in.

Feigning innocence, Larry asked what I meant by that.

"You know very well what I mean. You wouldn't go with me to take Ebert's picture when I wanted one,' I complained.

"I could see he was busy, but you rushed up and took his photo anyway. It was not a pretty sight," Larry reminded me.

"Not for Ebert, anyway," I admitted. "He informed me my picture taking was ruining his videotaping, so I told him **his** videotaping was ruining **my** picture of him. He was not amused."

"But I was," Larry added. "From a safe distance. And don't forget I did get a great shot of you and Billy Crudup after you introduced him at his session there."

"That was sooo sweet of you," I cooed, and we both laughed. Glancing at a roomful of smiling faces, I knew our silly banter entertained everyone.

Kelly asked if we liked our new home. Knowing how much their mom and dad love movies, he and Sue had picked out a house for us located within five minutes of the town's new multiplex theater. "It's just great," I replied. "We've been seeing about three films a week at Tinseltown."

No doubt about it. Whether living in San Diego or Pueblo, movies assumed a major importance in our lives.

The Telluride Connection

Because driving from Pueblo to Telluride, the site of one of the world's most highly regarded film festivals, takes only about four hours, Larry and I decided not to miss this acclaimed festival while living in Colorado. Although suffering from the high altitude of that picturesque mountain community, we enjoy interacting with valuable film contacts there. For the past 28 years, this historic Colorado mining town has been **the** place to be during Labor Day weekend for actors, filmmakers, and movie buffs.

Our first Telluride experience surprised us in many ways. We had no idea what to expect. Unlike other film festivals, the program is a closely guarded secret until opening day. And we knew nothing about the tradition of standing in line, sometimes for over an hour, to get a good seat for the movies and events we wanted to see. Fortunately, our good friend David Kimball from Denver's Landmark Corporation took us under his wing and helped with our orientation. Otherwise, we might still be lost in Telluride searching for the gondola and the Chuck Jones (he's the Bugs Bunny artist) Theatre.

Showing up early for one of those lines turned out to be a stroke of luck for me. On Labor Day morning, Billy Crudup appeared in a special "Conversation Session" at the Telluride Court House. Shelly Westerman, a sound editor for *Jesus' Son*, tipped me off about Crudup's schedule while standing in line for a film the night before. Because I wanted to interview the young actor after seeing his amazing performance in *Jesus' Son*, I researched his background on the Internet. Hoping to catch Crudup before the program, Larry and I arrived shortly after 8:30 a.m. and were the first ones in line for the 10 a.m. session.

After a few minutes, a petite brunette showed up and began asking Tom Goodman, the program coordinator, questions about Crudup. Davia Nelson, from PBS (*Lost and Found Sounds*), had been recruited to moderate the session at the last minute. Eavesdropping on them, I interrupted and recited everything I knew about Crudup's films, awards, and so on. "Would **you** introduce him for me?" Nelson pleaded.

Without pausing for even a second, I agreed. Crudup, stunned by my in-depth introduction, sought me out after the program and thanked me personally. However, I almost spoiled this memorable experience with a flippant response. While talking with Crudup, a member of the audience came up to speak with the star. He wanted Crudup's opinion concerning who was a better actor, Skeet Ulrich or Billy Crudup. Crudup answered with a smile, "Skeet Ulrich, of course."

I added that Ulrich was "the poor man's Johnny Depp"—to which the man replied, "Really? I'll tell him that. I'm his father."

Mortified, I apologized, calling Larry over to bail me out. "I'm just kidding, sir. I've always admired your son's acting. Haven't I, Larry?" I begged. My helpful spouse came through for me again. "Right! She gave Skeet Ulrich high marks in her review of *Chill Factor*," he declared.

In addition to Crudup, we met Richard Farnsworth, David Lynch, Roger Ebert, Catherine Denueve, Peter Sellars, and Ally Sheedy during our first trip to Telluride. On opening night, Walt Disney's *The Straight Story* had its American premiere there. Farnsworth, Oscar nominee for *Comes a Horseman*, told me after the screening that the Alvin Straight role meant more to him than his previous favorite, *The Grey Fox*. Portraying a WWII veteran who travels across America's heartland on a John Deere lawn-mower to reconcile with his ailing brother, Farnsworth gave a brilliant performance in this poignant movie, which sadly proved to be his last.

Deneuve, an Oscar nominee in 1992 for *Indochine* and look-ing just as beautiful in person as on the big screen, received one of the festival's special tributes. Although famous for her many serious roles during the past 35 years, she spoke most warmly about her film musicals, especially the classic *Umbrellas of Cherbourg*. "I love everything about musicals," the Grand Dame of European film responded to my question about this genre. "You feel like you have wings on, and everyone on the set seems so happy!"

Peter Sellars, the festival's guest director, presided impishly over Denueve's award session. Noted for his *Nixon in China* opera, Sellars beamed with joy at the French icon's enthusiasm for musicals. After the program, he came up to me and gave me a big hug. "Thanks so much for asking that question," he said. Wow, did I feel special! But the next day, Larry told me he saw Sellars hugging everyone on the street, so that feeling didn't last long.

Although Lynch, another festival honoree, seemed out of reach because of his "bodyguards," I caught up with him right after his tribute program. Because a young critic friend of mine, Greg Muskewitz, views Lynch as the greatest director alive today, I was eager to talk with him. Complimenting the filmmaker on his fine direction of *The Straight Story*, I then asked for an explana-tion of the theme behind his disturbing *Lost Highway*. "It's based on a condition called psychogenic fugue," he said. That didn't help much, but at least it came from the master himself, and I had something to report to Greg.

One of the festival's big disappointments came with the premiere of Woody Allen's *Sweet and Lowdown*, starring Sean Penn. While the jazz music was heavenly, the film itself didn't soar. Larry summed it up best by saying, "Allen rushed his movie to Telluride before he had time to put in the funny parts."

The following year we were fortunate to attend the festival's world premiere of *Chinese Coffee*, a movie directed by and starring Al Pacino. Pacino introduced his film, but he didn't stay to watch it. He should have, for the positive audience responses would have pleased him. *Shadow of the Vampire*, an extraordinary satire about obsessive filmmaking, also screened that year. After viewing this unusual movie, I interviewed one of its stars, Willem Dafoe, who later earned an Academy Award nomination for his portrayal of "a vampire playing an actor playing a vampire." Soft-spoken and thoughtful, Dafoe charmed me with details about his amazing physical and emotional transformation for this campy role. (Dafoe's complete interview appears on pages 84 to87.)

Because of the casual atmosphere at Telluride, actors and other film folks mingle informally with non-show biz participants. Danny Glover, appearing in connection with his movie *Boesman and Lena*, seemed appreciative of the help I gave him regarding the festival schedule. He had just arrived when we met. Suffering from a leg injury, he couldn't stay for the entire program. Former child star George "Foghorn" Winslow, the kid with the basso-profundo voice in *Gentlemen Prefer Blondes*, visited with us about his current film work under the name of Micajah Mott. He just finished *Bedazzled* and *Little Nicky*. We also had a friendly chat with Peter Riegert (*Crossing Delancy*) at the opening night party. He mentioned that *By Courier*, a short film he directed, which also earned an Oscar nomination, would be screening at the festival.

The following year, much of the excitement at Telluride's Annual Film Festival happened off-screen. More than usual, Larry and I faced situations filled with suspense, adventure, humor, and exotic food. During that hectic 2001 Labor Day weekend, we got lost in the mountains at midnight, sampled Indian cuisine prepared by a famous director, and received unsolicited advice from Roger Ebert. Before explaining all that, here are my reactions to some of the films we saw at the 2001 filmfest:

Lantana. This unusual missing-persons thriller from Australia reminded me even happy marriages can fall apart. I was impressed by the intense performances of the film's ensemble cast, especially Anthony LaPaglia's (*Murder One*) portrayal of a detective with more on his mind than solving a crime.

The Cat's Meow. Peter Bogdanovich directed this version of an incident on William Randolph Hearst's yacht that resulted in the death of producer Thomas Ince. The movie is notable mostly for Kirsten Dunst's mature turn as Marion Davies. When introducing his film, Bogdanovich referred to Dunst's performance as "a gift to us all." I agree. Still, Edward Hermann seemed too pathetic as Hearst, and I had trouble accepting Eddie Izzard as Charlie Chaplin.

A Shot in the Heart. Although made for HBO, the Telluride audience got first viewing of this new twist on the Gary Gilmore story. Giovanni Ribisi is heartbreaking as the younger brother of convicted killer Gilmore, superbly acted by Elias Koteas. Under Agnieszka Holland's expert direction, this television film appears destined for recognition come Emmy Award time.

Speedy. My sides still ache from laughing so much at Harold Lloyd's great silent comedy, especially those carnival mishaps and that amazing street brawl scene. Now I know why Lloyd ranks as one of filmdom's comic geniuses.

The Mystic Masseur. I didn't want this delightful Merchant Ivory film to end. It focuses on one man's burning desire to become a writer. "Put my picture on the cover," Ganesh insists to the printer of his first book, a catechism about the Hindu religion. The movie showcases Aasif Mandvi's (*The Siege*) acting versatility as his character ages. It also shows why Om Puri (*East Is East*) received one of the 2001 festival tributes. Although portraying a manipulative and dominating father-in-law, the veteran Indian

actor still evoked my sympathy for the character he played. Ismail
Merchant directed with his trademark classy touch.

Because I had interviews scheduled, I couldn't attend the
screening of *Mulholland Drive*. And, wouldn't you know it, Larry
talked of nothing else after seeing this latest David Lynch film.
I'm sorry I missed it.

Fortunately, I **didn't** miss the "Conversation Session" with
Peter Bogdanovich. He's a fabulous storyteller. Joking about mistakes of the past, Bogdanovich confessed his arrogance after the
success of *The Last Picture Show*. "I decided to make a musical
even though I knew nothing about them," he said. "When Gene
Kelly called me to offer his help, I turned him down because I
thought I could handle it. Well, of course, *At Long Last Love*
flopped miserably."

For me, the highlight of the festival came as the result of an
invitation to a midnight supper celebrating *The Mystic Masseur*.
However, finding hosts Ann and Vincent Mai's mountain home
became an adventure with almost as much suspense as an Alfred
Hitchcock film. No matter how many wrong exits or twists and
turns stood in our way, Larry and I were determined to attend the
party. Our persistence paid off. Greeted by Ismail Merchant himself, who served as master chef for the occasion, we then mingled
with such VIPs as James Ivory, Salman Rushdie, Faye Dunaway,
Aasif Mandvi, Peter Sellars, Om Puri, and legendary tabla player
Zakir Hussein. Although Roger Ebert failed to appear, he called
The Mystic Masseur "a lovely film" after its screening. I told him
Larry and I identified with the main character because our first
book had been published during the past year. "Be sure to put
your picture on the cover just like Ganesh did," he quipped. "Too
late for that, Roger," I replied.

The opening of a new 500-seat theater called "The Galaxy"
made it possible for more participants to see the movies of their
choice in 2001. But it was still necessary to stand in line for an
hour prior to the showing of most films. Only festival patrons
avoid a long wait for admission. They pay over $2000 for a spe-
cial festival pass and are seated before everyone else. At one
event, Larry decided to take a closer look at this distinguished

group. Leaving his place in line, he checked them out as carefully as possible. "I sense no tension among the patrons, and they sure smell good," he reported.

At last our goal in life became clear. If we earn more money by taking on extra jobs, writing another book, and mortgaging our house, someday we too might become relaxed and sweet-smelling patrons of Telluride's Annual Film Festival.

Taos, Too

Taos, New Mexico, another picturesque community within driving distance from Pueblo, also hosts an annual filmfest—the Taos Talking Picture Festival. Larry and I enjoyed attending this event in 2000 and planned a second visit in 2001. Instead of giving out trophies and plaques, Taos honors outstanding filmmakers in more creative ways. At the 2000 program, Anjelica Huston not only won the coveted Maverick Award for her vision and independent spirit as director of *Bastard Out of Carolina*, she also received a painting by one of her favorite artists. And, newcomer Daniel Yoon, winner of the Taos Land Grant Award for demonstrating passion and inventiveness in his debut film, was given five acres of New Mexico land.

Because so many people stood in line to see the Huston presentation, we worried about getting seats. But I soon spotted another one of John Huston's daughters working her way through the crowd. As Anjelica's sister, Allegra, walked by me, I noticed she was shivering. "I wish I'd brought my sweater," she complained. Shameless as always, I called out, "Here, Allegra, take this coat. I already have a jacket." Allegra, who was scheduled to moderate her sister's Q&A session, wore my coat during the entire afternoon's program. And we walked in right behind her—almost like part of the family.

Huston, looking casually elegant in a simple blue denim outfit, had no trouble captivating the standing-room-only crowd attending the screening of her film. But she warned the audience, "This was my innocent effort before I thought seriously about directing. I don't expect you to enjoy it. I'll just be happy if you endure it."

Originally made for TNT, Huston's "innocent effort" caused quite a stir when completed. Because it tells a disturbing story of child abuse and rape, the film contains some intensely violent scenes. Although asked to eliminate these scenes, Huston refused.

"If I had cut those scenes, there would have been no movie," she explained. "When Ted Turner wouldn't allow the film to be seen on any of his networks, I was so disappointed I went to bed for a few days," Huston recalled. "But I'll always be grateful to him for the opportunity to make that film," she added. Later, her controversial movie was accepted at the Cannes Film Festival and played on Showtime. Huston's second film as a director, Agnes Browne, was released to widespread critical acclaim.

The following night at a party honoring all award recipients, I discussed some of my favorite Huston films with the Oscar-winning actress (*Prizzi's Honor*). Under the category of "stupid things I've done," I regret demonstrating to Huston a funny curtsy she performed while playing Cinderella's wicked stepmother in *Ever After*. I thought I really blew it with her. But she just laughed and said, "I'll be sure to remember you!" And she did. A few months later, I received a personal note thanking me for the articles I wrote about her.

Eeny, meeny, miney, mo—which films to see among so many offered? That was the question Larry and I asked each other at our first Taos festival. We certainly chose the right one in the case of *Post Concussion*. Directed by Land Grant recipient Daniel Yoon, this semi-autobiographical film takes viewers into the strange world of a workaholic executive who must change his life after suffering a brain injury. "Finishing this project was a real challenge for me, especially since I have no background in film," Yoon admitted modestly. But his photogenic mother, who appeared in his film and attended the festival with him, told me her son had lots of help from his friends. Clearly, this entertaining seriocomedy represented a labor of love by the Yoon family and their supporters. I'm convinced it should be seen nationwide. Distributors, are you listening?

Our plans to participate in the Taos Talking Picture Festival 2001 and to meet this year's Maverick Award honoree, Elizabeth Taylor, fell flat. Actually, I'm the one who took the fall. When I broke the news about not being able to cover the festival because of my accident, one of my editors said, "Just make something up." Following that intriguing advice, I turned in this "Trippin' to Taos" piece (for the May 2001 Colorado Senior Beacon):

Now I know why people call mini-carpets "throw rugs." One recently threw me face-first onto the edge of my bathtub. Results? A broken arm and head injury. Meeting me as I staggered out of the emergency room, my husband took a concerned look at my sling, cast, and turban bandage. "How **was** Sarajevo?" he asked.

"That's not funny, Larry," I moaned. "It really hurts, and because of a stupid accident, we're going to miss the Taos Talking Picture Festival this year." However, dear reader, one should never underestimate the power of imagination.

That's how, while recuperating, I took a magic carpet ride to Taos for the April film festivities held in that picturesque New Mexico town. (Skeptical? Just blame it on the head injury.)

Dinner with a living Hollywood legend emerged as the highlight of this fantasy trip. Everyone knows Elizabeth Taylor is the last of the Great Movie Stars, so it was a thrill to see her in person. She received the Festival's Maverick Award, an honor given each year to a cinema artist "who has retained his or her unique vision over the course of a distinguished career." Although Liz already owns two Oscars (for *Who's Afraid of Virginia Wolfe* and *Butterfield 8*) and was dubbed Dame Elizabeth by the Queen of England, this remarkable woman deserves as many awards as she can collect after fifty-five years as a Hollywood leading lady.

Immediately following her festival tribute, Larry and I joined Liz for dinner at the Holiday Inn Don Fernando.

She looked lovely in a white jacket that contrasted dramatically with her dark hair and famous violet eyes. After congratulating her on such an amazing film career, I told about what my mother did when MGM was searching for a child to star in

National Velvet. "She sent the studio a picture of me on a horse," I said.

"I wonder how many other mothers did the same thing?" Liz mused. "But I think you're lucky you didn't get the part. I hurt my back during filming *National Velvet*, and that was probably the beginning of all my health problems."

Larry pointed to my cast and added, "Betty Jo has had her share of those too. Looks like both of you are real survivors."

"And *you* are a real sweetheart," Liz tossed back at him.

Suddenly, it dawned on me that Liz is between husbands now. No wonder I breathed a sigh of relief when dinner ended. After all, this is *my* fantasy, not Larry's.

Mile High Memories

Most Colorado press screenings and personal appearance tours take place in Denver. That means Larry puts on his chauffeur's cap and drives me to the Mile High City for many of these events. One of my favorite actors, Aidan Quinn, came to Denver to promote his film *This Is My Father*. His brother Paul, the film's writer/director, tagged along. I teased them by saying, "Most siblings would do anything to avoid working with each other after they grow up. What made you decide to take on this project together?"

Aidan pointed out his cinematographer brother, Declan (*Leaving Las Vegas*), also worked on the film. "It was a family labor of love," he declared.

"Because we know each other so well, we really saved time," explained Paul. Clearly excited about his first outing as a director, he admitted to a sense of awe about his two famous brothers.

Looking more relaxed and nonchalant than his younger brother, Aidan added, "We get along well, but we work intensely. Like most brothers, we get irritated at each other sometimes."

Filmed mostly in Ireland, *This Is My Father* features Aidan as a poor Irish farmer who falls for a young lass outside his social class. For this role, the actor drastically altered his handsome appearance. Watching him in this film, it's hard to believe he's the same leading man from *Desperately Seeking Susan, Practical Magic,* and *Blink.* "Paul made me gain weight, and my make-up man gave me a prosthetic eye piece," Aidan revealed.

After the discussion, I told Aidan how much I admired his performance, partly because of my Irish roots. I related how my Grandmother Donahue stowed away on a boat when she was only 14 years old to come to America. "She wanted to get away from her brothers in Ireland who mistreated her," I said.

I'll never forget the concerned look in Aidan's piercing blue eyes as I talked to him about my grandmother's experience. He leaned closer and asked, "What did they do to her?"

"She refused to tell us," I replied.

Aidan shook his head and frowned. He made me believe he actually wanted to know the answer to his question. Now, that's what I call acting. Or maybe he's just a very nice man.

If a contest were held to name the strangest movie screened in Denver during our first year back in Colorado, *Passion in the Desert* would win hands down—with nothing even close as competition. My sister-in-law Donna, another movie addict, attended this screening with me. After the film ended, we couldn't wait to jump in the car. As soon as the doors closed, we stared at each other, then burst out laughing. "Did we just witness our first animal porn movie?" I asked Donna.

"Maybe," she answered. "I've never watched someone fall in love with a leopard, smear mud all over himself, and walk on all fours to impress her before."

I told Donna one critic gave this movie a "family safe" seal of approval. "He must have meant the Addams family," she said.

When the *Air Bud* sequel screened in Denver, critics were invited to bring children along with them. Our little group included two grandsons, Sam and Taylor, and a granddaughter, Leslie— all three in elementary school at the time. Although traveling a long distance in a car with young children can be a trial, this trip was a treat instead. Even at their ages, all three grandchildren already loved films. Because we played our "I'm thinking of a movie" game, the time flew by. It amazes me to this day how many answers turned out to be Jim Carrey films.

At the theater, a drawing was held to give away a huge *Air Bud* movie poster, and Taylor won! He became the only youngster in Colorado who owned a poster signed by the canine star—with a furry paw print, of course.

EPISODE FIVE: FADE OUT

Life on the Web

A new world awaits movie fans on the Internet, and I'm excited to be part of it. Although still doing film and video commentary for James Grasso's *Colorado Senior Beacon*, I began writing online reviews of films spotlighted by Movie Index, a group reporting the amount of violent acts, sexual situations, and strong language in particular films. Under the direction of Assistant News Director Greg Boyce and with the expert technical help of Webmaster Mark Lubischer, my ReelTalk Movie Reviews now appear as a special feature of KOAA Online, an NBC-affiliate television Web site.

After writing for print media during the past five years, I faced a challenge in adapting my style to the Web's more informal emphasis. I needed help—but who ya gonna call? The Online Film Critics Society seemed like a good place to start.

Harvey Karten, founder of OFCS, pulled no punches in evaluating my early online reviews as "woefully inadequate." Ouch, that hurt! But he gave me suggestions on how to improve. Following Karten's advice to add more depth and personal reactions, I finally earned a bit of praise from him. He called my *American Psycho* critique "one helluva good review" and referred me to a mentoring program sponsored by his organization.

That's how I became acquainted with Ian Waldron-Mantgani, the famous "UK Critic," who served as my mentor for the next few months. Like *Harold and Maude*, a vast age difference made our relationship quite unusual. Ian, besides living across the ocean in Liverpool, had not even graduated from high school. And yet, here he was, teaching a grandmother—one who once worked as a college dean and vice president, no less—how to write better. Although I found out about Ian's youthful age by checking out his Web site, I don't think he knew how old I was when we started. Frankly, I got a big kick out of the entire situation, realizing something like this could happen only in cyberspace.

Ian helped me understand the importance of including more details and fewer puns in my reviews. I beamed like a grade school student receiving high marks every time I read his positive e-mail comments about my later reviews. These are my favorites:

"Impressive piece. Detailed, informed, and most importantly, sincere." (*Bring It On*)

"Fantastic opening paragraph. Witty, to the point, doesn't ramble, concise. Masterpiece!" (*Hollow Man*)

"Bursting with enthusiasm and has clear, vivid descriptions and evidence for its points. I knew nothing about the film when I read the review, and its title sounded pretty dumb, but now I can't wait for it. Well done! (*The Tao of Steve*)

When Ian recommended me for OFCS membership, I was elated. I applied right away, only to discover the group had closed its membership for the year. Or so they wanted me to believe.

Next, I turned to Cinemarati, a new Web alliance for online film commentary. One of its members, MaryAnn Johanson took me under her wing. Known as "The Flick Filosopher" and named "one of America's finest online movie critics" by *Variety*, MaryAnn inspired me to break out of the mold and try different writing approaches. For example, because of her influence, my review of *Bridget Jones's Diary* for KOAA Online took the form of a letter to an imaginary British friend, as follows:

Dear Emily,

How many times have we agreed that *Bridget Jones' Diary* couldn't possibly be made into a decent movie? I remember the fits we threw when Texan Renee Zellweger got the title role. You wanted Kate Winslet and I preferred Toni Collette. Well, sweetie, I just saw the sneak preview and couldn't wait to tell you we were wrong! Please don't get angry with me, but I think the film is better than the book.

That little Zellwegger gal practically transforms herself into our darling Bridget. Of course, she's not petite in this movie like she was in *Nurse Betty*, having gained over 20 pounds to play the part. I'm glad she wasn't afraid to show off her extra weight in some pretty revealing scenes. I loved the way her full-bodied charms overwhelmed a skimpy bunny costume in the disastrous "tarts and vicars" party sequence. She also sounds terribly British, so we needn't have worried about her American accent ruining everything.

I think you'll enjoy the performances of Hugh Grant and Colin Firth, too. Grant is terrific as Daniel Cleaver. He's just as slimy and seductive as we imagined Bridget's flirtatious boss to be. What a change from that shy bookstore owner in *Notting Hill*! And casting the dignified Colin Firth as Mark Darcy, Bridget's stuffy childhood friend, was a stroke of genius, if you ask me. Did you realize this is the same bloke who played **the** Mr. Darcy in BBC's *Pride and Prejudice*? Oh, crikey, you're the one who told me author Helen Fielding considers her book an updating of Jane Austen's classic, so you probably know all about Mr. Firth, too.

We were correct about one thing, Emsy. The role of Bridget's newly liberated mum doesn't suit Gemma Jones, the actress we admired so much in that television series about *The Duchess of Duke Street*. Your idea about Brenda Blethyn being better for the comedy bits is right on target. Brenda would have chewed the scenery in Mum's TV spots for all she's worth, just like she took over the screen in *Little Voice*, whereas Gemma just smiles and looks wide-eyed.

Call me sacrilegious, but I believe most of the story changes worked very well here. The best example is when Mark Darcy helps Bridget cook a meal for her friends. The big event ends in chaos anyway—thanks to an unwelcome appearance by Daniel Cleaver. Although this incident isn't in the book, I quite approve of the way it highlights the humor and apparent hopelessness of Bridget's relationship problems.

I know we made fun of Bridget's plans for self-improvement and weight loss while reading her amusing diary. We laughed at her whining over being a 30-something "Singleton" among a world of "Smug Marrieds."

But I'm warning you, Emily, the movie makes all that seem more poignant and real. I felt so relieved when Bridget finally discovered true friends and lovers liked her "just the way she is."

Anyway, Emsy, please see *Bridget* soon. I'm dying to hear your reactions!

Your v. g. friend,
Betts

With over one billion total Web pages available, people throughout the world can communicate with each other almost instantaneously, and that includes movie fans. (My favorite movie Web sites are listed on pages 75 to 78.) Filmmaker Francis Ford Coppola established a complete motion picture production studio on the Web with his Zoetrope Virtual Studio. I've received film-related Internet messages from all over the U.S.A. and from as far away as Argentina, Canada, France, Australia, England, and India. As I mentioned before, age is no barrier. One of my e-mail buddies is Adam Hakari, a 16 year-old movie critic in Wisconsin's Twin Cities area. He called his first Web site *Confessions of a Teenage Movie Fanatic*, and his passion for films almost equals mine.

Reel Reflections

I often wonder what caused my life-long addiction to movies. Even now, as much as I hate those repetitive special effects, loud soundtracks, and crude attempts at humor that ruin so many of today's movies for me (*The Mummy Returns, Any Given Sunday,* and *Road Trip* come to mind as prime examples), I can't wait to get my next film fix. Going on these make-believe journeys while sitting in a darkened theater still makes my endorphins kick into high gear. While saddened and dazed over the terrorist attacks on the World Trade Center and the Pentagon, I sought refuge from reality inside my favorite movie theater, thereby proving the degree of my addiction. Because confession is good for the soul, I admit enjoying films mostly for their escapist entertainment qualities. But I also love to be enchanted by cinematic artistry, enlightened by a great story, and inspired by memorable performances.

Film critic Diana Saenger says much the same thing in *Everyone Wants My Job! The ABC's of Entertainment Writing* (Picadilly Books, Ltd., 2000) when she observes, "The power of film makes us laugh, cry, or get angry. . . (Movies) are probably the most influential medium in our world. They showcase our history, offer us escapism, and become a part of our everyday lives. . . Films guide us in how to think and behave." (Pages 71 to 75 contain titles of other cool books about movies.)

When I think about films that did **more** than entertain me, that list is long enough to make up another book. In fact, author Raymond Teague mentions many of them in *Reel Spirit—A Guide to Movies That Inspire, Explore, and Empower* (Unity House, 2000). According to Teague, films have become our cultural storyboard for spiritual exploration and renewal. His book lists 400 movies that offer life-enhancing lessons for modern viewers. In addition to films with an obvious religious theme, like *The Ten Commandments*, some wonderful surprises are included. Who would expect to see such movies as *National Lampoon's Christmas Vacation* and *Stuart Saves His Family* in a book about spiritual messages? But here they are, along with *The Life of Brian, As Good As It Gets, Gone with the Wind, Sleepless in Seattle*, and other intriguing listings.

Steve Martin's character in *Grand Canyon* declares, "All life's riddles are answered in the movies." Hyperbole, yes. But many important questions have been answered for me by the movies.

What happens when a person is consumed by obsession? Watching Jimmy Stewart stalk Kim Novak in *Vertigo* showed the dangers involved. Is there a universal longing for home? Judy Garland's search for the way back to Kansas in *Wizard of Oz* proves that to be true. Can someone be too ambitious? *Citizen Kane* dispels all doubts. What's it like to be different and made fun of because you are? Films like *Simon Birch, Edward Scissorhands,* and *The Elephant Man* gave me an inkling of those feelings. How can a teacher motivate students? *Stand and Deliver* and *Dangerous Minds* offer valuable tips through super perform- ances by Edward James Olmos and Michelle Pfeiffer respective- ly. What are the symptoms of alcoholism? Lee Remick's per- formance in *Days of Wine and Roses* reveals more than any text- book, and so on. Because acting, writing, music, photography, and technical know-how all come together in a movie, filmmaking is the central art of our time. When everything works, something magical happens. A masterpiece that dazzles the senses while touching your heart or tickling your funny bone reaches the big screen. Film gems like *To Kill a Mockingbird, Moulin Rouge, Adam's Rib, Kolya, Waiting for Guffman, Casablanca, Little Voice, The Godfather, Topsy-Turvy, Raiders of the Lost Ark, Witness, Blazing Saddles, Night of the Hunter, Laura, Silence of the Lambs, Gladiator,* and *Singin' in the Rain*, come along too rarely—but they are worth waiting for.

If I had to pick a recent year with the most disturbing film releases, it would be 1998. During that 12-month period, movie- goers saw the bloodiest battle scenes ever filmed in *Saving Private Ryan*. They viewed filmdom's most gross-out comedy sequences in *There's Something about Mary*. They also watched Oprah Winfrey urinate in the fields in *Beloved*, Warren Beatty spout obscene rap lyrics in *Bulworth*, James Woods survive the screen's goriest vampire bloodfest in *John Carpenter's Vampires*, and practically everyone in *Very Bad Things* engage in illicit sex, murder, and dismemberment. "Cinematic shock treatment" emerged as the significant trend in movies that year, probably to gain attention from an audience exposed daily to television pro- grams also becoming more and more graphic. Movie moguls wor- ried that people used to viewing programs like *South Park,*

Millennium, Cops, and *The Profiler* for free might balk at paying for milder entertainment at the multiplexes.

Still,1998 also saw the release of some wonderful films. Who can forget the incredible heroism of tiny *Simon Birch* and *Mulan*'s courageous efforts to save her father from military service? Or the remarkable singing performance of Jane Horrocks and Michael Caine's deliciously smarmy attempt to make her a star in *Little Voice*? Or Adam Sandler's hilarious rendition of "Love Stinks" in *The Wedding Singer*? Or the passionate dancing of those Irish sisters in *Dancing at Lughnasa*? Or Drew Barrymore, as a very assertive Cinderella, picking up and carrying her Prince away from awestruck bandits in *Ever After*? Or that sexy sword fight between Antonio Banderas and Catherine Zeta-Jones in *The Mask of Zorro*?

One fellow critic dismissed my reviews as being too fan-oriented. Perhaps she's right. I admit it's hard to be objective about such filmmakers as Baz Luhrmann, Jonathan Mostow, and Ridley Scott. I'm blown away by the exciting visuals of Luhrmann's *Stricly Ballroom* and *Moulin Rouge*, the heart-pounding suspense in Mostow's *Breakdown* and *U-572,* and the you-are-there feeling of Scott's *Blade Runner* and *Alien*. I confess to being overwhelmed by admiration for stars like Billy Crudup, Annette Bening, Antonio Banderas, Kurt Russell, Russell Crowe, Jennifer Lopez, Johnny Depp, Reese Witherspoon, Michael Caine, Harrison Ford, Samuel L. Jackson, and Jackie Chan. I can't help it if my regard for their exceptional talent shines through in my critiques.

Still, I try to offer more than an opinion when writing a review. I like to give the reader something to think about in terms of what matters in the film, but with a different twist whenever possible. Because I see almost two hundred movies a year, it's easy for me to include comparisons and contrasts of cinematic elements and performances in my articles. When people disagree with me about a film, I want them to have a better understanding of their own values, beliefs, and feelings after reading my work. But most of all, I hope readers are entertained. (A selection of my ReelTalk reviews can be found on pages 117 to 246.)

In *Screening History* (Harvard University Press, 1994), author Gore Vidal confessed that as he looked back over his life, he realized the only thing he ever really liked to do was go to the movies. That makes two of us.

—THE END—

"If we bring a little joy into yer humdrum lives, it makes us feel as though our hard work ain't been in vain fer nothin'."

—Jean Hagen in *Singin' in the Rain* (1952)

ADDED ATTRACTIONS

Still Shots from Larry's Gallery

Having a movie addict in the family can't be easy for loved ones. The best thing to do is join them. I'm thankful my husband realized this. He's been a great enabler—taking me to films as often as possible, driving me to interviews and festivals, and serving as a photographer for my articles. Here are a few of his photos.

**"I was the biggest box office star in the world for two decades."
—Mickey Rooney at Palm Springs International Film Festival
(1995).**

Allegra Huston (L) introduces big sister Anjelica at Taos Talking Picture Festival 2000.

Willem Dafoe (Center) ponders a question from Leonard Maltin at Telluride Film Festival (2000)

Angelina Jolie (R) and Jonny Lee Miller (L) enlighten Betty Jo Tucker about *Hackers* (San Diego, 1995).

Filmmaker M.Night Shyamalan gets serious regarding *Wide Awake*, his first feature movie (San Diego, 1998).

Larry Tucker (L) helps music man Saul Chaplin with *The Golden Age of Movie Musicals and Me* book signing (San Diego, 1995).

The sublime Hope Davis and director Greg Mottola praise *The Daytrippers* (San Diego, 1995).

Yes, it really is Guy Pearce, and he's talking about *L.A. Confidential* (San Diego, 1997).

Billy Crudup converses with Davia Nelson about filming *Jesus' Son* (Telluride, 1998).

Brendan Fraser (center) makes big hit at *George of the Jungle* world premiere in San Diego's Wild Animal Park (1997)

RESOURCE FIXES FOR MOVIE ADDICTS

When you love movies as much as I do, you want to read everything you can about films and filmmaking, either in books or on the Internet. Listed below are some of my favorite books and Web sites.

Must-Read Books:

***The Art of The Matrix*. Edited by Spencer Lamm (Newmarket Press, 2000)**
An intriguing look at the painstaking process of producing a major special effects extravaganza. (Yes, I did admire those special effects in *The Matrix*. Too bad I still can't figure out what the story was all about.)

***Casablanca: Script and Legend/The 50th Anniversary Edition*. Howard Koch (Overlook Press, 1992).**
The original script, 25 classic stills, and a behind-the-scenes account of what went into making a film that keeps turning up on lists of America's best-loved romantic adventures—no matter how much "time goes by."

***Cinematherapy: The Girl's Guide to Movies for Every Mood*. Nancy Peske and Beverly West (Dell Trade Paperback, 2000).**
Authors make amusing comments about the healing power of numerous "chick flicks." Tongue-in-cheek classifications include

such categories as "Phony Gals that Piss Us Off" (*Pretty Women, Fatal Attraction*) and "Dresses to Die For" (*Age of Innocence*).

Nothing too deep here. Still, Peske and West remind us of some oldies-but-goodies to check out again, like *It Happened One Night* and *Pride and Prejudice*.

Comedy Is a Man in Trouble: A History of Slapstick in the Movies. Alan Dale (University of Minnesota Press, 2000).

A survey of physical comedy in the movies from the days of Charlie Chaplin, Harold Lloyd, and Buster Keaton to today's masters, including Jim Carrey and the Farrelly brothers. (Where are the funny women? Don't ask Jerry Lewis.)

Everyone Wants My Job! The ABC's of Entertainment Writing. Diana Saenger (Picadilly Books, Ltd., 2000).

Helpful advice from a professional critic about how to review films, conduct interviews, market your work, and perform other tasks associated with this competitive field. Author sprinkles each chapter with celebrity quotations and anecdotes that make her book a delight to read. No wonder people want Diana's job. But she does caution wannabes about the hard work involved.

For Keeps. Pauline Kael (Dutton-Penguin Books, 1994).

In this impressive compendium, America's most renowned film critic, the late Pauline Kael, presented the best of her New Yorker reviews and other writings on movies from 1965 through 1991. More than 275 reviews are arranged chronologically, forming a 30-year history of the movies. (At over 1200 pages, *For Keeps* also makes a terrific doorstop.)

The Golden Age of Movie Musicals and Me. Saul Chaplin (University of Oklahoma Press, 1994).

A fascinating memoir by the man who served as songwriter, vocal arranger, pianist, musical director, or producer on more than sixty films during the Hollywood musical heyday. Chaplin writes candidly about the major performers and filmmakers he met while working on such movies as *High Society, On the Town, Seven Brides for Seven Brothers, American in Paris,* and *The Sound of*

Music. (Gossip tidbit: no love lost between Chaplin and Al Jolson, despite their collaboration on "The Anniversary Song.")

Great Movie Lines. Edited by Dale Tamajan (Fawcett Columbine, 1993).
Just for fun. This little treasure for trivia fans contains lines from famous movies and asks, "How many can you identify? (I missed a bunch.)

The Groove Book of Hollywood. Edited by Christopher Silvester (Grove Press, 2000).
A comprehensive anthology of Hollywood's 90-year movie history beginning with those one-reel 1909 Westerns and ending with the blockbusters of 2000. (It's true. Movie addicts can enjoy and learn from history, too.)

The Liveliest Art. Arthur Knight (The MacMillan Company, 1957).
A panoramic history of movies through the late 1950s emphasizing the growth of film from an 1895 novelty to an important 20th century art form. (Obviously, Knight hadn't seen *Scary Movie* or *Road Trip* yet.)

The Making of the Wizard of Oz. Aljean Harmetz (Hyperion — Special 60th Anniversary Edition, 1998).
The inside story behind the filming of this American movie classic. Harmetz describes how the film survived four directors, serious problems on the set, and changes in casting to become an all-time family favorite. Buddy Ebsen as the Scarecrow? Shirley Temple as Dorothy? Cut Dorothy singing "Over the Rainbow"? And other close calls.

Memo from David O.Selznick: The Creation of Gone with the Wind and other Modern Classics, As Revealed in the Producer's Private Letters. David O. Selznick; Edited and selected by Rudy Behlmer; Series Editor-Martin Scorsese; Introduction by Roger Ebert (Modern Library Edition, 2000).

A veritable treasure chest of Selznick memos exposes the inner workings of Hollywood's studio system of the 1930s and 40s. (Memo to self: remember to delete all incriminating e-mail messages.)

Moviola. **Garson Kanin (Simon and Shuster, 1979).**

Fiction, yes. But in this ultimate Hollywood novel, the life of movie mogul B.J. Farber seems so real one can't help wondering who the author used as a model—Louis B. Mayer? Samuel Goldwyn? David Selznick? As the ninety-two year old Farber reveals his journey to success as the head of a famous studio, Hollywood's legendary past comes brilliantly to life on the pages of Moviola.

My First Movie: Twenty Celebrated Directors Talk about Their First Film. **Stephen Lowenstein (Pantheon, 2001).**

Selected directors discuss their reactions to the experience of making their debut movies. Ang Lee, P.J. Hogan, Mira Nair, Pedro Almodovar, and Kevin Smith are among the filmmakers interviewed. Joy, terror, struggle, and regret are mentioned by most of these directors in their recollections. (Sounds like my first date.)

Reel Spirit: A Guide to Movies That Inspire, Explore, and Empower. **Raymond Teague (Unity House, 2000)**

An analysis of spirituality in the movies. Includes almost 400 movies, with reviews of such films as *It's a Wonderful Life, The Lion King, When Harry Met Sally, Malcolm X,* and the *Star Wars* series. (Guess who this author considers the most admirable character in Hollywood films? Here's a clue—it's a woman.)

Screening History. **Gore Vidal (Harvard University Press—Reissue Edition, 1994).**

Vidal recalls the films he loved while growing up in Washington, D.C. during the 1930s and reflects on the movies that meant the most to him, such as *The Prince and the Pauper* and *Young Mr. Lincoln.* (Funny, I saw those films, too—but they didn't impress me as much as *King Kong* and *Frankenstein*. Could this explain our different career paths?)

Which Lie Did I Tell: Or, More Adventures in the Screen Trade. William Goldman (Pantheon, 2000).

Screenwriter Goldman (*Butch Cassidy and the Sundance Kid, Marathon Man*) tells how he fought his way back to the top of his profession in the 1990s, a period he calls "the worst decade in Hollywood history." (Hey, what about *Silence of the Lambs* and *Thelma and Louise*?) Among other interesting items, Goldman explains his disappointment with *The Ghost and the Darkness*, a film he wrote that didn't do well upon its release. (It did, however, frighten me beyond belief. Those mysterious lions invade my nightmares more often now than the hungry shark from Jaws.)

Writing with Hitchcock: A Collaboration of Alfred Hitchcock and John Michael Hayes. Steven Derosa (Faber and Faber, 2001).

Author describes how Hitchcock and Hayes worked together on four of Hitchcock's early films (*The Trouble with Harry, Rear Window, To Catch a Thief,* and *The Man Who Knew Too Much*). Biographical sketches of both men as well as a breakdown of all four films are included. (Did Hitch really say that actors are like cattle? No, his comment was "Actors should be treated like cattle." Just his way of getting attention from the press, according to Norman Lloyd, one of Hitchcock's former actors, at the Telluride 2000 Film Festival.)

Cool Movie Web Sites:

Academy of Motion Picture Arts and Sciences (www.oscars.org)—All about Oscar. Includes a history of the Academy Awards, past winners, schedule, and glorious photos.

Apollo Movie Guide (www.apolloguide.com).—Well-written film, video, and DVD reviews by Dan Jardine and Brian Webster.

Believe Me (www.believe-me.com/main.htm)—Honest movie reviews by Jeffrey Huston, a critic who lets you know when he changes his mind after seeing a film more than once.

Cinephiles (www.cinephiles.net)—Comprehensive movie reviews and in-depth film analysis geared toward helping viewers appreciate cinema. Discussion boards also included.

Cinemarati (www.cinemarati.org)—A Web alliance for film commentary. Includes movie reviews, weekly articles, and lively Roundtable forum postings from online film critics and movie buffs.

Cozzi fan Tutti Celluloid Musings (www.cozzifantutti.com) —Humorous and perceptive movie reviews by Jill Cozzi and Gabriel Shanks.

Critical Eye (home.vicnet.net.au/~freeman)—Film and video reviews by Australian critic Mark Freeman, who's not a bit happy about that Crocodile Dundee image.

Film Festivals (www.filmfestivals.com)—Best site for keeping track of what's coming up at film festivals throughout the world.

The Flick Filosopher (*www.flickfilosopher.com*)—Creative film and video reviews by MaryAnn Johanson. Includes impressive "Movie-a-Day" feature.

Foreign Films (www.foreignfilms.com)—A guide to finding foreign films on the Web. Message board, user reviews, ratings, plot summaries, and interviews are also posted on this site.

Internet Movie Data Base (www.imdb.com)—Most ambitious movie web site to date. Catalog of information on over 250,000 films made and the people who helped make them.

ReelTalk Movie Reviews (www.koaa.com/community/entertainment/reeltalk)—KOAA TV's Web site where my own reviews, interviews, and film festival reports are posted.

Review Express (www.reviewexpress.com)—Spirited film, video, music, and book reviews by Diana Saenger. Interviews and "Justin's Journal" (comments by the USA's youngest movie critic) are also included.

Rotten Tomatoes (www.rottentomatoes.com)—Quotes and film reviews by the nation's top film critics. Site rates each movie as either "fresh" or "rotten" based on reviews submitted. (Warning: new forum feature can be addictive.)

The Snack Bar (www.ajhakari.com)—Passionate reviews of movies and video releases by Wisconsin teenager Adam Hakari.

UK Critic (www.ukcritic.com)—Ian Waldron-Mantgani's award-winning site contains articles, links, retrospectives and reviews of UK cinema releases.

Variety (www.variety.com)—Free to Variety subscribers. Others pay yearly fee which grants them access to daily publication plus archives.

Zoetrope Virtual Studio (www.zoetrope.com)—A complete motion picture production studio on the Web. Offers collaborative tools for writers, directors, producers, and other artists. Also features film-related discussion sections.

Studio Web Sites—Information on upcoming films is available from major movie studios online as follows:

Artisan (www.artisanfilms.com)
Columbia/Sony (www.sonypictures.com)
Dimension (www.dimensionfilms.com)
Disney (www.disneyfilms.com)
DreamWorks (www.dreamworks.com)
Fox Searchlight (www.foxsearchlight.com)
Lion's Gate (www.lionsgatefilms.com)
Metro-Goldwyn-Mayer (www.metrogoldwynmayer.com)
Miramax (www.miramax.com)
Paramount (www.paramount.com)
20th Century Fox (www.foxmovies.com)
Universal (www.universalpictures.com)
Warner Bros. (www.warnerbros.com)

INTERVIEWS

As a film critic, I've been fortunate to talk personally with a number of actors, directors, and screenwriters who were eager to discuss their careers and latest movies. Because artists are ultra-sensitive people, I decided to present the interviews in alphabetical order. (NOTE: no show biz ego was damaged in the conducting of these interviews.)

Joey Lauren Adams (*Forum Publications*, San Diego, April 24, 1997).

How far will filmmakers go to shock today's adult audiences? After seeing Miramax's *Chasing Amy*, some moviegoers may want to answer that question with a resounding, "Too far!" Although telling a very entertaining story, this comedy/drama contains possibly the most graphic language ever on film, making it difficult to watch at times despite a super breakthrough performance by Joey Lauren Adams (John Travolta's perky pie waitress in *Michael*). The convincing young actress plays a comic book artist with a lesbian life style who falls in love with a straight man and must struggle with the consequences.

During a recent interview at the San Diego Hyatt, Adams talked enthusiastically about her *Chasing Amy* role. Speaking in an unforgettable, almost gravelly voice, she admitted that the film's writer/director, Kevin Smith (*Clerks*), is her boyfriend and that he wrote the part especially for her. "The producers wanted a name star like Drew Barrymore, but Kevin stuck with me," she said proudly.

The petite Adams denied having any qualms about the strong language used by her character in *Chasing Amy*. "I'm a very frank and open person and can talk about anything," she affirmed. However, she confessed that her mother (who lives in the San Diego area) was uncomfortable with one of the scenes.

When asked about her favorite scene in the movie, the usually cheerful actress became rather serious. She explained that she had to show tremendous rage and emotion when her character tells off the man she loves after he complains about her past. Adams was so afraid she wouldn't do a good job that she blanked out right before the end of the scene. "When I came to, the crew was applauding and Kevin hugged me and said I did everything just right," Adams concluded softly. (She has won widespread critical acclaim for her work in this demanding scene.)

Adams smiled engagingly again as we talked about her musical talent. She plays the guitar, writes songs, and even sings one of her own compositions in *Chasing Amy*.

Calling herself a monotone, she claims she can only do her own songs. "But I did get a job once as a back-up singer in a country western band that toured China," she added impishly.

Adams, a native of Arkansas who lived for almost a year here in San Diego, said she hopes moviegoers will watch her new movie "with their hearts, rather than viewing it with any preconceived notions about lesbians."

While not for mainstream audiences, *Chasing Amy* brings a strong, unique female character to the big screen. It also provides insights into a controversial area of human relationships usually ignored by major filmmakers.

Annette Bening (*Uptown-Marquee*, San Diego, March, 2000).

Former San Diegan Annette Bening, named by the San Diego Film Critics as Best Actress of 1999 for her brilliant work in *American Beauty*, must be counting her blessings more than usual lately. In addition to her second Oscar nomination, she and husband Warren Beatty are expecting their fourth child soon. And, the versatile actress co-stars with Garry Shandling in a new comedy, *What Planet Are You From?*, scheduled for release the first week in March.

"Garry is a remarkable guy who's just naturally funny," Bening said in a recent telephone interview. "He's a very dear friend of mine, and it was a pleasure working with him. We had lots of laughs making this movie."

Matching wits with funnyman Garry Shandling should be no problem for Bening. Although she looks more delicate in person than on the big screen, the petite star has held her own with such powerful leading men as Harrison Ford, Robert DeNiro, Denzel Washington, Jack Nicholson, Michael Douglas, Kevin Spacey, and, of course, Warren Beatty.

Equally adept at drama and comedy, Bening can't say which she prefers. "I like to play a variety of roles. As long as the writing is good, that's the important thing," she pointed out. This attitude has helped her develop an enviable reputation for the diversity of her screen roles. Prior to *American Beauty*, Bening's dramatic portrayals have included a tragic Queen Mother in *Richard III*, an evil countess in *Valmont*, an unscrupulous con woman in *The Grifters*, and a mysterious government agent in *The Siege*.

Bening's delightful flair for comedy can be seen in *Mars Attacks* and *The American President* (which earned her a Golden Globe nomination). As a ditzy flower child in the former, she steals the show from Jack Nicholson. In the latter, her hilarious reactions to the President (Michael Douglas) when he phones her for a date bring down the house. Bening's parents (Grant and Shirley), who still live in San Diego, are not surprised at their daughter's success with comedy. Shirley Bening once told me, "Annette always kept us in stitches—she was a great mimic as a child."

How does Bening prepare for her roles? "It depends on the project," she explained. "Doing research helps, of course. It's a way to grow and learn more. For example, in *What Planet Are You From?* I play a recovering alcoholic, so I did some research in that area. But I don't like to talk about that a lot because it's not always important. Whatever works in the moment you're filming is best. I remember learning quite a bit about the CIA and the Middle East before shooting *The Siege*. But it depends on the project. And I don't have as much time to read now. I have to be more strategic with my time because I have kids."

Remembering fondly her early years in San Diego, Bening stated, "I lived in the San Carlos area. When I was in the 8th or 9th grade at Pershing Junior High, I saw my first play at the Old Globe Theatre. I recall it was by Shakespeare and I was so moved by it—by the vitality and energy of it. And somehow I understood it and just loved it. That's very important to me because I ended up with a life in the theater which is totally different from any-thing anyone in my family had done."

After honing her acting talent at San Diego Mesa College, San Francisco State University, and the American Conservatory Theatre, Bening garnered recognition early in her career. Before her Oscar nomination for *The Grifters*, she received a Tony nom-ination as well as the Clarence Derwent Award for Most Outstanding Debut Performance for *Coastal Disturbances*. Because of her love for live theater, she returned to the stage last year in a critically acclaimed Los Angeles production of Ibsen's *Hedda Gabler*.

Although Bening agrees it's sometimes difficult to combine marriage, family, and career, she seems to enjoy the challenge. "I consider myself lucky to be in a career where I can stop working for awhile and then start again," she declared. "I take a year and a half off when I have a baby, but I like to take time off between projects anyway—even when I'm not pregnant. Warren is a won-derful father. Still, it's the mother who has to take care of the nuts and bolts of child rearing. I don't mind. I always wanted to have children and a big family. I also like to work."

This interview served as an excellent example of Bening's skill at combining important parts of her life. She answered my questions on a cell phone while driving to pick up her kids. And, in spite of her success, Bening has not forgotten her San Diego friends. She concluded our conversation with, "Please tell every-one I appreciate that home town support."

Kaige Chen (*Uptown-Marquee*, April, 1999)

"I'm the only person who could have made this film," Kaige Chen explained matter-of-factly in a telephone interview from

Denver, Colorado. The award-winning director was referring to his awesome epic, *The Emperor and the Assassin*. He's probably right, for it's hard to imagine anyone but this renowned, hard-working Chinese filmmaker taking on such an ambitious project. Winner of the prestigious Palme d'Or at Cannes and a Golden Globe Best Foreign Film Award in 1993 for *Farewell, My Concubine*, Chen takes viewers back to the China of 2,000 years ago in his latest movie.

"This is a very special movie—a type of film you hardly ever see anymore," Chen declared. No doubt a movie like this would cost too much to film in most countries today. (At $20 million, Chen's film holds the record as the most expensive Asian movie to date.) There's also the controversial nature of the film's theme. Chen pointed out that *The Emperor and the Assassin* "tells the story of Ying Zheng's (Li Xuejian) brutal struggle to unify the country but also raises serious issues of human rights, betrayal, and corrupted leadership."

One of Chen's greatest challenges involved staging the movie's battle scenes. "We had 5,000 soldiers to move from place to place in big trucks as well as to costume," he recalled. "We had to get up in the middle of the night because we needed seven hours to put wardrobe on these soldiers. Some people joked with me by saying 'Now you are a real emperor on the set.' And I almost had that feeling."

Besides the problems of logistics, Chen had to decide how to film the battles without imitating other directors. "I didn't want to copy directors like Kurosawa, and I didn't want to show excessive bloodshed or the details of killing—I wanted the scenes to be more poetic," he said. He made the right decision, for by emphasizing the aftermath of violence, these incredible scenes carry tremendous impact.

Gong Li, a veteran of Chen's films, plays the role of courageous Lady Zhao and looks even more gorgeous than in *Farewell My Concubine* or in *Temptress Moon*. "Gong Li shows great dramatic power and understands her characters very well," Chen exclaimed. "It's not just on the surface. She's more concerned with feelings and emotions than with the lines her characters say."

Chen also complimented other cast members and rightly so. Li Xuejian delivers a dynamic performance as the ambitious leader who sacrifices everything for his political ends. In addition, playing a reformed assassin recruited by Lady Zhao to kill the Emperor, Zhang Fengi makes viewers believe completely in his redemption and honor. Surprisingly, the director cast himself in the role of a banished Prime Minister who turns out to be the Emperor's real father.

According to Chen, he assumed this role as a kind of homage to his own parent, now deceased, who was also a film director in China. When Chen was 14 years old, he denounced his father as part of the Cultural Revolution, but his father forgave him. "I was obsessed with that—with the sacrifices made to unify the whole country," he admitted. "There's a connection between me and my father and the Emperor and Prime Minister as depicted in my film."

Chen plans to direct a love story for Miramax Films soon. It's based on Martin Cruz Smith's novel, *The Rose*. "I think Miramax wants one of its rising young stars for the female lead and already has decided on the male lead, but they haven't told me yet," he said cheerfully, perhaps relieved at not having more huge battle scenes to oversee.

A former basketball player for the Chinese army, Chen has very little time for the game now. "I work so hard, run around so much, then fall apart," he complained. After watching his monumental *Emperor and the Assassin*, it's easy to see why.

Willem Dafoe (*Colorado Senior Beacon*, October, 2000)

Because of his remarkable performance in *Shadow of the Vampire*, an extraordinary satire about obsessive filmmaking, Willem Dafoe became the sensation of this year's Telluride Film Festival. During an interview and special converstion session at that event, Dafoe shared his reactions about portraying an actor who appeared as a vampire in the silent German horror classic, *Nosferatu*.

"No one on the set ever saw me without the vampire make-up," he said. "I had to arrive three hours before everyone else to get made up, and I stayed later to remove the make-up. So, just like in our film, people started wondering if I was a real vampire!"

A campy movie about the making of *Nosferatu* in 1922, *Shadow of the Vampire* stars John Malkovich as director F. W. Murnau and Dafoe as the mysterious Max Schreck, who is portrayed as a real vampire in this fictionalized version of events. Dafoe, a completely unthreatening and friendly person in real life, obviously relished playing such a scary role. He endowed it with surprising flashes of humor—like clicking those clawlike fingernails when plotting something evil. "I liked the costume, the mask, the physicality of the character," he declared.

Even so, the unconventional actor had difficulty with one particular scene. "In the sequence where I'm drinking schnapps with the producer and writer, I have to catch a rubber bat that's swinging by me on a fishing pole, bite off its head, and just go right on talking," he explained. "Because it was 4 o'clock in the morning, we were about to lose the light and had to shoot the entire thing straight through without any re-takes. I felt considerable pressure to get that shot right the first time."

Joking about the image he projected while filming, Dafoe stated, "We were on location in a little Luxembourg village, and you can imagine how children coming home from school were frightened when they saw me as this horrible creature emerging from the forest."

Dafoe's portrayal of Schreck has garnered praise at other film festivals and is generating serious Oscar buzz. Nicolas Cage, a co-producer of *Shadow of the Vampire*, calls Dafoe's Schreck "the most compelling vampire I've seen on film." Director Elias Merhige credits Dafoe with putting his own spin on this character through much of the filming. "There were so many great things that came out of rehearsing with the actors that I had to just throw some of the storyboards out," he revealed. "Some of the stuff that was going on between Willem and John was so great that I had to include it."

Dafoe explained he hadn't met screenwriter Steven Katz before making this film. Still, Katz wrote the role of Schreck with

Dafoe in mind, claiming he "just has this quality—a mixture of the incredibly frightening and threatening with an erotic charge, too, that I knew was perfect for the part."

Dafoe, who has made over forty films, observed. "Katz was familiar with my work, and I admired his script right away. It was witty, complete, and strong."

Commenting on the popularity of vampire movies since *Nosferatu*, Dafoe said, "People love to get scared. They love to deal with the 'boogie man' and the undead. People are always, in various ways, avoiding their mortality, so the idea of the undead coming back to feed on the living is kind of comforting in a way. That's pretty cool stuff. It's close to our nightmares and day-dreams."

How did Dafoe prepare for this grotesque role? "So much had to wait until I got into the make-up," he said. "I didn't just have extreme make-up, but also a costume that was restricting. The shoes made me walk a particular way. The padding in the clothes also made me walk strangely. It was great because it's a huge mask which frees you up so much."

Still, Dafoe identified the footage of *Nosferatu* as his most important research tool. "It was a kind of touchstone and base," he explained. "*Nosferatu* is filled with creepy images that blur the boundaries between the real and the unreal. It's considered by many to be Murnau's greatest movie and served as the inspiration for dozens of vampire films, including the famous Hollywood version starring Bela Lugosi." According to Dafoe, Nosferatu was based on Bram Stoker's *Dracula*, but different names had to be used because of legal problems with Stoker's estate. The title was changed, and Count Dracula became Count Orlock. "The only thing I could find out about Schreck (who played Orlock) was that a biographer of Murnau said he was an actor of no distinction," Dafoe stated.

It's ironic that an acclaimed, Oscar-nominated actor (for *Platoon*) was selected to portray another actor referred to as one of no distinction. But Dafoe is used to doing unconventional roles in films like *Wild at Heart, Streets of Fire, Lulu on the Bridge,* and *eXistenZ*. He once complained about missing out on more tradi-tional parts because filmmakers view him as "an eccentric actor in dark little films, a kind of boy next door type—if you lived next door to a mausoleum."

This offbeat boy next door began his acting career as a teenage member of an experimental theater troupe in Milwaukee. Later, he joined an avant-garde theater company in New York and is still deeply involved with that project. "I enjoy acting on the stage. It's a contrast to the fragmented nature of film work," he said.

When asked about his upcoming movies, Dafoe modestly replied, "I think there are some ready for release." Yes, indeed. Just look at this impressive list—*The Animal Factory*, a prison drama directed by Steve Buscemi; *Bullfighter*, a millennium Western; *Pavilion of Women*, the film version of Pearl Buck's novel; and *Edges of the Lord*, a Holocaust story co-starring Haley Joel Osment.

Charles Dickens (*Forum Publications,* December, 1995).

In addition to the many film versions of *A Christmas Carol*, most of Charles Dickens' other novels have also been made into movies (*Oliver Twist, David Copperfield, A Tale of Two Cities*, and so forth). If Dickens were alive today, I'm certain he would be involved in the movie business and willing to share his opinions with us. That explains why my imagination went wild recently, giving me the opportunity to interview this great author concerning the movies of 1995. Here are some highlights from our unusual session:

TUCKER: Mr. Dickens, how would you summarize this past year in terms of film accomplishments?

DICKENS: Not to put to fine a point on it, I believe 1995 was the best of times and the worst of times for moviegoers.

TUCKER: What do you mean by "the worst of times," Mr. Dickens?

DICKENS: For one thing, it was the year movies became too unbearably loud. Now I admit to using considerable noise in some of my work (especially the ghostly visitations to Ebenezer

Scrooge), but the sound people for *Money Train* and *Strange Days* went completely out of control. My ears haven't been the same since seeing these films.

TUCKER: Was there anything else you disliked about the movies during 1995?

DICKENS: Well, although I'm no stranger to depravity—having covered such ugly violence as Bill Sykes' murderous rage in *Oliver Twist*—I still feel that during this past year movies reached new depths of bad taste with *Showgirls* and *Jade*, both written by our highest paid screenwriter, Joe Eszterhas. I offered my services as a script doctor on these films, but Joe turned me down.

TUCKER: What did you mean when you said 1995 was also the "best of times" for moviegoers?

DICKENS: Happily, this past year we saw a resurgence of intelligent, humanistic dialogue in such gems as *Smoke, Don Juan Demarco, Living in Oblivion, The American President, Leaving Las Vegas,* and *Circle of Friends.* I am very pleased by this trend and also by Sean Penn's writing and directing of *The Crossing Guard*—one of the most remarkable cinematic storytelling achievements of recent years.

TUCKER: What is so remarkable about that particular film?

DICKENS: Mr. Penn masterfully combines dramatic images, compelling dialogue, and intense background music to tell about a father's vengeance against a drunken driver who killed his daughter. I admire the way he includes the importance of redemption as a key element in this thought-provoking film. Of course, the themes in this movie are very familiar to me, although I dealt with them in a different way in *A Tale of Two Cities* and *Oliver Twist.*

TUCKER: Do you have any thoughts about what movies will be like next year?

DICKENS: I fear our eardrums will still face some hard times, but I have great expectations for more films based upon well-written screenplays.

Aaron Eckhart (*Marquee*, San Diego, August, 1997).

Watching total wickedness on the big screen can be pretty scary, especially when the evil-doer looks like an average, ordinary person one might see everyday at work. In Neil LaBute's controversial film *In the Company of Men*, newcomer Aaron Eckhart portrays this type of villain with chilling realism.

As Chad, an unscrupulous mid-level executive, Eckhart depicts one of the most deliberately malicious characters ever seen on film. Chad hates everyone, particularly women. In order to get even with the opposite sex, he manipulates a naïve colleague into joining his scheme to shower an innocent woman with attention, then dump her.

Waiting for my telephone interview, I can't help wondering if Eckhart is like the despicable Chad in real life. Eckhart's polite, soft-spoken apology for his late call immediately puts me at ease. He laughs a little when asked how his work as Chad has influenced his personal life. "After seeing the film, my girlfriend's mother complained to her that she couldn't trust me anymore," he says. "That's why I don't want my own mother to see the movie. She still thinks I'm such an angel."

Eckhart claims he was able to nail Chad's character so effectively because he reviewed case studies of sociopaths, studied their antisocial behavior, and went to upscale Wall Street bars where he listened to men talk about their wives and girlfriends. With a hint of dismay in his voice, he insists, "Chad is alive and well, I can tell you."

Will Eckhart get stuck in bad guy roles because of his stunning success as the malevolent Chad? "I hope not," he says. "In fact, if a remake of *The Fabulous Baker Boys* is ever in the works, I would like to play the Jeff Bridges part." Nevertheless, Eckhart has signed on for another unsympathetic role in the upcoming *Thursday*, a dark comedy from Propaganda Films.

Eckhart was indeed fortunate to land the career-boosting role in his first feature film. His only prior film experience involved small parts in television movies and a few commercials. However, LaBute knew him from their time together at Brigham Young University; so he took a chance. Eckhart admits his friendship with writer-director LaBute gave him the casting edge for *In the Company of Men.* "After reading Neil's script, I knew I just had to play Chad," he recalls.

No doubt the film's low budget of $23,000 also contributed to LaBute's decision to hire the unknown Eckhart. "We ate bologna sandwiches, and Neil even mowed the neighbor's lawn to help finish the film," Eckhart proudly declares, then points out that shooting took only eleven days. In an age of movie budgets closer to $100 million and with shooting schedules running into months, not days, that's quite an accomplishment, especially considering the impressive results.

When asked to summarize the message of this disturbing film Eckhart replies emphatically, "Watch your back. Don't trust anyone or anything." Sounds like good advice to me. Still, moviegoers can trust at least one thing—Aaron Eckhart will shock them with his unforgettable performance as the contemptible Chad in *In the Company of Men.*

Hector Elizondo (*KOAA Online*, August, 2001)

"I quit show business when I was a youngster," Hector Elizondo declared in his deep, velvety voice during a revealing phone interview. That's a surprising statement from the man who mesmerized television viewers with his portrayal of Dr. Watters in *Chicago Hope* and who has over 80 films to his credit. "I wanted to be a baseball player, not an actor," he added.

Describing how he was discovered by the legendary W,C. Handy (of "St. Louis Blues" fame), Elizondo told about appearing in a public school play when he was 10 or 11 years old. "I sang a song and they wanted an encore. Then someone told my mother, my father, and my uncle that a man wanted to talk with us. That man turned out to be Mr. Handy. A few days later, I was in a television rehearsal studio."

After appearing in a couple of kiddie shows like *Howdy Doody*, Elizondo retired. Changing his mind when he got older, he returned to acting and won an Obie Award for his live theater work in *Steambath* as well as a Golden Globe nomination for his portrayal of the helpful hotel manager in *Pretty Woman*. In discussing his numerous supporting roles, Elizondo revealed his three favorites to be the cross-dressing mobster's son in *Young Doctors in Love*, Matt Dillon's hardworking dad in *The Flamingo Kid*, and a trigger happy villain in *The Taking of Pelham One, Two, Three*. It's obvious he enjoys playing very diverse roles. "But I don't get to play bad guys much anymore," he complained.

Although Elizondo snagged the lead in television's adaptation of *Burden of Proof*, his first big-screen starring role didn't come along until *Tortilla Soup*, the American version of Ang Lee's *Eat Drink Man Woman*. According to Elizondo, who portrays a retired chef living with his three grown daughters, **Tortilla Soup** is a hard film to categorize. "It's a slice of life with lots of heart, but it's not a comedy," he said. "We played it straight and the humor came from that. I think everyone can identify with this father and his daughters. The father wanted these young women to make their reach exceed their grasp. It's contemporary but also very old-fashioned, a movie with many layers and great depth."

The preparation of delicious Mexican food assumes major importance in *Tortilla Soup,* but Elizondo didn't have to learn how to cook for his role. "I just had to learn how to look like I could cook," he said. "People should be sure to eat before they see this movie," he advised.

Recognizing that gorgeous women as well as yummy food fill the screen in his latest film, Elizondo quipped, "I had to do push-ups every day to keep up with them. They were loaded for bear. I had to watch my back all the time." The them referred to includes Elizabeth Peña, Jacqueline Obradors, and Tamara Mello as the chef's strong middle-class daughters. But there's also sexy Raquel Welch as a man-hungry grandmother and Constance Marie as her beautiful daughter.

In a sequence showing Elizondo and Welch dancing together, the actor's smooth moves are reminiscent of his elegant number with Julie Andrews in *The Princess Diaries*. Admitting he trained as a dancer, Elizondo seemed adamant about not wanting to do a musical. "It's a lotta trouble," he almost shouted. "I'd have to stay in bed a whole day to prepare for just one scene."

When asked what he would like people to know about him, Elizondo responded, "People know too much about me already." After a brief silence, he reconsidered and said, "That I'm grateful for the opportunities I have every day."

With all his success on stage, television, and in the movies, is Elizondo a happy man? "Happiness is like broken crystal, you can never find all the pieces," he explained.

"Some times are better than others. But the most important thing is making someone else happy."

That might be why Elizondo agreed to star in *Tortilla Soup*, a film destined to make his fans very happy indeed.

Judith Godreche (*Forum Publications*, December 19, 1996).

That old saying, "Sticks and stones may break my bones, but words will never harm me" certainly did not apply during the reign of Louis XVI in 18th Century France. *Ridicule*, a film chosen by France as its entry into this year's Oscar race for Best Foreign Language Film, reveals how cruel and humiliating remarks could destroy a person's life in the Versailles of 1783—a place where wit was a weapon used to gain access to the King.

In this fascinating costume drama, Judith Godreche plays Mathilda de Bellagarde, an intelligent young woman out of step with the games in vogue at the King's court. During a recent interview at a Hillcrest coffee shop in San Diego, Godreche explained, "Mathilda is a scientist, which was unheard of for a woman at that time. She's impulsive, passionate, has ideas and principles, and is not the simple country girl stereotype seen in so many period films."

Godreche said her film character falls in love with a county engineer seeking help from the King for his mosquito-infested region. Complications develop because, in order to get money for her own research, Mathilda agrees to marry a much older man. Almost as impulsive as the woman she plays, Godreche admits she left school at age 16 and ran away from home at 15, giving up her teenage years to the movies.

According to the lovely actress, she lives in a "real movie culture." She identifies Gene Tierney as her favorite actress and proclaims *Singin' in the Rain*, the first movie she ever saw, as her favorite film. "I've seen it twelve times," she said joyfully.

Although only 25 years old, this intriguing young star has already appeared in twelve movies and two stage plays. She has also co-written a movie script and, just last year, published her first novel, *A Stitch on the Side*.

The recently married Godreche appeared happy during her short visit to San Diego, and not simply because her architect husband came along with her. "I feel happy and free here because the journalists are not too heavy—they are more conversational," she said.

(In Japan, where Godreche is a well-known actress, she angrily dismissed a group of pushy reporters who wanted to film her even while she was eating.)

Tony Goldwyn (*Uptown-Marquee*, April, 1999)

Is it possible to talk with Tarzan, Neil Armstrong, and a member of a Hollywood dynasty all at once? Only if you catch up with Tony Goldwyn, grandson and son of movie moguls Samuel Goldwyn Sr. and Samuel Goldwyn Jr. This newest Goldwyn to make his mark in show business played astronaut Armstrong last year in HBO's miniseries *From the Earth to the Moon*. And he provides Tarzan's voice for Disney's animated feature out next summer. In spite of these and other acting accomplishments, Goldwyn preferred discussing *A Walk on the Moon*, his first film as a director.

"I wanted to branch out as an actor, to produce something I could act in, but as we worked on the script for this romantic comedy, I got so involved I decided to direct and produce instead," he said. Originally scheduled to play the sexy hippie who seduces a housewife during the summer of 1969, Goldwyn believed he was not right for the part. Admirers of his mesmerizing voice and leading man good looks will argue about that, but the minute Goldwyn saw Viggo Mortensen, he couldn't imagine anyone else in the role.

Mortensen's love scenes with Diane Lane scorch the screen. How did a new director get such impressive results? "Lane and Mortensen had great chemistry together to begin with," Goldwyn admitted. "We shot the scenes in order. I wanted them to be organic and real. And our cinematographer, Anthony Richmond, knows how to shoot love scenes, so Lane and Mortensen felt safe with us."

Goldwyn approached directing by fantasizing an actor's perfect director. "As an actor, I sometimes felt the director was sitting on my head, limiting what I could do," he confessed. "Characteristics I crave involve drawing people out, inspiring them, and respecting their expertise while collaborating with them and leading in a way that helps them take off."

Co-producer Dustin Hoffman served as Goldwyn's mentor for this project. "Dustin was an amazing teacher. But for him, nothing is ever finished. Even after the film was completed, he was still ready to shoot a new scene," quipped the fledgling director.

Why did Goldwn pick a film about the Sixties? After all, he was only nine years old in 1969. "I've always been fascinated with the period and feel it's been treated badly in films. I wanted to express that era in a more personal way. I chose *A Walk on the Moon* because it's a movie truly from the heart. You feel you've been through something and faced issues everyone can relate to," he explained.

Surprisingly, Goldwyn couldn't remember hearing any of his grandfather's legendary Goldwynisms (such as "Include me out"). Evidently, publicity surrounding these comments made the senior Goldwyn self-conscious about any misuse of the English language. Goldwyn also revealed that his grandfather and father influenced his choice of career only indirectly. "At first, I didn't want anything to do with movies," he recalled. "Of course, I absorbed so much from both of them. When I told my father I wanted to become an actor, he was worried. He thought it was a dangerous profession. But he was the first one who encouraged me to try directing."

Turns out that was sound advice. Tony Goldwyn enjoyed helming *A Walk on the Moon* and has already agreed to direct two more films. Once again, father knows best.

Rachel Griffiths (*KOAA Online*, July, 2000)

Interviewing Rachel Griffiths is a bit like chatting with one of your wittiest friends. Warm, out-going, and humorous, the delightful Australian actress even managed to joke about her hotel accommodations while on the phone from Denver during a press tour for her latest film, *Me Myself I*.

"Is 7:30 a.m. too late to take a shower in Colorado?" she asked facetiously. "There was no hot water in my room this morning! People in this part of the world must take showers during the middle of the night and use up all the hot water," she teased in her engaging Aussie accent.

Griffiths never expected fame in the movies. "I planned on being a theater actor," she stated. "Although my degree is in drama and dance, the school I attended was nothing like Julliard. It was a liberal arts college, and I was particularly interested in design. I worked on such things as lighting, sets, and so forth."

Speaking enthusiastically about her first real internship, Griffiths recalled, "It was with the Woolly Jumpers, an innovative theatrical group organized to bring drama to children who might not get a chance to see it otherwise. We worked on plays part of the year, then traveled to various areas to put on these productions."

In 1994, an impressive debut as Muriel's friend Rhonda in *Muriel's Wedding* launched Griffiths' movie career. She accepted roles after that in such films as *Cosi, My Best Friend's Wedding,* and *Welcome to Woop, Woop*. An Academy Award nomination for Best Supporting Actress in *Hilary and Jackie* came her way in 1999. As the real-life musical du Pres sisters, both Griffiths and Emily Watson won worldwide critical acclaim for their performances in this intense drama. Ironically, their success as *Hilary and Jackie* probably prevents them from working together again. "If we appeared with each other as any other characters, people wouldn't believe us," Griffiths explained.

How does Griffiths prepare for her movie roles? "It depends on the film," she said. "I worked out in a gym for six weeks for *Me Myself I*. I was getting paid a lot of money, so I wanted to make sure I stayed healthy. It was like training for a marathon, but I knew physically I had to stay more positive than I ever had done on any other film in order to be light and funny."

Because Griffiths is in all but three scenes of this romantic comedy, she faced a grueling shooting schedule. She also spent hours watching as many romantic comedies as she could. "I watched Tom Hanks, Meg Ryan, and Julia Roberts films because these are the masters of walking the line between making you laugh and making you feel something," she explained. "And, I watched *Ground Hog Day, It's A Wonderful Life, Harvey*—practically any movie like that about people who believe in something that might seem farfetched. I was worried the audience might find *Me Myself I* a little hard to believe, especially since my character meets another version of herself in this unusual film."

Although Griffiths maintains a busy working schedule, she makes time for such activities as cooking, surfing, and reading. "I become obsessed with certain things, so I read mostly non-fiction," she offered. "For example, I've read a tremendous amount about architectural theory and the history of architecture. Right now, because I've been traveling through the American Southwest, I've bought a lot of books on American Indians and American history."

Perhaps thinking this sounded a bit too serious, Griffiths added, "But I'm planning to take up sailing. That's my next project. And, of course, there's always time for dating." When asked about an internet report concerning her and American actor Eric Stoltz, she quickly responded, "Where did that come from? I'm not at all interested in becoming part of a famous show biz couple!"

Griffiths is interested in doing more than just acting in film. *Tulip*, a short movie she wrote and directed, earned accolades at festivals in Aspen, Palm Springs, and Melbourne. "It's not a happy-ever-after story," she admitted. "I was taken with the idea of how a person could adjust to the loss of a partner after living together for 60 years. These ideas come to me and captivate me. I'm getting back to where I was in my college days when it was all about storytelling to me. If I love the story and it feels right to tell it through film, that interests me. I plan to do another short film this year, but it will be very different from *Tulip*."

Movie fans will be happy to learn that Griffiths has three full-length features coming up in which she plays a major role. "The thing I like best about being in films is the opportunity to work internationally with the best actors around," she exclaimed. In *Blow*, her co-star is Johnny Depp. According to an admiring Griffiths, "He's an artist before he's a star. He respects himself and the material and doesn't freak out. I always appreciate Johnny Depp's work." In *Very Annie Mary*, Griffiths appears with Ioan Gruffudd, the young Welsh actor who made such a hit in television's *Horatio Hornblower*. "He's beautiful!" she exclaimed. Griffiths also complimented the skill of British actors Alan Rickman and Natasha Richardson, her colleagues in an upcoming comedy entitled *Blow Dry*.

As a movie fan herself, Griffiths enjoys going to the cinema. Her current favorites? "I saw *American Beauty* several times," she responded. "And good for Hilary Swank. She gave such a brave performance in *Boys Don't Cry*. I also loved *Erin Brockovich*. I just hope Julia Roberts finally gets the recognition she deserves for this movie. Julia has infinite skill at making what she does look effortless, but I know how difficult it is to do comedy after making *Me Myself I*. I can agree with that actor who whispered from his death bed, 'Dying is easy. Comedy is hard.'"

It wouldn't be too surprising if both Julia Roberts and Rachel Griffiths receive the recognition they deserve when the next Academy Award nominations are announced.

Lauren Holly (*Pre-Vue Entertainment Magazine*, Winter Issue, 1998).

It's hard to imagine glamorous Lauren Holly as a waitress in a small town. Yet that's the acting challenge facing her in *No*

Looking Back, Gramercy Pictures' new film written and directed by Edward Burns. Holly puts to rest any doubts about her ability to relate to a working class woman. "The role may be a departure for me in my professional career, but it is the closest one to myself I have ever played," she says. "I'm not the Little Miss Hollywood some people think I am. I grew up in Geneva, a small town in upstate New York, and even worked in a cannery at one time."

Holly claims her enthusiasm for acting "started at birth." Her grandparents and great-grandparents gave her lots of attention when she was a child. "During family gatherings, they would form a huge circle with me in the middle, and I loved the spotlight," she admits.

While Holly was studying the flute in London during one of her father's sabbaticals (both parents were college professors), she had to take drama. "That's when I became seriously interested in acting, but I though of it only as a hobby," she recalls. "Then, while attending Sarah Lawrence College, I decided to audition for guest directors' plays. Even though I got a part in *Seven Minutes in Heaven*, a Francis Ford Coppola film, during my senior year, I still planned on going to graduate school to become a corporate lawyer."

Instead, Holly has worked steadily as an actress since 1985. "I'm like a kind of Energizer Bunny that keeps going and going and going," she quips.

It was her appealing portrayal of the spunky policewoman Max in television's acclaimed *Picket Fences* series that led to various movie offers. She appeared in such films as *Band of the Hand, The Adventures of Ford Fairlane, Dragon: The Bruce Lee Story,* and *Down Periscope*. She then went on to star with Jim Carrey in *Dumb and Dumber,* with Harrison Ford and Craig Kinnear in *Sabrina*, with Ray Liotta in *Turbulence*, and with Kinnear again in *A Smile Like Yours*.

Sometimes receiving as much media coverage for her off-screen romances as for her films, Holly has become a frequent target for gossip columnists. "It goes with the territory, but I wish the bad things written about me didn't bother me so much," she confides. Her affair with Jim Carrey during the filming of *Dumb and Dumber* resulted in a marriage that fell apart almost as fast as they both could say "I do." After being linked romantically with both Kinnear and Burns, Holly faces rumors about a reconciliation with Carrey. "We're very close and talk together practically every day, but we're just good friends," she explains.

In her role as Claudia—a character who feels trapped in her job, in her town, and in her relationships—Holly draws on personal life experiences. She describes Claudia as "an antsy woman with a lot of dreams" who is torn between a routine relationship with a long time live-in boyfriend (Jon Bon Jovi) or a more exciting life with an old flame (Ed Burns) who comes back to town after an absence of several years. Ultimately, Claudia must make some difficult decisions about her future.

Holly knows something about such feelings. She herself has been trapped by type-casting. "I really hope other filmmakers see this film and realize what I can do," she says. Writer/director/co-star Ed Burns centered his first two films, *The Brothers MacMullen* and *She's the One*, around men. *No Looking Back*, on the other hand, revolves around women. Holly is positive it will make women feel uplifted and empowered. An admirer of Ed Burns, Holly enjoyed working with him. "I think Eddie is a wonderful filmmaker," she says. "Even though he made me audition the entire script."

Jane Horrocks (*Forum Publications*, December, 1998).

The voice on the phone belongs to Jane Horrocks, one of England's most popular stars of stage, screen, and television. She has won extensive critical support in such diverse roles as Bubble, the public relations assistant in television's *Absolutely Fabulous*, an anorexic teenager in Mike Leigh's *Life is Sweet,* and Lady MacBeth on the London stage. Just listening to her charming British accent makes one long for a spot of tea and crumpets.

Horrocks talks about her new film, *Little Voice*, with warmth and candor. "I had no previous singing training," she admits. This comes as quite a surprise, for the role she plays requires her to imitate a variety of famous singers. "I've been able to mimic vocalists since I was a very young child," she explains. "I performed for my family and friends, but it took no conscious effort on my part."

When playwright Jim Cartwright offered to write a play showcasing her vocal talent, Horrocks felt "frightened to death." But her fine work in *The Rise and Fall of Little Voice* earned accolades from London theatrical audience and critics alike. For the film version, director mark Herman knew no one else could do justice to the role.

Of all the voices Horrocks does, Judy Garland is her favorite. "There's nobody like Judy for me," she declares. "But she is the most difficult to do because her voice is pure magic."

Horrocks wants everyone to know all the songs in *Little Voice* are performed live because "it gives the cinema-going audience a real theatrical experience usually difficult to express on screen."

Other *Little Voice* cast members get high praise from Horrocks. She regards Michael Caine, who plays a down-at-the heels agent, as "a true professional and marvelous to work with." She admires Brenda Blethyn for "doing such a terrific job as the domineering mother, even though she had only one day of rehearsal because of prior commitments." Regarding handsome Ewan McGregor, Horrocks exclaims, "I wondered how you could make him look plain enough for his role. It's a tribute to Ewan and the make-up artist that he comes across so convincingly as a shy phone repairman."

Horrocks also captivates the audience as a character unlike herself in real life. "Thank heavens I'm not a bit like Little Voice. I didn't have a miserable upbringing. I had wonderful parents," proclaims this concerned mother of a 17 month-old son. Ending the interview with a description of the film's message, the intelligent actress points out, "This story shows there is hope for everyone. Miracles can happen, and people can find themselves at the end of the day."

Moviegoers who see Jane Horrocks in *Little Voice* will find one of these miracles.

Donal Logue (*Uptown-Marquee*, September, 2000).

After receiving an Outstanding Performance Prize this year at Sundance for *The Tao of Steve*, Donal Logue admitted feeling "so scared I just wanted to go back to Los Angeles and start building things on my house." Logue won this award for his first leading role—one that's being compared to Michael Caine's star-making turn in Alfie.

Discussing his critical success in a recent telephone interview, Logue said, "I always think if something feels good in my heart and soul, it will work for everyone, and I felt this way about *The Tao of Steve.*

Previously, Logue has done supporting work in over forty films, playing such diverse roles as the priest who was one of Julia Roberts' spurned lovers in *Runaway Bride* and the mad vampire Quinn in *Blade*. But he claims his greatest acting challenge was a recurring television appearance as cabdriver Jimmy McBride for MTV in the mid-1990s. "Even though it was mostly improvisation, I had to write about a hundred pages a day," he explained.

Logue didn't start out to be an actor. He studied history at Harvard and planned to go into teaching or law. So how did he get involved in acting? "On a dare from my roommate," he recalled.

While at Harvard, the future thespian took what he calls "a rather snooty course." It was titled Intellectual History. "I had no idea this philosophy class would be helpful to me as an actor later," he stated. "But it gave me a better understanding of Dex, my character in *The Tao of Steve*. By twisting the ideas of great philosophers, Dex believes he's developed a foolproof theory of dating. He and his friends think becoming Steve, as in Steve McQueen, is the ultimate Tao."

For Logue, the major benefit of an acting career is working with interesting colleagues. "I've been lucky to work with lots of nice people, ands that's great because being in scenes is like only 1/90th of the time—the rest involves being with people," he explained.

Evidently, Mel Gibson is one of those "nice people." Logue has appeared with Gibson in two films, *The Patriot* and *Million*

Dollar Hotel. "Mel is a great prankster," he said. "I know a million jokes, but whenever I start to tell one, he already knows it. He doesn't do the super pranks he used to though, like running one for as long as four months and getting everyone involved. Mel has a serious side, too. He's turned me onto some wonderful books, like Graham Greene's *The Power and the Glory.* Also, while we were on location together, my son was born right before his seventh child was due, and he was great about giving me rides back to L.A. to see my family."

Another colleague receiving Logue's praise is Skeet Ulrich. Both are in *Takedown,* an upcoming film about computer hacker Kevin Milnick. "Skeet is a sweetheart. He had cast approval for the film and wanted me, so I like him right away. He's a big family man with dogs and everything," Logue reported cheerfully.

In addition to *Takedown* and *Million Dollar Hotel,* Logue's versatile talent can be seen later this year in *Steal This Movie, The Big Tease,* and *The Opportunists.*

Elias Merhige (*KOAA Online,* October, 2000).

Elias Merhige, director of *Shadow of the Vampire,* an engrossing movie about the making of the silent 1922 German classic *Nosferatu,* admits being frightened by the latter film at an early age. "I saw it for the first time when I was 11 years old, and it scared the hell out of me," he said during a recent interview while attending the Denver International Film Festival. "The unnatural movements of the vampire gave me chills. Then I saw it nine times more before shooting *Shadow of the Vampire* and sixteen times after that."

Amazingly, Merhige maintains he always finds something new and different each time he views *Nosferatu.* "It was directed by F. W. Murnau, an artistic filmmaker I truly admire," Merhige declared. In *Shadow of the Vampire,* John Malkovich plays director Murnau and Willem Dafoe portrays the mysterious actor Max Schreck. Schreck, which means "shriek" in German, is depicted as a real vampire in this scary, satirical film. Murnau has promised him the neck of the heroine when he completes his "acting" assignment. Merhige claims he prepared storyboards from Steven Katz's script, then had to throw some of them out because of the "great stuff" going on between Malkovich and Dafoe during rehearsals.

"When you have great actors like John and Willem, it's like a painter given two rare pigments—and you have to decide whether to stick with your original idea or take a chance and expand in new directions," Merhige explained. "In this case, what kept me awake at night was how to get the very best out of these talented actors. John and I did a lot of talking and rehearsing together months before shooting. This changed many of my ideas. And Willem made discoveries about his character, such as clicking his long claw-like fingernails, after getting into the make-up and costume. He's a very tactile actor. He inhabits the costume and the mask completely."

The biggest challenge Merhige faced in filming *Shadow of the Vampire* related to time. "We shot the film in 35 days, so I felt considerable scheduling pressure. I was like a military strategist, always reviewing things and trying to comprehend the best use of time when there really wasn't enough of it," he recalled. Nevertheless, the harried filmmaker expressed a great deal of pride in the finished product. "I'm pleased this film communicates the levels of meaning, passion, and humor I wanted to create," he stated.

Merhige described the message of his film as showing that creative art can be carried to an extreme conclusion. "Any creative person can be very powerful," he said. "It doesn't have to be an artist like Murnau. It can be a scientist, a politician, or so forth. But creativity is neither good nor evil. A person can use or abuse the creative process."

It's no wonder Merhige was selected to direct *Shadow of the Vampire*. Unlike most current directors, he actually has experience working on a silent movie. His first film, *Begotten* (named by Time Magazine as "One of the Top Ten Films of the Year"), was a silent film. "I did the special effects, cinematography, and directing in a way that kept me involved with the flesh and blood of my actors," he explained. "This was an amazing process. It taught me how the silent movie director was directly engaged in the moment of creation and that with sound, the director becomes somewhat disengaged."

Evidently, *Shadow of the Vampire* kept Merhige completely engaged despite being a "talkie." His extraordinary satire of obsessive filmmaking won the Grand Prize at the Festival d'Avignon 2000 and has been well received by audiences at film festivals in Cannes, Telluride, Toronto, and Denver.

Pat O'Connor (*Forum Publications*, December 24, 1998).

Imagine having a spirited conversation with one of Ireland's friendliest leprechauns. That gives you some idea of how much fun a phone interview can be with Pat O'Connor, director of the movie version of Brian Friel's acclaimed play, *Dancing at Lughnasa*. O'Connor's great sense of humor can't hide his serious reasons for wanting to helm this deeply moving story of five unmarried sisters in 1930s Ireland.

"What I intended to do was to illuminate the human character and celebrate the best side of what we are," he declared in his lilting Irish brogue. "By the end of this film, I wanted people to experience a sense of loss, but I also wanted them to feel uplifted because of the dignity and integrity of the characters they've come to care about."

Audiences do care about these women who gain strength and courage from each other despite their individual eccentricities and deplorable economic conditions. O'Connor said Oscar-winner Meryl Streep was compelled to appear as the oldest sister. "She is a very intelligent actor," he said. "She knew this was an ensemble piece, not a star turn for her, and that's the way she wanted it."

In addition to Streep, this talented director of such popular films as *Circle of Friends, January Man,* and *Cal,* assembled the best people possible (Sophie Thompson, Kathy Burke, Catherine McCormack, Brid Brennan, Michael Gambon), then rehearsed them together for two weeks so they would get to know each other. "I also got close to them," he said. "I always feel like an actor when working with actors, so they trust me. I don't let technology get in the way of directing."

One of the film's most exciting sequences shows all five sisters slowly joining in an exuberant display of Irish folk dancing. O'Connor didn't want to shoot it during the day or at night, searching for the perfect lighting. "We did it during three consecutive twilights and used three cameras to get close shots and wider shots," he explained. "I wanted to emphasize the passion of the dance, not the choreography. That's why I told the women to forget the steps after they learned them and concentrate on the emotion they were feeling." The result is one of the year's most memorable cinematic experiences.

O'Connor said his "abiding interest in life" centers on films about ordinary people. "I want people to remember this film like I remember the movies of John Ford and John Huston," he said.

Oscar®, (*Colorado Senior Beacon*, March, 2000).

Whether March comes in like a lion or a lamb, it traditionally brings questions about which stars and moviemakers will win the coveted annual Academy Awards. This year is no exception. But even Oscar himself can't reveal the winners until March 26th. He can, however, share other interesting information with his many fans. Ad so, dear reader, thanks to a reporter with a vivid imagination, your Senior Beacon presents the following interview with Hollywood's most famous Golden Boy.

BEACON: Congratulations, Oscar, on 72 years of honoring the best in film achievement. Do you mind telling us how you got your name?

OSCAR: I was born with the name Academy Award of Merit, but that's quite a mouthful. Believe it or not, no one knows for sure where my nickname came from. I seem to recall an employee at the Academy telling people I looked like her Uncle Oscar. After that, everyone started calling me Oscar, and the name became official in 1939.

BEACON: You must have many fond memories after all these years. Which winners impressed you the most?

OSCAR: Katharine Hepburn tops the list. Did you know she holds the record for most acting nominations and winning performances? She was nominated 12 teimes and won 4 Oscars as Best Actress.

BEACON: That is remarkable! Do you also have a favorite host of the Academy Awards televised ceremonies?

OSCAR: We've had some great ones, haven't we? Whoopi Goldberg looked terrific last year in all those funny costumes, but the emcee who makes me laugh most is Billy Crystal. And he'll be hosting for the seventh time this year. I hope he does those amusing song parodies of the nominated films again, don't you?

BEACON: You betcha—or something just as entertaining. Are you planning anything special for the first Academy Awards program of the new millennium?

OSCAR: Yes, indeed. I started my own Web site (www.oscar.com) this February. It carries all kinds of Internet activities and information about the Academy Awards, including some fun trivia items.

BEACON: Such as?

OSCAR: Well, if you want to know things about the Academy of Motion Picture Arts and Sciences—such as how many members there are or how the nomination and voting process works, just click on this Web site. In addition, if you like trivia, you can find answers to questions like what actor was nominated in two categories for the same performance, which sisters received nominations in the same category during the same year, or who was the only star with a write-in campaign organized for her.

BEACON: Don't keep us in suspense, Oscar. Please answer some of those questions now.

OSCAR: Okay, but you'll have to check out my Web site for the full stories. Let's see now. There must be close to 6,000 voting members of the Academy. Competition takes place in 24 categories. Each member can submit nominations for best picture, but only actors can nominate actors, only directors can select best director nominees, and so forth.

BEACON: And those trivia answers?

OSCAR: Aha! I thought that's what you really wanted. So— Barry Fitzgerald was nominated for Best Actor and Best

Supporting Actor in 1944 for *Going My Way*, but the rules now prohibit acting nominations in more than one category for the same performance. Two pairs of sisters received nominations for the same award in the same year: Joan Fontaine and Olivia de Havilland vied for Best Actress in 1944, and Lynn Redgrave competed against Vanessa Redgrave in 1966. Fontaine was the only one who won. Bette Davis' supporters organized a write-in campaign for her 1934 performance in *Of Human Bondage*. That's also illegal now.

BEACON: Thanks so much for sharing all this with our readers, Oscar. You have a wonderful memory. Here's hoping we can talk again sometime.

OSCAR: How about next year?

Oliver Parker (*Uptown-Marquee*, June, 1999).

He's a versatile director who writes his own screenplays and chooses projects with universal, provocative themes. His extensive work as an actor and theater director helps him understand the needs of each cast member. Who is this ideal filmmaker" It's not George Lucas, Steven Spielberg, or even James Cameron. It's Oliver Parker, the man behind *An Ideal Husband*, a new romantic comedy inspired by one of Oscar Wilde's wittiest plays.

"I try to avoid a directing formula," Parker declared in a recent interview. "It goes actor by actor," he explained in his appealing British accent. "For example, Cate Blanchett (who plays Gertrude in *An Ideal Husband*) likes to work one on one with copious notes, while some actors just want to be comfortable and steered toward their performance. I try to create an atmosphere where everyone can be relaxed. As a actor, I felt I did my best under those conditions. As a director, I just stay on my toes and work out what each character needs. There's always so much pressure involved in making a film. Why add more?"

After successfully adapting and directing William Shakespeare's *Othello* (with Laurence Fishburne and Kenneth Branagh), why did Parker select an almost forgotten Wilde play for his second major movie project? "I wanted to blow the dust off something that had been incarcerated in an academic prison," the talented filmmaker confessed. Parker's clever movie version opens up the action by adding outside scenes of London and the House of Commons during the late 1800s. But more importantly, it emphasizes the emotional involvement of the characters, becoming a romantic comedy instead of the farcical melodrama Wilde originally created.

"I want people to know this movie is not a stuffy period piece," said Parker. "It has a sexuality and vibrance that break through these misconceptions. It deals with contemporary themes, delivering its message in a lighthearted way." Because making a movie takes so much time out of his life, Parker takes on only projects that connect with him and his passions. "I like to deal with significant themes such as acceptance of contradictions and complexity—nothing is black and white," he stated.

Parker's choice of *An Ideal Husband* certainly meets this criteria. It tells the story of a respected Member of Parliament whose career and marriage could be ruined when a seductive blackmailer threatens to reveal a secret from his past. His ultra-ethical wife and playboyish best friend attempt to save him. Serious subject matter, right? Yes, but, as Parker pointed out, "I want the movie to be a little like those slightly screwball comedies of the 40s."

What can you expect from someone whose favorite films include Hitchcock's *North by Northwest* and the Marx Brothers movies? According to Parker, "It's all about the right balance between drama and comedy. I hope I got it right, but I'm always haunted by alternatives."

Parker got many things right in *An Ideal Husband*, especially the casting of Rupert Everett (*My Best Friend's Wedding*) as Lord Goring, the politician's devil-may-care best friend. "Rupert is such fun to work with," Parker exclaimed. "He's very witty, very funny, very spontaneous—a curious mix of self-consciousness and style. And he has a charming, disarming quality of speaking his mind. It was great to see him just swan through this movie."

What's next for this creative British filmmaker? A little change of pace seems in order, so he's thinking of joining forces with another outstanding director, John Sayles (*Lone Star, Limbo*), to film a murder mystery set during the postwar period. What a winning combination that should be for moviegoers everywhere!

Bob Saget (*Pre-Vue Entertainment Magazine*, Spring, 1998).

Chevy Chase. Don Rickles. Norm Macdonald. Artie Lange. Even the bravest filmmaker might tremble at the thought of directing these outrageous comics in the same movie. Yet someone had to do it for *Dirty Work*, MGM's new comedy about love, hate, revenge, and cold hard cash. Why did Bob Saget, popular former host of *America's Funniest Home Videos*, take on this awesome challenge?

"I come well-prepared to direct a group of comics," Saget explains. "After all, I am one of them. After spending twenty years in stand-up comedy, I understand the comic's tilted mind."

Dirty Work marks Saget's motion picture directorial debut, although he has been involved in filmmaking since he was only nine years old. "My father gave me an 8 millimeter camera he bought from a butcher," he recalls. "I used this meat-cam (that's what it smelled like) to put all sorts of people on film."

Saget went on to film school, won a student Academy Award for his documentary short film, and achieved success as a television actor, writer, director and producer.

Dirty Work features Norm Macdonald (formerly of *Saturday Night Live*) and Artie Lange (*Mad T.V.*) as unemployed losers who set up a revenge-for-hire business. The company motto is "Don't get even . . . let Dirty Work, Inc. do it for you!"

"All of us worked very hard to make the funniest movie ever," Saget boasts. "When someone ad-libbed and it was funny, we left it in." Not surprisingly, Saget allowed the legendary Rickles free rein and used his best bits in the final cut. "Norm, who also co-wrote the screenplay, worked with me every step of the way," Saget acknowledges. "He imprinted this film with his trademark edgy irreverence."

Clearly, Saget loved directing *Dirty Work*. He insists "the world needs to see more of Norm Macdonald. There's no one quite like him. In fact," he pauses with perfectly honed comedic timing, "Norm and I are lovers and are raising a child together." Ba-da-bing! He just couldn't help himself.

Tony Shalhoub (*Forum Publications*, September 26, 1996).

Tony Shalhoub admits he would like to be more like Primo, the Italian master chef he portrays in the new comedy/drama *Big Night*. Although not of Italian descent, Shalhoub is best known as the Italian cab driver in television's popular situation comedy *Wings*. "I admire Primo's simplicity, his artistry and certainly about his work as well as his inability to compromise his principles," said Shalhoub in a recent interview at Mr. A's Restaurant in San Diego.

Shalhoub explained he didn't want Primo to be just another version of Antonio, the character he plays on *Wings*, so he gave him a different tempo and style. He actually trained with a real chef for several months in preparation for this important role.

Landing this movie part can be traced to Shalhoub's past when he and Stanley Tucci (*Murder One*), the co-writer and co-director of *Big Night* appeared in a play together. "I must have done something great in a previous life because after Stanley and his cousin wrote the screenplay, I didn't even have to read for the role," he said.

Big Night is a remarkable film about the bond between two brothers who leave Italy to open a restaurant in America. Shalhoub described it as a labor of love. "Stanley was tired of playing Italian Mafia types and wanted to do a movie dispelling this stereotype," he stated. Shalhoub understood and supported Tucci's motivation, having himself been offered many terrorist roles due to his Lebanese ethnic background.

According to Shalhoub, Tucci also hoped to show how important food is in bringing people together, perhaps because of its significance in his own large Italian family. In *Big Night,* chef Primo proclaims, "To eat good food is to be close to God," and "Knowledge of God is the bread of angels." Then, because Tucci encouraged Shalhoub to improvise some of Primo's lines, he adds, "I'm not sure what that means, but I know it's true."

Rob Sitch (*Colorado Senior Beacon*, May, 1998).

Every once in awhile, a small film comes along that puts big budget films to shame. Australia's *The Castle*, shot in 11 days for less than a million dollars, is that kind of film. Rob Sitch, who served as director and helped write the script, says, "When we won the Audience Award from Africa's Zimbabwe Film Festival, we knew our movie was not just for Australians. The unbelievable charm of it sneaks up on everyone."

In a telephone interview during Sitch's U.S. press tour, he explained, "We wanted to do a comedy about happy families. It seems lately laws must have been passed against films about them." After seeing so many movies about dysfunctional families, viewers are in for a treat as they watch Darryl Kerrigan (Michael Caton) struggle to save his family's ramshackle house from being taken over by airport expansionists. And what a family! Darryl himself may be the most upbeat, positive father ever depicted on film. He even compliments his wife's cooking at each meal in hilarious scenes based on Sitch's own father. "He did the same thing every night!" the filmmaker declared.

Darryl's wife (Anne Tenney) spends her time with "crafts," making ridiculous doo-dads her husband thinks are amazing. "The couple's grown children, eccentric in their own way, care deeply about their parents and each other—even the son in jail for armed robbery," said Sitch.

A member of Australia's famous Working Dog creative team, Sitch modestly claims he is not necessarily the best director of the bunch. "The five of us have been working together on television shows for 12 years, and we all write and all direct, but I was selected this time because we only had 11 days to shoot and I'm the fastest worker," he admitted.

According to Sitch, the most difficult scene to film in *The Castle* involved presentation of the Kerrigan case to the High Court of Australia. "It's ironic this judicial body is called the people's court but no filming is allowed there," he complained. "We took a long time writing this key scene. After the film was released, we received a message from the High Court notifying us that the judges were reserving any decision concerning the case. At least they have a sense of humor," quipped Sitch.

Sitch, who earned a medical degree, knows quite a bit about humor. (Just imagine a bizarro Patch Adams.) He and his Working Dog colleagues met while putting on comedy sketches 16 years ago at the University of Melbourne. They went on to win accolades in Australian television for such groundbreaking satirical shows as *The Late Show* and *Frontline*. With *The Castle,* their first movie venture, these talented Aussies have presented a gift of heartwarming laughter to viewers throughout the world.

Mark Steilen (*Uptown-Marquee*, March, 2001).

"It's been crazy the past few years," Mark Steilen exclaimed while taking a break from fixing a scene for his latest movie. The former Mesa College English teacher was referring to his life in Los Angeles since the mid-1990s. He's currently directing *Basketcase*, a Warner Bros. film which he also co-wrote with partner Bennett Yellin.

"The Farrelly brothers are producing this film," Steilen said with unabashed enthusiasm. "I was lucky enough to do some polishing on *Dumb and Dumber* and *There's Something About Mary*, so they've been kind enough to shepherd me through the Hollywood maze. These guys are the most loyal, most brilliant people to work with, and they know how to have fun too."

Basketcase, set to co-star Denis Leary (later replaced by Vince Vaughn) and Will Ferrell, is Steilen's second directorial assignment. He also helmed and wrote *The Settlement*, a dark comedy about the downfall of shady businessmen who buy out insurance policies from the dying. "My executive producer, Skip Yazel, asked me if I could make a movie for a quarter of a million dollars," Steilen recalled. "I told him 'Absolutely!' and took on the job. Then when John C. Reilly, William Fichtner, and Kelly McGillis signed on, more money came in. We ended up with a $650,000 budget. Happily, HBO and Blockbuster bought the film, so with a little luck, everyone will get their money back."

Listening to Steilen talk about his new film is a treat in itself. Calling *Basketcase* "a very sweet, funny movie," he reports that Leary and Ferrell play an odd couple who could win two million dollars if they shoot two baskets during a particular halftime. "But Ferrell's character suffers from agoraphobia," Steilen revealed. "He won't even leave his apartment. Leary has just five days to get him out and teach him to shoot on the basketball court."

For his thesis film in the UCLA Directing Program, Steilen chose a more serious topic. *The Trip Back* is based on a story from Robert Olen Butler's *A Good Scent from a Strange Mountain* (which later earned a Pulitzer Prize). Steilen explained that although Broadway and film actor B.D. Wong did the voiceover for this movie, his Mesa students served as actors and technical crew. "Because the story deals with Vietnamese expatriates, a Vietnamese student, Hien Ngyen, translated my script and co-starred with Viet Hung. A Norwegian student, Snorre Sivertsen, was the sound technician, and the lighting guy, Jin Zhao, was from Shanghai. Some of these students are now professionals in the movie business. In fact, I'm using the same sound man for *Basketcase* as I did for *The Trip Back*."

Appearing more the proud teacher than ambitious filmmaker, Steilen declared, "One of the most satisfying things for me is looking across the set and seeing people who were once students of mine still working with me—only now I'm relying on their expertise."

Although born and raised in Spokane, Washington, Steilen admits having a soft spot in his heart for San Diego. He returns often with his wife and two young children. San Diegans who worked with Steilen haven't forgotten him either. Dennis Howard, his first English Department Chair at Mesa, remembers his talented colleague as "an intense, energetic young man who rarely sat down." Fortunately, those same characteristics should continue to help Steilen build his career as a successful filmmaker.

Fred Willard (*KOAA Online*, November, 2000).

"The world needs comedy," funnyman Fred Willard declared in a recent telephone interview. That's why this acclaimed comedian plans to keep playing such roles as the hilarious real estate agent in *Waiting for Guffman* and the ignorant commentator in *Best in Show*, two outrageous mockumentaries by filmmaker Chistopher Guest. "I'd like to try action-adventure, but that's too much work," he quipped.

Well-known for his improvisational talent, Willard explained how he approached his *Best in Show* character. "I was told Buck Laughlin was a former athlete who had done some sportscasting but didn't know anything about dogs and was too lazy to find out. Then I just came up with things I thought a man like that would say."

Willard's interpretation of Laughlin certainly hit pay dirt. His amusing comments about how someone should do a calendar of "women bathing their dogs" and the need for a bloodhound owner "to wear a Sherlock Holmes cap" had critics attending a Denver press screening howling with delight. The veteran Second City sketch artist seemed pleased about how much of his work remained in the final cut of *Best in Show*. "I was surprised, especially since many of my *Guffman* scenes didn't make it to the finished movie," he admitted.

Born in Cleveland, Willard confessed to causing minor disturbances with his comic antics while in school there. "When the kids laughed at me, I always asked the teacher why I was in trouble when the others were the ones making the noise."

Like many comics, Willard found laughter the best way to cope with pain as a child. "When I was 11 years old, my father died just four days before Christmas," he stated. "That had quite an impact on me and my attitude toward life. I'm a lot like Dick Cavet, who says, 'Whenever I go to a restaurant, I expect it to be closed.'"

Turning back to his childhood days, Willard recalled wanting a B.B. gun as a youngster. His mother wouldn't allow it. "You'll never be completely happy until you put someone's eye out," she warned him. "Well, she was right," he said. "I've never put some-one's eye out, and I've never been completely happy."

Commenting on his own child-rearing techniques, Willard explained, "We gave our daughter everything she wanted. We nur-tured her and never made her suffer. Now she's all grown up and a mom herself. But she doesn't want to work at being an actress or do comedy. Where did we go wrong?"

Although Willard really wanted to be a baseball player, choos-ing acting as a career has brought him success in films, live the-atre, and television. Highlights of his work include being a found-ing member of a classic improv group (Ace Trucking Company) and performing recurring television roles on *Mad About You, The Tonight Show with Jay Leno,* and *Roseanne* (for which he received an Emmy nomination). He has appeared in such diverse movies as *Idle Hands, This Is Spinal Tap,* and *Roxanne.*

Willard has also provided voices for characters in *The Simpsons* and *King of the Hill.* In addition, his one-man show, *Fred Willard: Alone At Last* (with a cast of twelve!) received two Los Angeles Artistic Director Awards, for Best Production and Best Comedy. "I even played the President of the United States once, just like Harrison Ford," Willard mentioned. "It was in a recent television movie, *The Pooch and the Pauper.*"

Willard's upcoming projects include the films *Teddy Bears' Picnic, The Wedding Planner, Chump Change,* and *Dropping Out.* One of his most hilarious performances can be seen on video now in *Waiting for Guffman.* I recommend it highly—but not for the kiddies.

If the report of this interview seems a bit jumbled, it's because Willard kept me laughing too much to take good notes. But he's absolutely right. The world does need comedy. And comedy needs talented comedians like Fred Willard.

REELTALK MOVIE REVIEWS

So far, there's plenty to rant and rave about in movies released during 2000 and 2001 A.D. I'm particularly amazed by the progress made in special effects these past two years—as show-cased in sci-fi films like *A.I., The Cell, Hollow Man,* and *X-Men.* 2000 A.D. also saw the birth of the world's first full-length clay-mation movie, *Chicken Run*, a film that won the hearts of kids and adults alike. But the following year, *Final Fantasy*, the first com-pletely computer-generated film, failed miserably (probably, I imagine, to the delight of most live actors). While quality movies such as *Almost Famous, Cast Away, Erin Brockovich, Gladiator, O Brother, Where Art Thou?, Moulin Rouge,* and *Shrek* boded well for the future of filmmaking during the 21st Century, too many releases like *Road Trip* and *Scary Movie* emphasized bad taste and crude humor in place of creativity.

Still, I managed to see practically all of them—the good, the bad, and the ugly—for a total of almost 400 films during this 24-month period. And, yes, I do need a new set of eyeballs and eardrums. (Any interested donors out there?)

Since the beginning of 2000 A.D., my ReelTalk Movie Reviews have appeared regularly on KOAA Online (http://www.koaa.com). This section includes selected ReelTalk reviews of films released during 2000 and 2001. For the reader's convenience, they are listed alphabetically according to the fol-lowing categories: action/adventure, comedy, drama, horror, musical (only four in this group—bummer!), romance, and thriller. Because I'm writing this book during the month of September, it's too soon to tell what impact the recent terrorist attacks on New York, Washington, and Pennsylvania will have on Hollywood filmmaking. Studios are already pulling some violent movies, including Arnold Schwarzenegger's terrorist-themed *Collateral Damage*, from the 2001 release schedule.

Reviews for films released after September are not included here, but I have high hopes for such upcoming flicks as *Harry Potter & the Sorcerer's Stone*; the Coen brothers' *The Man Who Wasn't There*; *From Hell* (starring Johnny Depp); *The Royal Tenenbaums* (with Anjelica Huston and Gene Hackman), and the first part of the *Lord of the Rings* trilogy.

ACTION/ADVENTURE:

CROUCHING TIGER, HIDDEN DRAGON

Because of the widespread acclaim for *Crouching Tiger, Hidden Dragon*, I decided to give this martial arts fairy tale a second viewing. I wanted to see if I missed something. After all, no other Chinese movie ever received ten Academy Awards nominations, including Best Picture and Best Foreign Language Film, or surpassed all other foreign language films at the U.S. box office. Unfortunately, except for admiring Michele Yeoh's performance even more, my original reaction still stands. In my opinion, this fantasy is generally entertaining and beautifully photographed—but definitely overrated.

First, the good news. Yeoh (*Tomorrow Never Dies*) projects impressive nobility and strength as the head of a security company in 19th century China. Rising above the material, sometimes literally, Yeoh sails through the film with flying colors in the role of Shu Lien, a courageous woman warrior. Brave as she is, Shu is too frightened to reveal her love for legendary warrior Li Mu Bai (Chow Yun-Fat). And Bai has the same problem with his repressed feelings for Shu. "Where emotions are concerned, even great heroes can be idiots," one of their friends explains.

In her exceptional portrayal of Shu Lien, Yeoh combines dynamic action with poignant emotional moments. Gazing tenderly at Yun-Fat in their early scenes together, she gives no hint of her character's tremendous physical power to follow. Later, when fighting Jen Yu (Ziyi Zhang), the protégé of Bai's evil enemy Jade

Fox (Pei Pei Chang), Yeoh displays a sense of discipline lacking in the younger woman. Granted, that's an important part of the plot—but Yeoh is clearly the more convincing of the two.

Based on the book by Du Lu Wang, the movie focuses on efforts to recover a famous sword while helping a young girl find herself. With her petite model's figure and coal-black hair, Zhang is quite photogenic as the impulsive, physically gifted Jen. However, I found her mannerisms too exaggerated, especially in a lengthy flashback showing Jen's adventure with a sexy outlaw (Chen Chang). Another disappointment is the small part played by Yun-Fat (*Anna and the King*) in this film. Since most of the battle scenes are between women, this renowned Asian star gets little opportunity to demonstrate his considerable talent as an action hero.

As directed by Ang Lee, *Crouching Tiger, Hidden Dragon* combines elements of *Peter Pan, The Matrix, Star Wars*, and another of his Oscar-nominated movies, *Sense and Sensibility*. Warriors fly through the air, soar across rooftops, and battle with each other from swaying tree branches. They fight like Keanu Reeves and Laurence Fishburne, wield swords like Jedi Knights, and fear unrequited love almost as much as the characters in Jane Austen's novel.

Why didn't all this excitement knock my socks off? Probably because I prefer more down-to-earth martial arts activities and value overall plot consistency, no matter how farfetched the story. It's still a puzzle to me why someone who can fly would ride a horse to get help in an emergency, particularly when time is of the essence.

Oh, well—it's just a movie. And, on the plus side again, the film's most memorable line ranks as the greatest love declaration ever uttered on screen. "I'd rather be a ghost floating by your side than enter heaven without you," a wounded warrior tells the object of his affection. Be still my heart! That's even more romantic than "Here's looking at you, kid."

(Released by Sony Pictures Classics and rated "PG-13" for martial arts violence and some sexuality. This review also appeared in the Colorado Senior Beacon.)

FINAL FANTASY

Now let's get this straight. In the year 2065, humans will be battling phantoms from outer space who have taken over planet Earth. But even though they're fighting ghosts, the characters in *Final Fantasy: The Spirits Within* use the type of firepower that usually works with traditional invading forces. And this isn't a sci-fi comedy? Too bad. The movie might have been saved if played for laughs. Instead, it's just plain bewildering.

As the first full-length cyberfilm in the history of the world, *Final Fantasy* ranks as a millstone—er, milestone—movie. Computer generated images provide all its special effects, sets, monsters, and people. But, wouldn't you know it, those pesky humans just don't come out right. The leading man (or mannikin) looks like Superman but talks like Alec Baldwin (whose voice seemed more appropriate in *Cats and Dogs*). One of his sidekicks resembles the boy next door but sounds like an eerie Steve Buscemi from *Con Air*. Clearly recognizable voices of James Woods (*The General's Daughter*), Ving Rhames (*Bringing Out the Dead*), and Donald Sutherland (*Space Cowboys*) emerge from characters who appear very different from themselves physically. While this technique works for cartoon characters, my primitive brain rebels against such dissonance where humans are concerned.

Still, even if more commonplace voices had been used, the mechanical appearance of the film's humans would also be off-putting to me. Case in point: the movie's feisty heroine, Dr. Aki Ross, whose dialogue is spoken by the relatively unknown Ming-Na of *Mulan*. Not being distracted by Aki's verbalizations, I could concentrate on other aspects of her "performance." While her eyes and hair amazed me with their lifelike appearance, she reminded me of a wind-up doll, not a real person. Even the little mole on her face seemed too perfect.

I'm becoming more and more wary of films based on video games. (A big *Tomb Raider* disappointment remains fresh in my mind.) The inspiration for *Final Fantasy* came from a highly successful interactive game created by Hironobu Sakaguchi, who also served as the film's producer and director. "I have always wanted to create a new form of entertainment that fuses the technical wizardry of interactive games with the sensational visual effects of motion pictures," Sakaguchi declares. Although recruiting some of the same artists who worked on *The Matrix, Godzilla, Titanic,* and *The Fifth Element,* Sakaguchi failed to put together a movie with the visual thrills of such sci-fi classics as *Alien, Blade Runner,* and *Star Wars.* Yes, there are intriguing giant phantoms with filmy, serpentine tongues and tentacles, but they keep showing up over and over again. I don't think I'm alone in preferring a little variety in my futuristic creatures. Last year's sci-fi disaster was *Battlefield Earth;* I'll be surprised if *Final Fantasy* doesn't earn that distinction this year.

What does surprise me, however, is that Oscar-nominee Al Reinert (for *Apollo 13*) co-wrote (with Jeff Vintar) the nonsensical script for *Final Fantasy.* In an attempt to blend spiritual themes with environmental concerns and sci-fi adventure, these writers have come up with a plot that defies description. No wonder most of the film's characters complain "I don't understand" at one point or another. And that pretty much sums up my feeling about the entire movie. Just because you can do something doesn't mean you should do it. Although the technology for a completely digital movie exists, I don't understand why it was used to make a film as unsatisfying as *Final Fantasy: The Spirits Within.*

(Released by Columbia and Square Pictures; rated "PG-13" for sci-fi action violence.)

GLADIATOR

Ruggedly handsome and minus the extra pounds he gained for *The Insider* last year, Russell Crowe finally emerges as an A-list star in *Gladiator.* Yes, I know he received an Oscar nomination for *The Insider* and earned rave reviews for *L.A. Confidential,* but neither of those films reached audiences the way *Gladiator* is sure to do. Nor has the New Zealand-born actor ever been photographed so gloriously before.

Crowe plays Maximus, a Roman general who becomes a powerful gladiator bent on destroying a treacherous Emperor. Displaying a strong, silent stoicism, he's especially impressive during the film's gladiator training sessions. And, throughout most of the movie, Crowe projects a smoldering anger that held me spellbound. When his rage finally erupts in the arena, he commands the screen in the same way Robert De Niro owned it in *Raging Bull*.

Matching Crowe's exceptional performance is the movie's superb direction by Ridley Scott. Noted for creating unusual worlds that draw viewers into them (remember *Blade Runner* and *Alien*?), Scott does it again in *Gladiator*. His battle sequences and arena carnage scenes are so realistic I felt like I was a participant. Spectacular cinematography by John Mathieson (*Plunkett and Macleane*) enhances that you-are-there feeling.

The film's violent action in no way interferes with its compelling story (from a screenplay by David Franzoni, John Logan, and William Nicholson). Revenge is always a grabber, and *Gladiator* focuses on Maximus' desire to wreak vengeance on Commodus (Joaquin Phoenix)—the man who became Emperor after killing his own father (Richard Harris). Commodus also arranged for the brutal murder of Maximus' wife and young son, so it's easy to understand why Maximus wants to destroy him. Because Phoenix (*8MM*) oozes so much slimy evil as Commodus, I wanted to hiss at him like the villains in those old-fashioned melodramas.

Other excellent supporting cast members add to the film's quality. Oliver Reed (*Oliver!*) stands out as a veteran trainer of gladiators. (This was Reed's last movie. He died during filming.) Playing a benevolent impresario, Reed endows his character with an admirable combination of toughness and concern for his gladiator team. Derek Jacobi (*I, Claudius*) reeks with dignity as a Roman senator who believes in democracy. "I am not a man of the people; I am a man for the people," he explains. Connie Nielsen (*Mission to Mars*) portrays Commodus' frightened sister with Grace Kelly-like coolness. And, Djimon Hounsou (*Amistad*), as a fellow gladiator, shares some exciting scenes with Crowe in the Roman Colosseum.

Historical accuracy doesn't fare too well in *Gladiator*, even though some of the characters were real people in Ancient Rome. Filmmaker Scott explains, "I felt the priority was to stay true to the spirit of the period, but not necessarily to adhere to facts. We were, after all, creating fiction, not practicing archeology."

Happily, Scott's cinematic fiction captivated me as completely as its title character won the soul of Rome.

(Released by DreamWorks Pictures/Universal Pictures and rated "R" for intense, graphic combat scenes).

JURASSIC PARK III

Those dreaded Raptors are back with a vengeance in *Jurassic Park III*. More bad news—they've brought along even more deadly friends. Tremendous progress has been achieved since *Jurassic Park II*, so these genetically engineered creatures can now communicate with each other. Making matters worse, the other dinosaurs also seem to talk together. Because I'm not multilingual (and no subtitles were shown), I was forced to call on Dr. Dolittle for a translation. Having just seen the movie himself, the good doctor appeared eager to help. (**Warning**: spoilers from this point on.)

I asked Dr. Dolittle first about that huge Spinosaurus who destroyed an aircraft in one of the movie's early scenes. Passengers in danger included Dr. Grant (Sam Neill again from *The Lost World: Jurassic Park II*), his assistant (Alessandro Nivola from *Face/Off*), parents searching for their lost son (William H. Macy and Tea Leoni from *Fargo* and *Family Man* respectively), and their crew. "What did the creature say when he went after that group so viciously?" I inquired.

"Well, that Spiny was one scary dude," Dr. Dolittle replied. "He hadn't tasted food for awhile, so he felt happy about the possibility of a good meal. The Spinosauruses are carnivorous, you know. This one couldn't help commenting out loud, 'There's my dinner!'"

"Yeah, I noticed how angry he got when the T-Rex got in his way," I said. "And what about those Velociraptors who circled the humans when they discovered some dinosaur eggs were missing? From the sounds of so much crying in the theater during the screening I saw, there's a scene that really frightened most little children! The Raptors looked like they were carrying on a lively discussion, but I couldn't understand a word of it."

"Still, you had to recognize the Velociraptors wanted those precious eggs back. But what you probably missed is their argument about which of the people to eat first as well as who should begin the feast," explained Dr. Dolittle.

Trying to hide my amazement, I uttered a simple "I didn't pick up on that. No wonder those castaways showed such fear." Then, in an attempt to downplay my lack of inter-species communication skills, I added, "It was perfectly clear, however, when one of the bird-like Pteronodons wanted a terrified boy (Trevor Morgan from *The Patriot*) as nutrition for her young."

Dr. Dolittle nodded vigorously. "You're right. But did you catch the mother's warning to her chicks as she scolded them about not playing with their food?"

"No, I didn't. Hey, I couldn't even figure out what the flock of Pteronodons were shouting at those pitiful humans while flying away from their first nesting place."

Smiling at my naivete, Dr. Dolittle declared, "That's easy; they were all yelling, 'We're still gonna get you, sucka! Just wait for *Jurassic Park IV*.'"

(Released by Universal Pictures and Amblin Entertainment; rated "PG-13" for scenes of intense sci-fi terror and violence. Definitely not for the pre-school set.)

A KNIGHT'S TALE

Gadzooks! Methinks I witnessed the World Series of Jousting in *A Knight's Tale* and actually enjoyed every minute of it. Combining the heart of *Rocky*, the courage of *Gladiator*, and the fun of *Monty Python's Quest for the Holy Grail*, this action-adventure grabbed me with its opening scene of a medieval crowd clapping to Queen's "We Will Rock You" and held me in its clutches until the closing credits.

After watching such an unusual beginning, I couldn't wait to see what filmmaker Brian Helgeland (*Payback*) had in store for viewers next. Happily, it was surprises galore. Besides using background music from the 70s and 80s in many key scenes, guess who it is he recruits to help the film's hero (Heath Ledger from *The Patriot*) become a jousting champion? None other than Geoffrey Chaucer. "Chaucer's my name and writing's my game," the famous poet tells Ledger's character when they meet on the way to a tournament.

As played with delicious flamboyance by Paul Bettany (*Bent*), this Chaucer is very unlike the one I learned about when studying *The Canterbury Tales* in World Literature. After all, bawdy as his work is, the real Chaucer did become an esquire of the royal court. Of course, the events depicted in *A Knight's Tale* are supposed to have happened before he achieved success as a writer and as the comptroller of the port of London.

William (Ledger), the son of a poor thatcher, first encounters Chaucer walking naked along the road, having lost all his clothes because of a gambling addiction. Realizing the daring youth must prove he is of noble birth to enter jousting contests, Chaucer agrees to provide forged documents in return for food and cloth-ing. He then joins William and his two squires (Alan Tudyk and Mark Addy) as a loyal member of the team. Using his talent with words to improvise amazing tournament introductions for William (who jousts under the name of Sir Ulrich von Lichtenstein of Gelderland), Chaucer becomes a ringmaster, press agent, sports promoter, and friend—someone any modern sports icon would be lucky to have working for him.

Chaucer also advises William about romance. In one of my favorite scenes, he composes a beautiful letter from the lovesick lad to Lady Jocelyn (newcomer Shannyn Sossamon), by slightly changing phrases offered by each of the team members. (Shades of *Cyrano de Bergerac*?) In addition, the poet instructs William how to talk to Jocelyn, even giving him quotes from the Bible. But he fails at teaching the ambitious young man to dance. It takes an independent female blacksmith (Laura Fraser) to accomplish that difficult task. Thank heavens she succeeded, or I wouldn't have had the pleasure of watching William and Jocelyn do their swingin' movements to the tune of David Bowie's classic "Golden Years." A similar melding of modern music and attitudes with medieval customs continued to delight me throughout this spirited movie.

Ledger's appealing performance is another of the film's many treats. Although I liked this Australian-born actor even better as the rebel teenager in *10 Things I Hate About You,* I found it quite easy to accept him here as a man who wants to reach for the stars and change his destiny. Ledger projects an intense underdog motivation reminiscent of Sylvester Stallone in *Rocky*—plus an inner strength similar to Russell Crowe's *Gladiator.* And, best of all, like *Monty Python*'s Black Knight, he convinced me his character wouldn't quit, no matter what. The evil Count Adhemar, played almost too seriously by Rufus Sewell (*Dark City*), doesn't stand a chance against such an eager adversary. I had a great time cheering William on, even while laughing at his social weaknesses.

Verily, I'm a sucker for movies about knights and their ladies. In days of yore, the sumptuous film version of Sir Walter Scott's *Ivanhoe* (1952) made me hungry for more. Films like *Prince Valiant* and *Camelot* are among my favorites. But *A Knight's Tale* is the first flick of this type to draw me in as more than a spectator and give me that welcome "you-are-there" feeling. Maybe that's why my husband had to stop me from joining the crowd on screen in one of those jousting tournament WAVES.

(Released by Columbia Pictures and rated "PG-13" for action violence, some nudity, and brief sex-related dialogue.)

THE MUMMY RETURNS

While watching *The Mummy Returns*, I felt like I was riding on a roller coaster that only goes downhill, making it impossible to enjoy the thrill of it all. Likewise, in this eagerly-awaited sequel (starring hunky Brendan Fraser again), special effects and action sequences were hurled at me so fast and furiously, I had little time to savor any of it. In fact, I was more irritated than entertained.

Most youngsters probably won't share my negative reaction, especially kids addicted to video games. POW! PUNCH! ZAP! BOOM! Creature after creature explodes or evaporates on screen in practically every scene. Granted, most of these fantastic demons are something to see. There's a gang of wild pygmy skeletons, hordes of jackal-headed warriors, lots of lively decaying corpses, plus a giant scorpion with the face of a famous wrestler (The Rock). And, as the title indicates, the powerful Mummy Imhotep (Arnold Vosloo) comes back from the dead to fight an equally evil Scorpion King who wants to take over the world.

How does Fraser's soldier-of-fortune character get involved again in such shenanigans? He's married now to *The Mummy*'s Egyptologist Rachel Weisz (*Enemy at the Gates*), but the couple is far from "settled down." She's still fooling around in ancient Egyptian tombs and he's helping her. Their precocious son (played with great comic timing by newcomer Freddie Boath) tries on a non-removable antique bracelet once belonging to the Scorpion King. Unfortunately, that little trinket holds the key to all kinds of miracles, which explains why it's sought after by unscrupulous agents who follow the family to their home in London. The child is kidnapped, so Mom and Pop hop a hot air balloon back to Egypt to rescue him. In the process, they decide to knock off all those nasty supernatural devils as well.

"It's the usual story," claims Fraser. Well, if that's the case, I wish the story were an unusual one. I wanted to see more than superficial romantic interactions between Fraser and Weisz, who projected such wonderful chemistry together in *The Mummy*. Or how about the hint of an attraction between Weisz and Oded Fehr (*Deuce Bigelow, Male Gigolo*), who plays such an intriguing man of mystery while narrating the story with his deep, appealing voice? Instead, human relationships take a seat way back in the bus to make room for special effects, relentless action, and excessive mumbo jumbo about reincarnation.

And what can I say about poor John Hannah? He puts in another appearance as Weisz's ineffectual brother, but this fine actor (witness his superb performance in *Sliding Doors*) adds nothing to the movie. His character just whines most of the time and carries an Egyptian scepter around with him. I can't help imagining filmmaker Stephen Sommers, who also wrote and directed the original film, saying to himself, "I must use everyone from *The Mummy* or a curse will be placed on me."

I'm most upset with Sommers for not letting us stop and smell the sand. For example, beautiful cinematography by Adrian Biddle (*Aliens*), especially those colorful shots of the desert sky at sunset, just flies by. Such lack of sensible pacing seems inexcusable to me. Sadly, my cup runneth over with disappointment at this bombastic sequel. I was expecting an exciting adventure film like *Raiders of the Lost Ark, Lawrence of Arabia,* or, yes, even *The Mummy.* With apologies to Mr. Shakespeare, all I got was a flick full of sound and fury, signifying nothing.

(Released by Universal Pictures and rated "PG-13" for adventure action and violence.)

PLANET OF THE APES

While watching Tim Burton's version of *Planet of the Apes,* I wanted desperately to recast the movie with the stars of *Gladiator.* Instead of Mark Wahlberg as the lost astronaut, Russell Crowe would be my choice. Like Charlton Heston in the original, Crowe could run around shirtless. Betcha he'd refuse to wear those Raggedy Andy-like duds Wahlberg sports in most scenes. Next, I'd put Joaquin Phoenix in the part of the villainous ape general. Not that Tim Roth does such a bad job, but Phoenix could do it without make-up. Finally, as the beautiful blonde lady, I'd go for Connie Nielsen in place of fashion model Estella Warren, who seems uncomfortable wearing her tacky *One Million B.C.* costume.

Now that I think of it, the plot needs fixing too. Less frenzied action and more character development would help. I do love action scenes, but I want them to take place after a suspenseful build-up. And the action should involve characters we care about, like in *Gladiator* and, of course, in the original *Planet of the Apes.* However, Burton (*Sleepy Hollow*) claims her wasn't interested in doing a remake of the 1968 movie. "But I was intrigued by the idea of revisiting that world," he says. "The original has a life of its own, and we're trying to be respectful of it. We hope to get the best out of it and in the process introduce new characters and other story elements, keeping the essence of the original but inhabiting that world in a different way."

Unfortunately, Burton's efforts failed to hold my interest after the first 15 minutes. Granted, the opening credits and space station sequence offered great promise. As the beginning of the film,

Danny Elfman's (*Batman*) stirring drumbeat music enhanced dramatic graphics of simian warriors and teased me into thinking something wonderful was about to appear on the big screen. Maybe that's why I was so disturbed later by campy dialogue making fun of the first film-like "Get your stinking hands off me, you filthy human!"

I was also bothered by the ape civilization depicted as still rather primitive and by the humans shown as white, except for one token black. What's the unconscious message here? Highlighting the evils of slavery is one thing, but emphasizing the inherent inferiority of a particular species (or race, symbolically) doesn't seem to jibe with this premise. In the earlier film, the apes were technologically advanced, so there was no question about equality of intellect.

But, hey, I'm getting too serious here. And *Planet of the Apes* does feature some stunning visuals, particularly those warrior simians in attack mode, running on all fours. In terms of performances, there are a couple of gems. Helena Bonham Carter (*Fight Club*) actually breathes life into her role as the liberal daughter of an ape senator (David Warner) who sympathizes with the humans. Her expressive eyes shine through all that impressive make-up by Rick Baker (*The Grinch*). Paul Giamatti (*Duets*), as a sleazy orangutan businessman, enlivens his scenes with perfect comic timing. Discovered hiding during one of the conflicts, he insists, "I was just about to make my move." I almost believed him.

And now, a word about the film's mysterious ending. I'm sworn to secrecy (under threat of being forced to watch the movie again if I reveal it). But I will mention that this conclusion, though confusing and unsatisfying, is just as surprising as the original. Okay, here's a clue. It involves a different famous landmark. Which reminds me, I'd change that—and make it the Colisseum.

(Released by 20th Century Fox and rated "PG-13" for action and violence.)

SHAFT

Striding down the middle of a rain-soaked New York City street, the tall man in a long, black coat moves confidently against on-coming traffic. Going against the tide this way is nothing new for Shaft (Samuel L. Jackson), a fearless African-American police detective. Like his uncle before him, he sometimes breaks the rules to fight injustice—whether it's in the form of crime, corruption, or prejudice. His latest battle involves all three of these elements, plus a spoiled yuppie murderer.

The incredibly charismatic Jackson (*Rules of Engagement*) is a worthy successor to Richard Roundtree, who became a cultural icon after starring in the original *Shaft* in 1971 (and who appears as Jackson's uncle in this current film). Projecting an impressive combination of attitude, intensity, and wit, Jackson takes charge of this role and makes it his own. Not quite the ladies' man of his uncle's reputation, the new John Shaft is more flippant and aggressive. Sleek as a panther and twice as deadly, he seldom misses his target. Even his words sting like bullets. When he arrests Walter Wade (Christian Bale from *American Psycho*), the son of a real estate mogul, the suspect asks indignantly, "Don't you know who my father is?" Shaft shoots back, "No, do you?" He also has no qualms about insulting a powerful drug lord. After Peoples Hernandez (*Basquiat*'s Jeffrey Wright) brags about his Egyptian cotton suit, Shaft stuns him with, "You wouldn't know Egyptian cotton if the Pharaoh himself delivered it to you."

Both Wade and Peoples are fascinating villains to watch. From backgrounds as far apart as the politics of Rush Limbaugh and Fidel Castro, they form an unlikely pair of conspirators. Bale plays racist killer Wade with a devilish silver-spoon smirk, and Wright gives an unforgettable performance as the mercurial Peoples—even if his Dominican accent could use subtitles at times. Bound together by their desire to get back at Shaft, Wade wants Peoples to find and kill Diane Palmieri (Toni Collette), the only witness to his crime, while Peoples hopes Wade will lead him to "upscale" customers for his product.

Joining Wade and Peoples in their dastardly plans are two corrupt police officers (Dan Hedaya and Ruben Santiago-Hudson). Is it any wonder Shaft trusts no one except his loyal partner Carmen Vasquez (Vanessa Williams) and his helpful pal Rasaan (Busta Rhymes)? In Williams' case, her limited time on camera is a crime in itself. Justice is not served by a lack of romance between this lonely-looking lady and the sexy Shaft. Although not a love interest either, Oscar-nominee Collette (*The Sixth Sense*) has the juiciest female role in Shaft. Her mesmerizing portrayal of a woman in constant fear ranks as one of the best supporting performances so far this year. It's no surprise when her character elicits Shaft's only tender reaction in the entire film. After Palmieri finally admits seeing Wade's brutal beating of a young black man (Mekhi Phifer), the tough cop says to her, "These last two years must have been hell for you."

Fed up with police force restrictions and the fallible justice system, Shaft decides to resign and work with his uncle as a private detective. (The franchise cometh?) "I'm too black for the blues and too blue for the brothers," he explains. As directed and co-written by John Singleton (*Boyz N the Hood*), the new Shaft still includes an overuse of "mf" expletives. It also raises those usual blaxploitation issues. Still, with an Armani-clad Jackson filling the leading role and that classic *Shaft* music in the background, this action-packed update should ensure *Shaft*'s popularity well into the new millennium.

(Released by Paramount Pictures and rated "R" for strong violence and language.)

SHANGHAI NOON

Not since Mel Brooks' hilarious *Blazing Saddles* has there been such an outrageous Western as *Shanghai Noon*. Jackie Chan and Owen Wilson make the perfect odd couple in this action-packed comedy about the kidnapping of a Chinese princess during the mid-1800s.

Chan (*Rush Hour*) plays a member of China's Imperial Guard sent to America to bring the princess (Lucy Liu) back home. Motivated by duty, honor, and a strong sense of responsibility, he unwittingly partners with Wilson (*The Haunting*), a bumbling outlaw more interested in gold than in the Golden Rule. As usual,

Chan's Kung Fu clowning worked its magic on me, keeping me amused and astonished during his remarkable martial arts scenes.

But Wilson is the big surprise here. He's incredibly funny as a cowboy who can't make a life of crime work for him, yet still suffers from delusions of adequacy. His off-beat character is a cross between Robert Redford in *Butch Cassidy and the Sundance Kid* and Woody Allen in *Take the Money and Run*. Writing much of his own dialogue, Wilson says such comical lines as "John Wayne is no name for a cowboy" (after Chan tells him his name is Chon Wang).

Nothing succeeds like excess, so instead of just one dastardly villain to hate, *Shanghai Noon* gives viewers three of them. That adds to the fun, of course. Roger Yuan (Red Corner) is particularly menacing as the greedy and powerful kidnapper. Xander Berkeley (*Air Force One*) projects steely-eyed evil as a psychotic sheriff. The third bad guy, a sadistic outlaw played by Walton Goggins (*The Apostle*), is just downright mean. Naturally, they all get their comeuppance.

Yes, all the cliché Western scenes are included in this spoof of the genre—from saloon brawls and lynchings to train robberies and Indians. But here's a switch, the Indians are the good guys (and gals). And what would a Western be without horses? In *Shanghai Noon*, a very special horse steals a scene or two from the great Chan. Trainer Claude Chausse taught the animal, called Fido, to sit on his haunches just like a dog and to drink a bottle of whiskey for one sequence.

Jackie Chan movies always feature fast-paced action as well as humor. *Shanghai Noon* is no exception. In particular, Chan's closing struggle in the bell tower of an old church is a masterpiece of comic timing and physical activity. Knowing that Chan performs all those daring stunts himself makes a scene like this even more exciting.

Kudos to first-time director Tom Dey and to writers Alfred Gough and Miles Millar (*Lethal Weapon 4*) for their fine work on this entertaining film. It's an old-fashioned, rollicking good time.

(Released by Touchstone Pictures and Spyglass Entertainment; rated "PG-13" for action violence, some drug humor, sensuality, and language.)

SPACE COWBOYS

Four daring test pilots from yesteryear outshine today's brightest astronaut stars in *Space Cowboys*, a sci-fi action thriller starring Clint Eastwood, Tommy Lee Jones, Donald Sutherland, and James Garner. Although it's sad to see one's favorite movie heroes age right before your eyes, this involving film proves why these four senior citizens have maintained successful acting careers for so long.

Eastwood, whose craggy face still exudes that *Dirty Harry* macho, plays Frank Corvin, former leader of Team Daedalus, a group of pilots who trained to be the first in outer space. Neither he nor the rest of his team took it well when they were replaced by a chimp in 1958. Frank also designed the guidance system for a space satellite that is now malfunctioning. Because NASA's technicians know nothing about this "ancient" guidance device, Frank is drawn back into the space program to fix it. The only way to do this, he insists, is by traveling to the satellite and repairing it there.

Refusing to take on this assignment unless his Daedalus team-mates are involved, Frank coaxes each one to come along. He finds Hawk (Jones), a rambunctious old flyboy, at a small airport in Arizona. He's now a crop duster and sometime stunt pilot. Projecting a sarcastic devil-may-care attitude, Jones (*The Fugitive*) makes Hawk one of the film's most intriguing charac-ters. Noted for putting his foot in his mouth, he cracks disparag-ing jokes to people about their loved ones, then learns the indi-viduals he's talking about are deceased.

After one of these embarrassing conversations, he tells Frank, "Have you noticed that everyone seems to be dead lately?" In spite of Hawk's flippant attitude, NASA Mission Director Sara Holland (Marcia Gay Harden) takes special interest in him. She soon discovers he's still grieving over the recent death of his wife.

Frank has little trouble persuading Jerry (Sutherland) to rejoin the team. Jerry gets his thrills now by designing and testing roller coasters—and by pleasing women of all ages. Portraying an eld-erly Don Juan, Sutherland (*Instinct*) clearly relishes this role. When Team Daedalus appears on television's *Tonight Show*, Jay

Leno refers to Jerry as "the babe magnet" of the group—and Sutherland's broad smile at this remark seems completely genuine.

Tank (Garner), the wittiest member of Frank's team, has a surprising new vocation. He's a minister, but one with difficulty keeping the congregation's attention unless talking about flying. Frank recruits Tank by explaining, "You'll have material for three or four more sermons." Garner (*My Fellow Americans*) has lost none of his great comic timing with age. Amusing as ever, he delivers the film's funniest lines. At the beginning of the space launch, his character announces, "I'm going to recite the Shepard's prayer now. Alan Shepard, that is. Dear Lord, please help us not to screw up!"

Becoming a team again is not easy for this over-the-hill gang. They must deal with past differences, work with a treacherous former boss (James Cromwell), undergo grueling physical preparation activities, and face taunting by the much younger NASA astronauts. But they give as good as they get. After receiving cans of Ensure to drink with their lunch, they send jars of Gerber's baby food to the jokesters. When Ethan (Loren Dean), the competitive astronaut assigned to help Frank, complains about not understanding the old guidance system in spite of his two masters degrees, Frank says, "Maybe you ought to get your money back."

Eastwood also served as director of *Space Cowboys*. In this capacity, he wisely focused on character and human relationships instead of on high-tech gimmickry. Even so, the film's outer space scenes depicting repair of a gigantic satellite hiding a dangerous secret are extremely well-done. Visually impressive, the clunky, aged satellite contrasts dramatically with the sleek, modern spacecraft of the crew sent to save it. Floating in space against a silvery moon backdrop, the white-suited astronauts look small and insignificant as they perform their daring feats, reminding us of the immensity of the universe. And then, like a bad dessert after a delicious meal, the movie's last scene almost spoils everything. To the tune of "Fly Me to the Moon," a final panning shot of the moon's surface reveals something we don't want or need to see.

(Released by Warner Bros. and rated "PG-13" for language.)

SPY KIDS

Children of all ages will have a hard time resisting *Spy Kids*, a live-action comedy starring Antonio Banderas and Carla Gugino as retired secret agents whose pre-teen son and daughter must save them—and the world. Although gadgets galore almost overwhelm the film's characters and plot, this whimsical spoof of spy thrillers offers plenty of fun for the whole family.

In a fast-paced and well-edited opening, Ingrid Cortez (Gugino) tells her children a bedtime story about how two notorious spies met, fell in love, and were married. Little do Carmen (Alex Vega) and Juni (Daryl Sabara) realize it's a true story about their own parents. "They aren't cool enough to be spies," Carmen says.

After Gregorio (Banderas) and Ingrid are called back into duty, they are kidnapped by Fegan Floop (Alan Cumming), the host of a television program who turns secret agents into bizarre characters for his popular kiddie show. Discovering their parents' true identity, Carmen and Juni decide to use all the spy equipment they can find to bring their family back together. And what an amazing arsenal they manage to collect! Exploding bubblegum, silly-string cement, jetpacks that resemble backpacks but zoom like rockets, a submarine pod that transforms into a boat, a spy car with video screens, and a mini-spy plane with video-game controls are among the inventions used in their daring exploits.

Filmmaker Robert Rodriguez, whose claim to fame lies in creation of such violent movies as *Desperado* and *From Dusk to Dawn*, let his inner child run wild in writing and directing this espionage fantasy. "I wanted to make a movie that had the kind of imaginative elements of all those movies I loved growing up such as *Willy Wonka* and *Chitty Chitty Bang Bang*—which was written by Ian Fleming by the way," explains Rodriguez. The visual wonder of Spy Kids exceeds his goal. Floop's surrealistic castle and his Thumb-Thumb robot guards win hands down over a flying horseless carriage and those musical Oompah Loompahs.

Cumming, a Tony-winner for *Cabaret*, displays his unique singing talent in the film's only musical number. His flamboyant potrayal of a villain who just might be more concerned about show business than destroying the world is a gem. The movie's other "bad guys" include Tony Shalhoub (*Big Night*) as Floop's quietly evil assistant, Robert Patrick (from television's *X-Files*) as a humor-challenged corporate executive, and Teri Hatcher (*Tomorrow Never Dies*) as a betrayer who gets her comeuppance in the form of an extremely bad hair day.

Although each actor seems to be having a great time in this rambunctious movie, Vega (*Deep End of the Ocean*) and new-comer Sabara don't always connect as brother and sister. Vega frowns most of the time, and Sabara's klutziness doesn't ring true. They also lack the comic timing needed for these key roles. In contrast, Banderas (*The Mask of Zorro*) and Gugino (*Snake Eyes*) can do no wrong. Funny and sexy, they bring Gregorio and Ingrid to life in every scene together. In addition, while wearing sophis-ticated disguises before settling down to raise a family, this stun-ning couple makes the ultimate fashion statement for spydom.

Ingrid, Gregorio, Carmen, and Juni learn that keeping the Cortez family together is more important than any spy mission. Does this mean they won't accept other assignments as secret agents in the future? Of course not. A sequel is already in the works.

(Released by Dimension Films and rated "PG" for action sequences.)

TOMB RAIDER

Movies featuring women as heroes usually perk me up con-siderably, even when the story includes dark themes or tragic moments. Whether it's Sigourney Weaver battling the space mon-ster in *Alien*, Ingrid Bergman inspiring her troops as Joan of Arc, Drew Barrymore taking charge of her life as Cinderella in *Ever After*, or a young Chinese girl named Mulan defeating the invad-ing Huns, I cheer them on. That's one of the reasons I looked for-ward to seeing Oscar-winner Angelina Jolie as Lara Croft in *Tomb Raider.*

Jolie (*Girl Interrupted*) is among the first stars I interviewed after becoming a film critic, so that's another reason. Charming and out-going, she's my only interviewee who insisted the photographer take a photo of the two of us together. Although I view having photos taken with celebrities as unprofessional, I'm glad it happened. Imagine the thrill that picture gives my grandchildren today!

Expecting Lara Croft to make my list of admired film heroines, I came away from *Tomb Raider* feeling sadly disappointed. Yes, Jolie looks gorgeous in her archeologist mini-pants, and her stiff-upper-lip British accent sounds perfect to me. She also shares a couple of provocative moments with her own father, Jon Voight (*Pearl Harbor*), who plays Lara's dad, a famous archeologist gone missing in the field. (Actually, "provocative" might be too strong a word here, but I couldn't help wondering if Voight got the job strictly because of his relationship to Jolie.) Regrettably, Jolie's Lara lacks the human vulnerability of those great female characters I mentioned above, even the animated Mulan.

Because we know Lara Croft is a video-game icon—one that can't be destroyed (at least in this movie)—nothing suspenseful results from her *Indiana Jones*-like quest to find both pieces of an ancient triangle with the power to reverse time. While watching the young archeologist overcome various obstacles during her tomb-raiding adventures, no matter how many grotesque statues came to life and tried to stop her, I couldn't believe she was in any real danger.

Another weak spot in *Tomb Raider* concerns its lack of a respectable villain. I found Iain Glen's (*Beautiful Creatures*) attempts to appear sinister and evil are about as convincing as John Travolta's laughable portrayal of the Psychlo thug in *Battlefield Earth*. Glen reminded me of someone who should be introducing Masterpiece Theatre, not plotting to become the ruler of the universe. Call me perverse, but I simply must have a vicious villain I can hate adequately in these action flicks. Give me someone like Gary Oldman as Mr. Zorg in *The Fifth Element*, Tim Roth as Archibald Cunningham in *Rob Roy*, or even Alan Cumming as the dastardly emperor in *Titus*, and I'm happy.

Just like in *The Mummy Returns,* incredible special effects overwhelm almost everything else in *Tomb Raider*. Lara fights giant machine creatures! Lara zaps a regiment of soldiers invading her high-tech English mansion! Lara jumps on a granite juggernaut and rides it like a bucking bronco! Lara saves the world in a blaze of explosions! Perhaps some other amazing stuff happened, but I dozed off a few times, so I'm not sure. Please accept my apologies. After all, unlike Lara Croft, I'm only human.

(Released by Paramount Pictures and rated "PG-13" for action violence and some sensuality.)

U-571

Before going to see *U-571*, be sure to get a good night's rest and take plenty of vitamins. If not, you will be completely wiped out by the end of this exciting movie. Just as he did in *Breakdown* (starring Kurt Russell and Kathleen Quinlan), director Jonathan Mostow keeps viewers on the edge of their seats with one frightening incident after another. In addition, superb sound effects, visually thrilling scenes, and stirring background music enhance the entertainment value of Mostow's second film, a World War II action thriller.

Most of the thrills take place inside a submarine where Lieutenant Andrew Tyler (Matthew McConaughey) is forced into command after the death of his captain (Bill Paxton). "Although my primary goal in making *U-571* was to recreate the experience of life aboard a WWII submarine during war, I also wanted to show audiences how young men in this environment rose above their fears to accomplish incredible feats of heroism," Mostow claims.

The heroism dramatized in U-571 invoves a group of U.S. sailors sent on a daring mission to capture Enigma, a German decoding device. Disguised as Germans, they board an enemy submarine, then become trapped there after their own ship is destroyed. They must use their wits and courage to survive torpedoes, depth charges, and the horrific silence between each explosion. Every crisis inside the sub comes across as incredibly terrifying and realistic. Viewers familiar with *Das Boot* will recognize the work of Gotz Weidner, who also did production design for that classic German submarine film. Both movies make you feel as if you are experiencing the events while they are happening on screen. It's almost too scary!

Kudos also to the cast. McConaughey (*EdTV*), in a welcome change of pace, shows just a hint of his twangy accent that is so annoying at times. Paxton (*A Simple Plan*), though only in the first part of the movie, is perfect as a captain to emulate. Harvey Keitel (*The Piano*) does a fine job as an "old salt" who's been through World War I and knows the ropes. Believe it or not, he actually keeps his clothes on throughout the entire film! Effectively playing other "ordinary men who do extraordinary things in extraordinary times" are Jon Bon Jovi, Jack Noseworhy, David Keith, Jake Weber, Thomas Guiry, T. C. Carson, and Erik Palladino. As a German taken prisoner, Thomas Kretschmann gives a chilling performance. (One criticism of this film is its negative portrayal of all Germans. Still, the setting is World War II, and that's the way most Americans felt then.)

Is this movie historically accurate? Not really. The British, not the Americans, captured the first Enigma machine. Lt. Commander David Balme, an intrepid British officer, actually led the boarding party onto the real submarine in May of 1941. But even Balme, who visited the set of *U-571* and viewed the completed movie earlier this year, calls Mostow's work of fiction "a magnificent film."

(Released by Universal Pictures/Studio Canal in association with Dino De Laurentis and rated "PG-13" for war violence.)

VERTICAL LIMIT

From its gripping opening sequence to its emotionally-charged ending, *Vertical Limit* kept me on the edge of my seat. Although primarily an action-adventure showcasing the excitement of mountain climbing, this fast-paced movie is also a compelling drama about love, family, and courage. Delivering his most touching performance to date, Chris O'Donnell stars as a nature photographer obsessed with rescuing his estranged sister, a woman trapped in an icy grave on the world's second highest peak.

After a tragic accident takes the life of their father, Peter (O'Donnell) and Annie (Robin Tunney) go their separate ways. While the three were climbing together, Peter made a split-second decision to save Annie and himself—a decision that resulted in the father's death. Peter is devastated by Annie's unwillingness to forgive him. Ironically, when they meet three years later, he must climb K2, the world's most feared mountain, to save her life again.

O'Donnell (*The Bachelor*) projects an intriguing sensitivity and daring in this starring role. "There is no doubt in Peter's mind about what he has to do," the young actor explains about the character he plays. "There's not a chance he's not going after her and giving it his all. If it kills him in the process, that's fine, because the idea of living without having tried would be harder for him. His only concern is to get her out."

Tunney (*End of Days*) endows Annie with a refreshing individuality and independence. "A lot of times when you're looking for roles in film as a woman, you're the girlfriend, or the wife, or the daughter, or the appendage," she declares. "But this woman is very independent, and that's hard to come by."

One of the big surprises in *Vertical Limit* is Bill Paxton's convincing work as a villain. His calculating, penetrating looks made me shudder almost as much as those scary cliff-hanging scenes. Paxton usually appears as the hero (in films like *U-571* and *Twister*), so it's a shock to watch him as the evil Elliot Vaughn, a selfish entrepreneur trapped in the cave with Annie. Wisely, Paxton disguised himself with a beard for this unsympathetic role.

In addition, Scott Glenn (*Absolute Power*) excels as a reclusive mountain man persuaded by Peter to lead the rescue team. Glenn's craggy face and gravelly voice seem perfect for this eccentric character. The fine supporting cast also includes: Nicholas Lea (from television's *X-Files*) as another trapped mountain climber; Izabella Scorupco (*GoldenEye*) as a member of the rescue team in it for the money; and Alexander Siddig (*Star Trek: Deep Space Nine*) as a courageous porter. Regrettably, although Ben Mendelsohn (*Cosi*) and Steve Le Marquand (*Two Hands*) have a great time playing comic brothers involved in the rescue, I had trouble understanding their Aussie accents.

With *Vertical Limit*, director Martin Campbell (*The Mask of Zorro* and *GoldenEye*) proves himself a master of the action-adventure film again. Working with cinematographer David

Tattersall (*The Phantom Menace*), he features realistic mountain shots that seem almost three-dimensional. Since I'm afraid of heights, I even felt a bit of vertigo during some scenes. Fortunately, Campbell concentrated this time as much on relationships as on special effects and visual thrills. As a result, *Vertical Limit* is a movie filled with drama, suspense, and humanity.

(Released by Columbia Pictures and rated "PG-13" for intense life/death situations and brief strong language.)

X-MEN

Movie adaptations of comic books are not renowned for depth of character development. That's why the sensitive depictions of Wolverine and Rogue in *X-Men* are such a pleasant surprise. In addition, the movie's concerns regarding prejudice and alienation are quite impressive. (Fans of sci-fi action needn't be turned away by these comments. *X-Men* also features spectacular clashes between mutants with fantastic super powers.)

Neither Wolverine (Hugh Jackman) nor Rogue (Anna Paquin) know why they are different from other people. He is blessed, or cursed, with deadly metal claws that appear during times of great stress. She is unable to touch anyone without siphoning off that person's strength and memories. When these two outcasts meet, it seems impossible they could form such a strong bond of friendship. Wolverine resembles a cross between Lon Chaney's Wolfman and the young Clint Eastwood. Rogue just looks like a normal teenager in trouble. But both are mutants, representatives of the next stage of human evolution. They are destined to work together in helping wheelchair-bound Xavier (Patrick Stewart) save mankind from destruction by Magneto (Ian McKellen), his former friend and colleague.

In spite of the film's dazzling special effects and superb acting by McKellen and Stewart, Jackman's animal magnetism takes over *X-Men*. The charismatic Australian actor, making his American film debut, projects a combination of humor and machismo that adds extra excitement to all his scenes. Granted, he's the one with the snappiest dialogue. When Xavier introduces

Wolverine to his oddly named mutant helpers, the feral recruit teases, "Cyclops. Storm. And who are you—Wheels?"

Stewart gives the telepathic Xavier that same nobility he brings to the role of Captain Picard in his *Star Trek* outings. In *X-Men*, he portrays the benevolent founder of a school where mutants learn to use their special powers in constructive ways. His three gifted assistants are the laser-eyed Cyclops (James Marsden), the telepathic/telekinetic Jean Grey (Famke Janssen), and Storm (Halle Berry), who can summon forth lightning and winds of hurricane force.

McKellen exudes *Richard III*-like venom as Xavier's opponent Magneto, one of the world's most powerful mutants. Believing it impossible for humans and mutants to coexist, he plots to destroy all humankind. Magneto's henchmen include the giant Sabertooth (Tyler Mane), the shape-changing Mystique (Rebecca Romijn-Stamos), and the long-tongued, high-jumping Toad (Ray Park). To complete their diabolical plans, Rogue must be captured, and her powers blended with Magneto's. As Rogue, Paquin appears to experience genuine terror in these frightening scenes. With her quivering voice and nervous facial expressions, she makes Rogue's dangerous plight seem quite real. (No wonder she won an Oscar as Best Supporting Actress in *The Piano*.)

What are humans doing while all this is happening? One of them, Senator Kelly (Bruce Davison), is seeking legislation requiring registration of all mutants. Capitalizing on the general fear and hatred of anyone different, he preaches a philosophy of segregation. "We have to know what the mutants are doing. They have to be watched carefully, " he insists. Davison (*Apt Pupil*) makes his McCarthyesque character so slimy no one is sorry when he gets an appropriate comeuppance from Magneto.

It's obvious there's enough material here for several movies. And that's the problem. Director Bryan Singer (*The Usual Suspects*) and first-time screenwriter David Hayter have included too many plot threads to follow in the film's 93 minutes. Consequently, some events seem confusing—such as why one particular machine disables Xavier but not Jean Grey and what causes Wolverine's amnesia. Also, there's not enough time to enjoy each of the mutant superheroes equally. Because Storm receives so much special-effects attention, she emerges as the most amazing of the group. (Her pearl-glazed eyes and flowing blonde hair help too!) But Toad gets short-shrift. He's in very few shots and contributes little to the mutant battles. Perhaps the *X-Men* sequel will focus on these neglected areas. Surely there will be one.

(Released by 2000 Twentieth Century Fox and rated "PG-13" for science fiction violence.)

COMEDY:

ALMOST FAMOUS

"One day, you will be cool," William Miller's big sister tells him in *Almost Famous*. Leaving home because of their mother's strict attitude, she whispers to the 11-year old, "Look under my bed. What you find there will set you free." What the wide-eyed youngster discovers is a stash of rock and roll records. Although listening to these records fails to make him "cool," it leads him to an adventure deep within the music world of the 1970s. Assigned by *Rolling Stone* magazine to cover the tour of Stillwater, a group on the cusp of fame, he becomes a rock journalist at 15. This engaging coming-of-age movie depicts William's struggle for objectivity in the midst of people he idolizes.

Unfortunately, I'm facing a similar dilemma with this review. Billy Crudup (*Jesus' Son*), who plays the lead guitarist of the rock band William (Patrick Fugit) must write about, is one of my favorite actors. I even had the privilege of introducing him at a special event during last year's Telluride Film Festival. It's not easy for me to be objective about his work—especially when he's so terrific in this film. (See what I mean?)

Anyhow, Crudup delivers another compelling performance here. In the role of Russell Hammond, he projects the charisma of a rock star, combining egotism with flashes of humanity. When his character confides in William that he is a much better musician than the rest of the band, Crudup does so in such a convincing way, it's like overhearing it backstage at a real rock concert. On the other hand, when he shouts how much he loves the group, he sounds a bit ingenuous, subtly revealing Russell's ambivalent feelings about his colleagues.

After befriending William, Russell tries to evade an interview with him. Speaking to the boy's over-protective mother on the phone, he uses all the charm he can muster, but it doesn't work on her. Oscar-winner Frances McDormand (*Fargo*) portrays William's college professor mom with so much authority, I wanted to snap "Yes, Ma'am!" right along with Russell whenever she issued an order. "I know all about your Valhalla decadence," she informs the rock musician, obviously worried about her son's involvement with people in the drug culture.

"Your mother freaked me out," Russell complains to the young reporter. But he can't help thinking about the things she said—such as "Be bold and make a statement; it's not too late to amount to something."

Helping Russell amount to something becomes a major task for William. He worries about Russell's treatment of Penny Lane (Kate Hudson), a young woman who follows the band everywhere. Even though the lad has fallen for her himself, he knows she loves Russell. Sadly, the guitarist is committed to someone else but leads Penny on anyway. Hudson (*200 Cigarettes*) simply glows in this key role. Her humorous and poignant scenes with young William are among the film's many highlights. Happily, Hudson inherited a flair for comedy as well as good looks from her famous mother, Goldie Hawn. She's especially amusing when tempting William to go with her to Morocco.

In addition to the wonderful Frances McDormand, Billy Crudup, and Kate Hudson, this involving movie includes flawless performances by Jason Lee (*Chasing Amy*) as Stillwater's volatile lead singer and Philip Seymour Hoffman (*The Talented Mr. Ripley*) as William's "uncool" journalism mentor who advises the youngster to be "honest and unmerciful."

Despite these fine actors, *Almost Famous* would not be the special movie it is without newcomer Patrick Fugit as William. Admitting his latest movie is autobiographical, filmmaker Cameron Crowe (*Jerry Maguire*) searched for the perfect boy for this part. After all, whoever was selected would be portraying the writer/director himself at that age. Fortunately, Fugit was an excellent choice. His William emerges as a funny, awkward, idealistic, and endearing young hero.

(Released by DreamWorks Pictures/Columbia Pictures and rated "R" for language, drug content, and brief nudity.)

AMERICA'S SWEETHEARTS

Better get this out of the way first. I love movies about movies. *Singin' in the Rain,* my all-time favorite film, puts a smile on my face every time I watch it. What those stars of silent motion pictures went through as a result of "talkies" taking over! It's great fun seeing a bit of cinema history presented in such an amusing way. And I always enjoy it when the spoiled prima donna portrayed by Jean Hagen loses out to a more deserving Debbie Reynolds.

Reminiscent of *Singin' in the Rain, America's Sweethearts* features Catherine Zeta-Jones as a super star who takes advantage of her sister/assistant both in their personal and professional lives. Julia Roberts, portraying the put-upon sibling, matches Zeta-Jones' flashy performance by displaying a quiet charm that won me over completely, even though I couldn't help wondering why she wasn't cast in the megastar role.

Making fun of all things Hollywood, this timely comedy co-written by *Analyze This* screenwriters Billy Crystal and Peter Tolan focuses on a studio publicist (Crystal) and his efforts to re-unite Zeta-Jones (*Traffic*) and John Cusack (*Being John Malkovich*), her estranged husband. These two have been big box office draws in a series of blockbusters, so it's important they get back together before their latest film is released. Crystal's job depends on it. He enlists the help of Roberts (*The Mexican*) in persuading Zeta-Jones to attend the press junket. Next, he bribes Cusack's wellness guru (Alan Arkin in a terrific cameo) to make sure the neurotic actor also participates.

I've never attended a press junket, so I don't know if any of the hilarious situations depicted here are true to life. But, as a veteran interviewer of stars during personal appearance tours, I can vouch for the number of stupid questions actors must answer (some asked by yours truly). I'm embarrassed to admit that a critic in one scene sounded just like me when inquiring about whether or not the two stars were getting back together. My interview with Lauren Holly after her much-publicized divorce from Jim Carrey seems all too similar now. (Sorry, Lauren.) No wonder actors sometimes lose control and can't resist giving ridiculous answers, like Cusack's character when he claims that he, his wife, and her new boyfriend (Hank Azaria from *Mystery, Alaska*) all make love together.

Studio heads and temperamental directors also take a ribbing in *America's Sweethearts*. Stanley Tucci (*Big Night*) makes the movie mogul he portrays look more ambitious and unethical than any mob boss. He even considers the idea of a star's suicide being good for his movie—"if it happens at the premiere." Christopher Walken (*Sleepy Hollow*) cracked me up as an eccentric filmmaker who edits all his movies in the unibomber's shack (which he purchased and moved to his estate.) His brief tap-dancing scene with Zeta-Jones is a special treat. I keep forgetting Walken started out in musical comedy on Broadway. What a shame he doesn't perform more song and dance numbers on screen!

All this talent would be wasted in *America's Sweethearts* without serious chemistry between Roberts and Cusack. Before seeing the movie, I was convinced they were miscast as the romantic leads. Fortunately, Cusack delivers a very funny and poignant performance as a man devastated by his wife's infidelity, yet drawn to her more sensitive sister. He appears like two different people with each of the women. Warmth comes through in his scenes with Roberts, an edgy nervousness with Zeta-Jones. As for Roberts, the way she looked at Cusack convinced me she cared deeply for him. Her glances, filled with tenderness and humor, say more than any words.

No, this isn't the greatest comedy about movies ever made. As mentioned before, *Singin' in the Rain* ranks number one in my book. *Bowfinger, State and Main, Silent Movie,* and *Won Ton Ton, the Dog Who Saved Hollywood* all evoke more laughs with less cynicism. Still, *America's Sweethearts* is a welcome addition to a genre so popular with movie addicts like me.

(Released by Columbia and Revolution Studios; rated "PG-13" for language and some crude and sexual humor.)

BEDAZZLED

The classic Faustian theme about selling one's soul to the Devil sets the stage for Brendan Fraser's tour de force performance in *Bedazzled*. This versatile actor is simply incredible as Elliot Richards, a lovesick nerd who becomes five very different characters during the film's hilarious wish sequences. I thought Fraser could never be any funnier than he was in *George of the Jungle*, but I was so wrong!

Ably assisted by glamorous Elizabeth Hurley (from the *Austin Powers* flicks) as Satan and lovely Frances O'Connor (*Mansfield Park*) as the object of his desire, Fraser uses his innate flair for comedy and considerable physical skills to make each character he portrays here as amusing as possible. In the opening scenes, he looks so pathetic it's hard to believe this is the same man who played such a convincing action-hero in *The Mummy*. When he changes into his other personas—a powerful Colombian drug lord, a debonair winner of the Pulitzer Prize, an ultra-sensitive suitor, a gigantic basketball star, and a U. S. President—he's just as amazing.

Director Harold Ramis (*Analyze This*) explains best what Fraser brought to this movie when he says, "Brendan has the soul of a misfit in the body of a hero. He is handsome, and has tremendous strength and energy, yet he can also be really goofy, completely self-effacing and humble."

Fraser's talent for appearing sincere as well as humorous serves him particularly well in one of *Bedazzled*'s wittiest scenes. After wishing to be the world's most sensitive man, Elliot weeps at the sunset and can barely look into his loved one's eyes without being overcome with emotion. Flattered at first, the woman leaves him for someone who doesn't respect her so much. As she walks away, Elliot looks at the sky and cries, "Will that damn sun never set!"

Although a remake of the 1967 film comedy starring Dudley Moore and Peter Cook, this *Bedazzled* emerges as edgier and even more outrageous. Casting a woman as the Devil adds a new twist to the legendary Faust tale, and Hurley's playful, sexy interpretation of the role works remarkably well. Fabulous costumes by designer Deena Appel give Hurley's Satan a kind of decadent Zeigfield Girl look. Seductive red dresses, a kinky red coat, a flamboyant red feather jacket, and shiny red snakeskin boots are among her haute couture choices. She does wear one white angel gown but insists, "It's a Halloween costume."

Watching the delightful interplay between Fraser and Hurley made me want to see more of these stars together on screen. Hurley's elegant British accent and saucy manner complement Fraser's comedic appeal. I loved how Fraser's Elliot appeared so indignant about the Devil's constant sabotage of his wishes and the way Hurley's Satan always gave him a look of mock surprise at this accusation. I think a Fraser/Hurley team would be terrific in updated versions of those old Gary Grant, Katharine Hepburn films like *Bringing Up Baby.*

Happily, winning Elliot's soul turns out to be no easy task for the naughty Devil. Good wins out over Evil, and Elliott not only learns to be more accepting of himself but also to be careful about what he wishes for. It's refreshing to receive this important moral lesson in such an entertaining way.

(Released by 20th Century Fox and rated "PG-13" for sex-related humor, language, and some drug content.)

BRING IT ON

"Cheerleaders are dancers gone retarded," claims choreographer Sparky Polastri in *Bring It On.* Hired to whip a high school cheerleading squad into shape for a crucial regional competition, he appears to use Bob Fosse and Adolph Hitler as role models. Played by Ian Roberts (*I Dreamed of Africa*), the outrageous Sparky emerges as a highlight of this energetic teen comedy. In addition, Kirsten Dunst's enthusiastic star turn as Torrance Shipman, the squad's highly motivated new captain, is something to cheer about.

A former cheerleader in real life, Dunst (*Drop Dead Gorgeous*) delivers a powerful physical performance that's right up there with Daniel Day Lewis in *The Last of the Mohicans* and Jennifer Lopez in *Selena.* Vivacious and perky, she bounces through this film like a human dynamo, performing those vigorous cheerleading routines to perfection. But she also acts up a storm as a San Diego teenager obsessed with leading the Toros, her five-time national championship squad, to another victory. When someone reminds her, "Don't worry, it's only cheerleading," Torrance replies "But I AM only cheerleading." With that one comment, Dunst made Torrance sound so sincere it saddened me—even in the midst of all the laughter.

Helping Torrance with her mission is new pal Missy Pantone (Eliza Dushku), a hard-core gymnast turned cheerleader. Dushku (Faith in *Buffy the Vampire Slayer*) projects comic sarcasm as a transfer student who informs Torrance that her predecessor "puts the itch in bitch" for stealing cheers from an East Los Angeles squad called the Clovers. After Missy takes Torrance to see this fantastic African-American group, led by its charismatic captain (Gabrielle Union of *She's All That*), fierce competition between the two squads ensues.

Cheering the Toros on, though sometimes reluctantly, is Missy's brother, portrayed by Jesse Bradford (*King of the Hill*), a young actor with the most charming crooked smile since Montgomery Clift. He's very amusing when flirting with Dunst in a cute teeth brushing scene—and almost matches her energy in one explosive guitar-strumming sequence.

There's not much of a story here, but that didn't bother me. I was too wrapped up in the film's exuberant cheerleading numbers and appealing characters. Also, I found the cheerleader tryouts hilarious. A variety of unusual teens competed for membership on the Toros squad. Ballet, stripper, and musical comedy wannabes were joined by some of the most unenthusiastic, clumsy students imaginable. It was great fun to watch each audition.

With so much going for this movie, it's disappointing that director Peyton Reed and screenwriter Jessica Bendinger included a disgusting vomiting incident, some risque cheers, and frequent jokes about gay male cheerleaders in their first feature film. Still, by focusing on a main character with a sense of honor, they elevated their movie above many recent teen comedies. I couldn't help admiring Torrance's attempts to make things come out right for both squads, in spite of their intense rivalry.

It's about time a movie celebrated cheerleaders and their incredible talents. Three cheers for *Bring It On*.

(Released by Universal Pictures and rated "PG-13" for sex-related material and language.)

CATS & DOGS

Imagine Mel Gibson's *The Patriot* with dogs playing American colonists and cats portraying their British foes. Throw in slapstick comedy to replace violent battle scenes. Add a few high-tech spy gadgets and hordes of brainwashed mice. Voila! It's *Cats & Dogs*, a summer movie treat for the whole family. While not as effective as *Chicken Run*, last year's hilarious poultry remake of *The Great Escape*, this live-action comedy worked for me—despite lackluster performances by its three human actors.

I took two young cat lovers to see *Cats & Dogs*, so I wasn't surprised by their reactions to the film's depiction of felines as diabolical villains. "How unfair!" one exclaimed. "Cats are better than dogs. They're easier to take care of and don't need constant attention," the other chimed in. Still, I noticed both of them laughing during most of the movie, even in scenes showing dogs getting the best of their age-old enemies.

How could anyone not laugh at deadly ninja cats foiled in their mission to destroy a scientist's laboratory? Or when a cuddly kitten suddenly switches into *Terminator* attack mode? Or at a gorgeous white Persian who imagines himself as the mastermind of world domination? ("Genghis Khan never wore a bonnet," the maniacal Mr. Tinkles complains while being dressed in a ridiculous costume by his human caretaker.)

Being a dog supporter myself, I cheered on the heroic canines in their efforts to stop power-mad Mr. Tinkles (voiced by Sean Hayes of *Will and Grace*) from taking over our planet. Beagles have always been a favorite breed of mine, so "Lou" (voiced by Tobey Maguire from *Wonder Boys*), a wannabe Secret Agent, had no trouble stealing my heart. With his big brown eyes and floppy ears, that little puppy charmed me in every scene. And Maguire's youthful voice seemed perfect for Lou, the film's main character.

Thrust accidentally into a family to protect the father's research on allergies to dogs, Lou soon bonds with the professor's son (Alexander Pollock) and wins the mother's (Elizabeth Perkins) affection. But, even more important for the future of man's best friend, he also meets secret operatives in the canine cause. There's a German shepherd (voiced by Alec Baldwin) who teaches him the ropes, a mysterious maternal Saluki hound (voiced by Susan Sarandon), a Chinese hairless electronics expert (voiced by Joe Pantoliano), and a sight-challenged sheepdog (voiced by Michael Clarke Duncan). I'm amazed at how well each actor's voice coordinated with the personality and expressions of the animal portrayed—awesome, just like in *Babe*.

Unfortunately, as the human family, Goldblum, Perkins, and Pollock show little enthusiasm for their roles. Goldblum and Perkins add nothing to the stereotypes of the absent minded professor and his long-suffering wife, and Pollock (*Replicant*) failed to convince me of any genuine concern for his pets. (Just looking out into space doesn't cut it.) Goldblum (*Jurassic Park*) licks a dog's nose, develops hives from the contact, misses his son's soccer event—but has the same quizzical look for each situation. Perkins, so delightful as Tom Hanks' love interest in *Big*, delivers her lines like a member of Robomoms, Inc. She punishes a puppy or encourages her son with the same nonchalant expression.

Am I being too harsh? Did these actors realize their performances, no matter how fine, would be overshadowed by such photogenic animals and just give up? Perhaps. For, make no bones about it—this movie belongs completely to those incredible *Cats & Dogs*.

(Released by Warner Bros. and rated "PG" for animal action and humor.)

CHICKEN RUN

Using the term "chicken-hearted" for cowardly behavior will no longer be tolerated. Not after watching the brave chickens of Tweedy's Yorkshire Egg Farm hatch their daring escape plans in *Chicken Run*, the world's first full-length movie in clay animation. Filled with heroism, humor and heart, this wonderful film is a treat for the entire family.

Who are the movie's plucky heroes? First and foremost, there's Ginger (voiced by Julia Sawalha), the leader of the flock. A very intelligent chick, she could probably find a way out by herself but cares too much about all the others to desert them. Next, there's Babs (Jane Horrocks), a compulsive knitter. She thinks the low egg-producing hens, taken to the chopping block by evil Mrs. Tweedy (Miranda Richardson), are simply "away on holiday." There's also a Scottish chicken (Lynn Ferguson) with a flair for engineering, and a champion egg-layer (Imelda Staunton). An old rooster called Fowler (Benjamin Whitrow) completes the list of major conspirators—but he spends most of his time crowing about his "good old days" in the RAF, so he's not much help at first.

No matter how hard they try, nothing seems to work. Then, as if by magic, Rocky (Mel Gibson), a cocky rooster from America, drops into their lives and changes everything. He promises to teach them to fly. Just in time, too, for greedy Mrs. Tweedy plans on increasing her profits by becoming a chicken pie mogul instead of an egg farmer. Mr. Tweedy (Tony Haygarth), who suspects the chickens are up to something, can't dissuade her. "Chickens don't organize," she insists.

While the admiring hens fall for Rocky's fast-talking scheme, Fowler remains skeptical. "You Yanks are always late for the war," the old rooster complains. Watching Rocky supervise the inmates' pre-flight training, it's easy to see why chickens can't fly. Although performing vigorous, and sometimes hilarious, exercises, these unlikely aeronautical recruits never get off the ground under their own steam. However, a romance between Rocky and Ginger is in the air. Unfortunately, after Ginger discovers Rocky can't fly, their romance suffers a crash landing. Although disappointed and heartbroken, Ginger takes charge of escape plans again. Motivating everyone to work together, she oversees the building of an amazing aircraft—one that looks like a monster bird.

The expressive voices of actors doing key characters in *Chicken Run* contribute to its special charm. Gibson (*Braveheart*) gives Rocky an energetic Yankee accent that contrasts perfectly with the sweet British tones of Sawalha (*Absolutely Fabulous*) and Horrocks (*Little Voice*) as Ginger and Babs. Among the film's many other delights are a wild ride inside Mrs. Tweedy's gigantic pie-making machine, a rousing "Flip, Flop, Fly" musical number, and the comic antics of a pair of scavenger rats (voiced by Timothy Spall and Phil Daniels). In addition to all this fun, *Chicken Run* offers an important lesson about the value of freedom.

If the plot of this landmark movie seems a bit familiar, it should. With Ginger in the Steve McQueen role, this is a poultry version of 1963's *The Great Escape*. Nick Park and Peter Lord (creators of *Wallace and Gromit*), who produced and directed *Chicken Run*, must be great fans of that earlier movie. Park says he once did a sketch of a chicken digging under a wire fence with a spoon. He claims that simple drawing started him thinking how funny it would be to have chickens as central characters in an escape film. He was right.

(Released by DreamWorks Pictures in association with Pathe/Aardman Productions and rated "G.")

CROCODILE DUNDEE IN LOS ANGELES

Ace crocodile hunter Mick Dundee becomes disoriented and does some pretty silly things whenever he leaves the Australian Outback. In *Crocodile Dundee in Los Angeles*, he mistakes a skunk for a dog, tries to kill a fake snake with his monster knife, and causes chaos on a movie set. Laugh? Like the kiddies say, I thought I'd never start. This fish-out-of-water character, introduced to the world by Paul Hogan in 1986, is no longer funny. In fact, if I were Australian, I might feel embarrassed by him today.

Here's why. Dundee (Hogan) doesn't even know who Mel Gibson is. He watches television with his son (Serge Cockburn), has a live-in lover and partner (Linda Kozlowski again) who works for a major news organization, and conducts tours for vacationers from all over the world. Yet he thinks people at a Hollywood party are asking him about Mal Gibson, an acquaintance back home, so he regales the awed guests with outrageous stories about that Gibson. I firmly believe only an Australian in a coma for the past fifteen years would be oblivious to the fame of Dundee's Oscar-winning fellow countryman. (Okay, I know Mel Gibson was born in the U.S., but he moved to Oz at an early age.)

In another scene, Dundee tells his buddy (Alec Wilson) a far-fetched story explaining how America uses passport pictures at crosswalks to keep track of traffic violators from another country. I cringed at the sight of that big, burly Aussie proving himself as mentally challenged as Dundee by swallowing this ridiculous lecture. Do these filmmakers have no shame?

Oh sure, they endow their hero with some admirable traits. Dundee willingly travels to the City of Angels to be with Kozlowski on her temporary assignment there. He helps her investigate a movie smuggling scam. He teaches their son how to survive in the Outback and does his best to take care of the youngster while in the big city. He's good-humored and loyal. But all this pales in significance to the insulting depiction of Dundee's stupidity in an urban environment.

Inconsistencies regarding Dundee's skill with animals also troubled me a lot. Here's a man who stops a ferocious lion or wild boar in its tracks with just eye contact and a pointing finger, but he doesn't know anything about skunks. And he can't tell an amusement park python from a real one. Sheesh!

I found the original *Crocodile Dundee* fresh and lively. I still smile when remembering how Mick frightened a mugger by pulling out his huge weapon and warning him, "That's not a knife. This is a knife." The first sequel wasn't too bad either. But that was over twelve years ago. Thanks to the wonders of modern technology, the world has become much smaller since then. People in all kinds of rustic settings, probably even in Dundee's own Walkabout Creek, belong to the "global village" and are much more sophisticated now.

Isn't it about time for the outdated Crocodile Dundee to retire? (Released by Paramount Pictures and rated "PG" for some language and brief violence.)

DISNEY'S THE KID

As an eight-year-old, or thereabouts, I wanted to be a movie star, a private detective, or a Rockette when I grew up. Instead, here I am sitting at a computer in the wee hours of the morning typing up this movie review. If my eight-year old self magically appeared, how could I explain what happened to those childhood dreams? In *Disney's The Kid*, Bruce Willis (*The Sixth Sense*) plays a man facing just such a dilemma when he meets himself as a child.

Portraying Russ Duritz, a highly successful image consultant, Willis impressively projects a Scrooge-like unwillingness to get close to anyone. From his cold demeanor to his twitching eye, he is totally convincing as an adult in deep psychological trouble. Bachelor Russ keeps so busy telling famous clients how to behave, he has no time for friends, family, or romance. He even demands a "5-minute" quick fix from his psychiatrist—while refusing to sit down in her office.

Two days before Russ' 40th birthday, his life changes dramatically. Like Scrooge's ghost of Christmas past, the child Russ once was appears in his plush upscale home. Rusty (Spencer Breslin) represents everything the adult Russ has repressed. The boy is chubby, playful, and curious. "What makes the moon look orange sometimes when it rises?" he asks with a sense of wonder. When Russ can't explain, the child complains, "I always knew I'd grow up to be stupid."

Rusty, who wants to be a pilot, can't understand what Russ does for a living. When he finally figures it out, he tells Russ, "You help people lie about themselves so they look like someone they're not." Adding to the child's disappointment is Russ' lack of companionship. "I'm almost forty years old and I don't have a wife or a dog? I'm a loser!" he shouts.

Willis and Breslin put their hearts and souls into these performances. Funny, pathetic, and furious, they draw us into their problems while reminding us of our own childhood ambitions. The amazing Willis, who even lost weight in order to be more of a contrast to Breslin, only falters in one scene. He hams it up too much when his character thinks he's going crazy. Although the role of Rusty fits movie newcomer Breslin (already a t.v. commercial veteran) perfectly, he says a few lines that seem inappropriate for his age. Maybe some eight-year-olds use words like "obviously," but none that I know do.

Anyone familiar with the outcome of Charles Dickens' *A Christmas Carol* can predict the impact of Rusty's visit on Russ' future. Screenwriter Audrey Wells, who co-wrote the hilarious *George of the Jungle*, has given this classic theme a whimsical, modern twist, and director Jon Turtletaub (*Phenomenon*) moves things along with a lively pace. Supporting actresses Emily Mortimer (*Scream 3*), Lily Tomlin (*Tea with Mussolini*), and Jean Smart (*Guinevere*) are just marvelous. In the role of an employee who loves Russ, Mortimer is a delight with her charming British accent and pixie face. Smart displays warmth and charisma as a television personality who helps Russ discover his inner child. Not surprisingly, Tomlin gets most of the laughs with her portrayal of Russ' sarcastic assistant. When he asks her to make Rusty disappear, she jokes about "magical assistant powers," claiming she should have worn her magic bra and panties.

While not a laugh-a-minute movie like *Chicken Run*, Disney's *The Kid* put a smile on my face and a song in my heart. Even though adults may appreciate this modern fable more than children, it ranks as one of the year's best family films.

(Released by Walt Disney Pictures and rated "PG" for mild language.)

DOWN TO EARTH

A good story can be told over and over again. And that goes for movie plots, too. *Down to Earth*, starring comic Chris Rock, is the second remake of a 1940s movie called *Here Comes Mr. Jordan*, and it's almost as entertaining as Warren Beatty's *Heaven Can Wait*, a 1979 Oscar-nominated film. Changing the hero from a sports figure to a wannabe stand-up comedian makes this third version a perfect showcase for Rock's unique brand of humor.

When Lance Barton (Rock) is run over by a truck and arrives in a nightclub called Heaven, he finds out his death is a mistake. That's why his inept guardian angel (Eugene Levy) and Sinatra-fan head angel (Chazz Palminteri) agree to help him find a new body back on Earth. The only one available at the time is an elderly white billionaire who has just been murdered by his wife (Jennifer Coolidge) and her lover (Greg Germann).

Of course, this is a ridiculous concept, but I just couldn't stop laughing at the idea of an African-American comedian inside the body of a man like Charles Wellington. When Barton, in spite of his new persona, plans to enter and win an Amateur Night Contest at the famed Apollo Theatre, it seemed hilarious to me.

Although Rock has appeared in movies before, this is his first leading role. He stole a few scenes from Mel Gibson in *Lethal Weapon 4* and received favorable notices as Judas in *Dogma* and as a hit man in *Nurse Betty*. In *Down to Earth*, the Saturday Night Live veteran gets the opportunity to show his romantic side with Regina King (who plays Barton's beautiful love interest). While posing no threat to Denzel Washington or Wesley Snipes in this regard, Rock projects a wide-eyed vulnerability that's quite appealing.

Still, Rock is at his best in the movie's stand-up comic scenes, even when he's bad enough to be booed by the audience. Delivering such unfunny lines as "My girlfriend is so ugly she wears make-up to be on the radio," Rock adopts a very funny deadpan expression. But when he gets rolling with his famous racial barbs, the movie really rocks. "There are two kind of malls," he begins. "White people's malls and the ones white people used to go to." Sprinkled generously throughout the film, material like this from Rock's successful comedy routines added to my enjoyment. I also appreciated the movie's lack of bathroom jokes and obscene language.

Another plus for me in *Down to Earth* is the appearance of a strong female role model. King (*Enemy of the State*) exudes spunk and courage as a dedicated nurse who helps Barton spend Wellington's vast fortune to help others. This talented actress has a natural glow about her and reacts convincingly to the strange situations faced by the character she plays.

Nevertheless, *Down to Earth* includes one serious problem. Because viewers see Rock instead of Wellington most of the time, it takes a tricky leap of imagination that's difficult to sustain.

More glimpses of Wellington as others see him might have helped.

Although it's safe to predict no Oscar nominations for *Down to Earth*, this remake is definitely a must-see for Chris Rock fans.

(Released by Paramount Pictures and rated "PG-13" for sexual humor, language and some drug references.)

DR. DOLITTLE 2

ANNOUNCER: Welcome to Fantasy Network's award-winning "Reel Issues" program. Today's distinguished panelists include critic David Manning and the world-famous Muppet star, Miss Piggy. Now here's your host, Betty Jo Tucker from ReelTalk Incorporated.

TUCKER: Thank you, David and Miss Piggy for joining us to discuss the compelling issues presented in Eddie Murphy's new movie, *Dr. Dolittle 2*. David, let's begin with you. What did you think about this sequel in general?

MANNING: It's a real winner!

TUCKER: If I remember correctly, that's what you said about *The Animal*. You certainly seem to enjoy movies about our four-legged friends.

MANNING: Well, yes I do. I just can't help laughing at animals relieving themselves on bushes, trees, and legal documents. It must be my inner child trying to break free.

TUCKER: Miss Piggy, do you feel the same way?

MISS PIGGY: Moi? Of course not. I object strongly to so many animals running around without any clothes on. Fozzie Bear used to drive me crazy because of this nasty habit. As for going to the toilette in public, no Muppet would be caught dead doing that—not even Animal, and you know how tacky he is!

TUCKER: But, Miss Piggy, you must have been impressed with the amazing acting by the film's animal stars. Right?

MISS PIGGY: Well, I agree they performed a couple of entertaining stunts and said a few funny lines. But, in my expert opinion, some of the voices didn't ring true. None of these wannabe thespians can compare with my darling Kermie—naturally, who can? I did, however, like Ava, the girl bear. Her voice sparkled just like Lisa Kudrow's. But Archie, the circus bear sent into the forest to mate with her, didn't sound convincing at all. I wonder if that was Steve Zahn in a big bear suit—not a real bear at all?

TUCKER: David, you know what it's like to be called a fake. Can you answer Miss Piggy's question?

MANNING: I certainly can. Archie is not a fake bear! A wonderful animal actor named Tank played that role, and very well indeed. I thought his rendition of "I Will Survive" stole the show.

TUCKER: Speaking of survival, let's talk about the movie's environmental message. Were either of you surprised at a comedy tackling such an important subject? Miss Piggy, why are you frowning at this question?

MISS PIGGY: Because I thought the women characters were depicted so unfairly! Instead of being willing to help Dr. Dolittle right away in his efforts to save the forest, his wife and daughter acted upset about what he was doing. I can't accept this. Most women, like moi, would jump at the chance to help those cute little forest animals.

TUCKER: David, do you have anything to add to Miss Piggy's criticism regarding this issue?

MANNING: Well, I think Miss Piggy is being Miss Picky here. After all, this is only a movie, not a feminist documentary. I believe these filmmakers deserve kudos for dealing with environmental protection in such an appealing way. Finally, I want to go on record complimenting Eddie Murphy's work. When he talks with the animals this time, he's even more amusing than in the previous *Dr. Dolittle* flick. Murphy truly is this generation's Bill Cosby!

TUCKER: A statement equal to your Heath Ledger praise for *A Knight's Tale*, David. I wouldn't be surprised if you're quoted in national newspaper ads again. Why are you shaking your head? No comment? Sorry, but I see our time is up anyway. My thanks again to both David Manning and Miss Piggy for their candid contributions to this stimulating discussion.

ANNOUNCER: Please join us next week when Fantasy Network's "Reel Issues" will feature guest panelists Roger Ebert and Pinocchio in an examination of the incredible story behind Steven Spielberg's *Artificial Intelligence.*

(Released by 20th Century Fox and rated "PG" for language and crude humor. This review is dedicated to The Flick Filosopher, one of America's best online film critics, for her inspiration to break out of the mold and try something different. DISCLAIMER: the fake critic David Manning is not associated with 20th Century Fox or with KOAA Online.)

HEARTBREAKERS

A glamorous mother and her sexy daughter use deceit and dirty tricks to defraud wealthy men in *Heartbreakers*, a comedy with very little heart and no soul at all. Although it's fun watching the usually wonderful Sigourney Weaver camp it up as a Russian vamp in one sequence, her feminine wiles seem exaggerated in most other scenes. She doesn't walk. She slinks instead— then bats those eyelashes incessantly when turning her attention to a male target. It's just too much. And Jennifer Love Hewitt needs more than low-cut, skimpy dresses to convince me she's a scheming con woman. A little acting might help.

As Max, the statuesque Weaver (*Galaxy Quest*) plays a mother who shows not even a modicum of concern for her daughter Page (Hewitt from television's *Party of Five*). In order to get a free hotel suite, she has no qualms about tripping Page in the lobby, thereby causing her to fall face-first on the marble floor. She also involves her daughter as "the other woman" in a series of marital scams. Max marries the mark, Page seduces him, and the bride collects a healthy settlement.

Heartbreakers treats men the same way last year's *Dr. T & the Women* depicted the opposite sex. They all come across as idiots. Ray Liotta (Goodfellas) plays a lecherous groom with the same finesse Harpo Marx might bring to such a role. He lunges at his secretary, pours ice down his pants, and kills fish with a gun. It's supposed to be funny, but I didn't laugh once. And Gene Hackman, portraying an elderly tobacco tycoon, just serves as the butt of age-ist dialogue like "His liver spots are glowing all over."

How the mighty Oscar-winner (*The French Connection, Unforgiven*) hath fallen!

Only Jason Lee (*Almost Famous*) emerges with any dignity amid all the nonsense. He's quite believable as a sincere, good-natured bar owner who likes to stargaze on the beach. But even this character is too gullible for words. He falls for Page despite her foul mouth and nasty disposition. Does his goodness and trust win her over? Only when she finds out his property is worth $3 million. Like mother, like daughter—at least until Page discovers true love and wants to reform.

Juvenile humor prevails in this misguided farce directed by David Mirkin (who did such a great job helming the hilarious *Romy and Michelle's High School Reunion*). There's much ado about the amount of phlegm produced by Hackman's character and, in scenes painfully reminiscent of *The Wedding Planner*, about a statue with an oversized sex organ. Some people in the sneak preview audience actually chuckled whenever Weaver hit Hackman in the back of his skull to make him think he was having sharp head pains. To me, there's nothing amusing about abuse like that, unless it's among the Three Stooges.

After watching *Heartbreakers*, I felt an overwhelming urge to rent videos of *The Grifters, The Sting, Shooting Fish,* and *Dirty Rotten Scoundrels*—all much better films about scam artists.

(Released by Metro-Goldwyn-Mayer and rated "PO-13" for sex related content including dialogue.)

HOW THE GRINCH STOLE CHRISTMAS (aka THE GRINCH)

Fantastic sets, colorful costumes, and Jim Carrey's performance of a lifetime bring *How the Grinch Stole Christmas* magically to life on the big screen. Director Ron Howard's movie version of this popular Dr. Seuss classic creates a world of wonder and enchantment for kids of all ages. I found myself captivated by everything about it.

First, there's Carrey's astounding interpretation of the Grinch. From his gruff voice and hairy green appearance to his wild physical antics and impossible grumpy attitude, Carrey simply is this incredible creature. I completely forgot *Ace Ventura, Andy Kaufman*, and Carrey's hilarious *In Living Color* personas while watching him in this film. From now on, I will remember the comic actor primarily for his Grinchiness.

Carrey's impeccable timing turns the simple task of checking a schedule into one of the movie's most amusing highlights. When the Grinch wonders if he's available for a Whoville event, he points a long green finger at his calendar and says, "Well, let's see. At 7 p.m, I wallow in self pity. At 8 o'clock, I gaze into the abyss, and at 9 o'clock I solve world hunger (but don't tell anyone about it)." Could anyone deliver such lines with the same silly sarcasm as Carrey? I don't think so.

Next, almost stealing a scene or two from Carrey are a wonder dog named Kelly and an appealing newcomer, Taylor Momsen. Kelly, a mutt with a bit of terrier, plays Max, the Grinch's only companion in his hermit's cave. Discovered in a dog shelter, this particular canine was cast because she reminded Howard (*Ransom*) of the animal in Chuck Jones' cartoon version of *The Grinch*. What a great casting decision! The photogenic Kelly looks so pathetic when the Grinch tries to turn Max into Rudolph the Red Nosed Reindeer and then forces the loyal mutt to drag a huge sleigh up a steep, snowy hill.

Momsen portrays Cindy Lou Who, a little girl who befriends the Grinch. Although barely hinted at in the original story, this character is extremely important in the movie. Cindy moves the story forward by her faith in the Grinch's innate goodness—which ultimately changes his nasty attitude and behavior. With her wide eyes and angelic face, Momsen projects innocence and honesty in this key role. And she's so darn cute! Her hairdos fascinated me, especially the one containing a cup of eggnog and a candy cane. She also has the sweetest laugh since Shirley Temple.

The whimsical village of Whoville is another treat contained in *The Grinch*. Even though Whoville is depicted as a series of haystack houses in the original book, production designer Michael Corenblith believed Theodore Geisel (Dr. Seuss) loved medieval architecture. Therefore, he used archways, bridges, stairs and spirals throughout the set, anchoring the gigantic Christmas tree in the middle of the town square.

Finally, an excellent supporting cast adds to the pleasure of seeing this wonderful film. Although not easy to recognize because of Rick Baker's make-up artistry, Bill Irwin (Mr. Noodle on *Sesame Street*) and Molly Shannon (*Saturday Night Live*) appear well-matched as Cindy Lou's caring parents. Jeffrey Tambor (*The Larry Sanders Show*) makes a perfect snobbish mayor, Christine Baranski (*Bowfinger*) unleashes her sophisticated charm as the Grinch's love interest, and Sir Anthony Hopkins (*Meet Joe Black*) provides a spirited narration of this well-loved holiday fable.

Like all fables, this one emphasizes an important lesson. After his attempt to deprive Whoville of its eagerly-awaited Christmas backfires, a reformed Grinch expresses that lesson best by saying, "Maybe Christmas doesn't come from a store—maybe it's truly a little bit more."

(Released by Universal Pictures and rated "PG" for brief crude humor.)

JOSIE AND THE PUSSYCATS

Note to self: Watch out for subliminal messages. They might be forcing me to buy things I really don't want or need—like that huge tub of popcorn I purchased in the lobby before seeing *Josie and the Pussycats*. Thank heavens I'm no longer a teenager like the ones depicted in this movie. Facing mindless manipulation through rock music every minute of the day and night, their salvation depends on the valiant efforts of Josie, Valerie, and Melanie, clueless members of a popular new all-girl band.

This is definitely risky business for the future of American teendom. I'd have to think twice before placing my trust in three such unlikely heroines. Josie (Rachael Leigh Cook) agrees to bookings in a bowling alley, even though the group earns only five dollars after renting bowling shoes; Valerie (Rosario Dawson) can't hide her jealousy of Josie; and Melanie (Tara Reid) keeps losing her soap in the shower while singing "If you're happy and you know it, clap your hands."

Still, this bouncy trio made me smile a lot, especially during their musical numbers. So what if all their songs sound pretty much the same? At least I understood the lyrics, which is more than I can say for some rock groups. And they are so very cute when all dressed up for their show biz gigs. Wish I could get my hands on that peacock-blue number Cook (*Antitrust*) wears in the closing sequence. It would be just the thing for next Halloween.

Thinking of Halloween reminds me that two very weird characters get most of the laughs in this movie. Alan Cumming (*Spy Kids*), playing an evil band manager, cajoles his musicians while planning their murders if they become suspicious about the subliminal messages hidden in their music. I found Cumming at his most amusing when trying to smooth over disputes among members of Du Jour, the boy-band featured in the movie's hilarious opening sequence. Faking concern in his smarmiest manner, he promises to take care of every problem mentioned by each band member, then rolls his eyes at the audience before putting his "final solution" into operation. His next victims—er, clients? Josie and the Pussycats, of course.

Although not as funny as Cumming, Parker Posey (*The House of Yes*) surprised me with her campy performance as the obsessed CEO of MegaRecords, a corporation trying to brainwash America's youth. Throwing a party for Josie, Val, and Melanie, she makes an entrance (à la Gloria Swanson in *Sunset Boulevard*) that cracked me up, and her true motivation for turning teens into mindless mall rats delighted me with its utter silliness.

Based on characters from Archie comic books, *Josie and the Pussycats* urges teenagers to be individuals instead of herd-like consumers. Ironically, in doing so, it contains more product placements than any movie I've ever seen. Have to stop now. Must go to Target for some Revlon cosmetics. And maybe I'll drop by McDonald's on the way home for an order of their delicious fries—or by Starbucks for a café mocha.

(Released by Universal Pictures and rated "PG-13" for language and mild sensuality.)

LEGALLY BLONDE

Blondes of the world, unite. You have nothing to lose but those "dumb blonde" jokes. Like this one. A blind man goes into a bar. He asks if anyone objects to him telling a joke about blondes. The bartender says, "I have blonde hair and weigh over 200 pounds." The woman sitting beside him adds, "I'm a blonde too. I'm a professional wrestler, and the bouncer is also blonde." The bartender inquires, "Do you still want to tell that joke?" "Nah," says the blind man. "I don't want to explain it three times."

If Elle Woods, as played delightfully by Reese Witherspoon in *Legally Blonde*, can't dispel this stereotype, no one can. She's just lost her boyfriend because she's "too blonde." Warner (Matthew Davis) tells Elle he plans on becoming a political figure, so he needs a fiance who's more "like Jackie, not Marilyn." Sure, they've had fun together, but it's time to get serious. After all, he's going to Harvard Law School in the fall. "If I'm gonna be a Senator by the time I'm 30, I need to stop dicking around," Warner explains.

What's a dumpee to do? Elle, who earned a degree in Fashion Design, decides to show Warner she's just as smart as he is. She'll go to Harvard too. Like Mae West in days of yore, Elle has no problem with self-esteem. Why should she? She's been a home-coming queen, an honor student, a runner-up for Miss Hawaiian Tropic, and president of her sorority. "I grew up in Bel Air, right across the street from Aaron Spelling," Elle declares when some-one suggests she's no match for the Vanderbilt crowd. Gaining admission to Harvard may be a piece of cake for this clever cook-ie, but being accepted by the faculty and students there presents more of a challenge for her.

While not as extreme, I had a similar experience attending my first semester of college in New York City. As the butt of jokes about my western twang, I found it ironic being made fun of by people who said they would meet me "at toity tird and tird" for lunch. Like Elle, my choice of dress also caused amusement among the natives. Of course, she looked gorgeous in her bright colors, high heels, and tight skirts—whereas my "saddle pants" did nothing for me. But I believe Elle and I represent sisters under all that denim and glitzy silk—both trying to be taken seriously in a conservative academic world. No wonder I desperately wanted her to succeed.

Witherspoon's quirky performance as Elle almost matches her unforgettable portrayal of Tracey Flick, the obnoxious over-achiever in *Election*. Because she was so convincing in that role, I've had trouble accepting her in other films (like *Cruel Intentions* and *American Psycho*). That's why I'm so surprised at the depth of my reaction to her fine work here. I love the way she infused Elle with energy while showing the young woman's growth as a law student. Also, her style and flair seemed so right for this char-acter. I could hardly wait for each new scene to see what she would be wearing next! But more subtle things, like her warmth toward a nerdy classmate and her convincing frown at Warner—as he sits by new girlfriend (Selma Blair) during classroom ses-sions—helped me think of Elle as a real person, not the flashy Malibu Barbie she resembles.

Legally Blonde is no *Paper Chase*. But it does deliver such serious messages as: don't judge a book by its cover; believe in yourself; and, most important of all, don't discriminate against people because of the color of their hair.

(Released by Metro-Goldwyn-Mayer and rated "PG-13" for language and sexual references.)

LUCKY NUMBERS

What are the odds against a supporting cast member outshin-ing megastar John Travolta and television funny lady Lisa Kudrow in any movie? Astronomical, but Bill Pullman does just that in *Lucky Numbers*. His amusing, low-key performance as a reluctant policeman enlivens this screwball comedy about "rig-ging" the Pennsylvania lottery. Travolta's portrayal of a financial-ly strapped weatherman and Kudrow's work as his ditzy accom-plice are fine too, but it's Pullman who made me laugh the most. Too bad he's in so few scenes.

Until Pullman (*Lake Placid*) comes on screen, Lucky Numbers is just your average crime caper flick—entertaining, but nothing special. Travolta and Kudrow play unlikable characters drawn together by a plan to win millions through a daring, but highly illegal, scheme. As Russ Richards, a popular television personality, Travolta makes fun of his own celebrity here.

Wherever Richards goes, people flock around him to have their pictures taken with him. He even has his own booth at Denny's.

Clearly, this role suits Travolta much better than the grotesque villain of *Battlefield Earth*, and the charismatic actor seems to enjoy it immensely. His enthusiastic weathercasts and glad-handing manner are very funny. But Travolta also projects a dark edge to his character's demeanor which helped me understand why Richards would go to such lengths to get the money he needs.

After watching Kudrow as the lovable Phoebe for so long in *Friends*, it's strange to see her portray Crystal, a woman who stops at nothing to get what she wants. "There's a limit to my classiness," Crystal says after killing someone. She has no conscience and almost no brains—a deadly combination indeed. But Richards needs her. She is the "Lottery Girl," the one who pulls the numbers and announces them to the television audience. Surprisingly, Kudrow succeeds in this challenging role. Although Crystal has a few hilarious moments (especially her clumsy highlighting of lottery information for the TV audience), there's a coldness in her eyes that telegraphs a complete lack of feeling for others.

Involved also in the scam are a devious strip club owner (Tim Roth), a loose-cannon thug (Michael Rapaport), a lecherous station manager (Ed O'Neill), and Crystal's hapless asthmatic cousin (Michael Moore). Unwittingly saving the day for law and order is Lakewood (Pullman), a cop trying to avoid any effort in connection with his job. Not one to bother with paperwork, he asks others on duty to fill in details of crimes he's been assigned to cover. In addition, he calls for "back-up" no matter how routine the incident. Despite Lakewood's faults, he's the only sympathetic character in *Lucky Numbers*. Pullman's quizzical expressions and laid-back manner won me over completely.

Director Nora Ephron (*You've Got Mail*) moves the action along nicely, except for tedious scenes between Travolta and Michael Weston, who plays an eager assistant at the weatherman's failing snowmobile showroom. That mentoring relationship didn't work for me, and I couldn't understand their frenetic conversations.

None of the culprits in *Lucky Numbers* suffer enough for their actions. Still, there's a very specific "crime does not pay" warning here. After seeing this movie, anyone planning to tamper with an official state lottery will think twice about it.

(Released by Paramount Pictures and rated "R" for violence, language, sexuality, and some drug use.)

THE PRINCESS DIARIES

Dear Diary,

Just got back from seeing *The Princess Diaries* and feel the urge to jot down my concerns. Here's another movie where teenage girls look like a bunch of unfeeling idiots or worse. Honestly, dear diary, if I didn't know some wonderful young women in that age group, I probably would avoid all adolescent females because of the way they are portrayed here and in other flicks like *American Pie* and *Josie and the Pussycats.* Is it possible Sissy Spacek started it all by wreaking bloody revenge on her classmates for making fun of her in *Carrie*?

In this new film, the predictable plot features movie newcomer Anne Hathaway as a klutzy high school student in San Francisco. She can't even get through a speech without getting sick and vomiting. Do the other girls empathize with her? Of course not. Only her annoying friend Heather Matarazzo (*Welcome to the Dollhouse*) offers a helping hand. The others tease her about her pitiful performance as well as about her appearance. Hathaway's bushy eyebrows, unkempt hair, and horn-rimmed glasses provide them with plenty of fodder.

What happens next really pushed my buttons, dear diary, causing me to vent on these pages instead of writing about my other adventures today. When Oscar-winner Julie Andrews (*Mary Poppins*) enters the movie as Hathaway's grandmother, who just happens to be the Queen of Genovia, she thinks Hathaway can't inherit the throne without improving herself, mostly the way she looks. That's when the elitist queen calls in beauty expert Larry Miller (*Nutty Professor 2: The Klumps*) to perform his cosmetic magic on her granddaughter.

I realize scenes like this worked in *Miss Congeniality* when Michael Caine transformed Sandra Bullock's plain FBI Agent into a glamorous beauty contestant. That made sense. One must be beautiful to enter such a contest. But how gorgeous does a person need to be to run a country? Golda Meier comes to mind. Okay, maybe she did resemble Ingrid Bergman a little, but I'll bet she didn't spend much time worrying about glamorous make-up, fashionable clothes, and the latest hairstyle.

A similar theme in *My Fair Lady* was also acceptable to me. However, Eliza Doolittle changed much more than her appearance as a result of Professor Henry Higgins' training. She became more trusting, developed cultural interests, and so forth. Andrews had to be painfully aware of this vast difference, having played Eliza for so many years in the Broadway production. I think that's why she seems so unhappy in a rip off of the Henry Higgins role here.

Yes, there are a few funny bits in the movie, but I'd seen them all before in the previews. Hathaway shows comic potential in a couple of slapstick moments—such as when she falls off a chair while trying to sit like an elegant lady. Also, I loved a brief dance number by Andrews and the wonderful Hector Elizondo (*Runaway Bride*), who played the queen's loyal assistant. These veteran actors brighten up the screen momentarily and made me wonder what they would've been like co-starring in *The King and I* instead of Yul Brynner and Deborah Kerr—or perhaps even now in a senior version of *Dirty Dancing*.

That's all for now, diary. Time to phone my teenage grand-daughters and remind them how terrific they are.

(Released by Walt Disney Pictures and rated "G" for general audiences—all ages admitted.)

SHREK

Consider the onion. It may be smelly and make you cry, but this popular plant offers much more than that. It has layers. In *Shrek*, the title character says ogres are a lot like onions. How does he know? Because he's one of them—an ogre, not an onion, that is. Despite being green and ugly, he's resourceful, fearless, and vulnerable to some very deep feelings.

Getting to know Shrek (voiced with a Scottish accent by Mike Myers) in this animated comedy brought back memories of my favorite fairy tale, "Beauty and the Beast." Predictably, Shrek turns out to be just as lonely and misunderstood as Belle's hairy friend, but watching a surly monster change into a loveable hunk gets to me every time. Speaking of fairy tales, *Shrek* pokes fun at practically all of them—at least the Disney versions. Even a sweet-singing bluebird (resembling the one in *Snow White*) meets an untimely end. Nursery rhyme characters take their lumps here too. For example, the Three Blind Mice bump into everything, and a Gingerbread Boy endures his worst nightmare as he faces a kind of milky torture.

When these imaginary creatures beg Shrek to save them from the evil Lord Farquaad (voiced by John Lithgow), it's an offer he can't refuse, especially since they've been banished and taken up residence in his very own swamp, a place he wants for himself alone. Shrek's mission? To rescue Princess Fiona (Cameron Diaz), the lovely "bachelorette" chosen by Farquaad as his bride after seeing her compared to Cinderella and Snow White in his confiscated magic mirror.

All Shrek has to do is fight a fire-breathing dragon guarding the tower in which Fiona is held prisoner. (In keeping with the film's intent to subvert our ideas about fairy tales, this dragon is unlike any seen or read about so far.) Not to worry. Shrek's helper on his important quest is a talking Donkey (Eddie Murphy) who expresses amusing thoughts about everything ("Did you say layers? Cakes have layers. Parfaits have layers. They're both so much better than onions!") and insists on humming annoyingly in an effort to bolster Shrek's spirits as well as his own. It doesn't take long to figure out that Donkey's cheeriness and excessive talking mask a loneliness equal to Shrek's. Donkey and Shrek are two sides of the same coin.

Like onions, cakes, and parfaits, the movie *Shrek* also has layers. Billed as a "fractured fairy tale," it offers plenty of laughs on one level. Peeling off that cover, something deeper emerges. The importance of friendship and true love are explored with unusual sensitivity in scenes between Shrek and Fiona and between Donkey and Shrek. "Friends forgive friends," Donkey teaches Shrek. From Fiona, this unjolly green giant learns that looks aren't everything to a loving significant other.

However, I'm bothered by the way filmmakers dealt with one issue concerning physical appearance. Although turning the "Beauty and the Beast" theme upside down, the movie loses much of its moral tone by its disparaging treatment of short people like Prince Farquaad. Perhaps this depiction is intended to satirize how this character compensates for his horizontally-challenged stature. Nevertheless, whenever the Prince came on screen, I half expected to hear Randy Newman singing in the background, "We don't want no short people round here." And it's too bad so many flatulence jokes were included. This clever film didn't need any of that at all, if you ask fuddy-duddy old me.

What movies may not need at all in the future are real performers in front of the camera. *Shrek*'s animation seems so life-like, it's scary. Thanks to a breakthrough software program called a "Shaper," the characters' body motions and facial expressions mimic human actions with eerie accuracy. If I were an actor who had just seen *Shrek*, I'd be afraid—very afraid—about my chances of living happily ever after, except as a voice-over.

(Released by DreamWorks and rated "PG" for mild language and some crude humor.)

TORTILLA SOUP

It never fails. Whenever we go out to eat, my husband asks, "Which Italian or Mexican restaurant will it be tonight?" Both of us enjoy the spicy cuisine of these two cultures much more than the blandness of our own English/Irish cooking. After leaving the film *Big Night*, which showed an Italian master chef preparing all kinds of delicious dishes, we rushed to the nearest Italian café and gorged ourselves on spaghetti primavera. We had a similar hungry feeling watching *Tortilla Soup*, only this time for the yummy Latino food served up by Hector Elizondo. As a retired chef who's lost his sense of taste, Elizondo's character must depend on someone else to let him know if everything is seasoned just right. How I would love that job!

Elizondo (*The Princess Diaries*) gets his first starring film role just right, too. I found him totally believable and charming as the single father of three adult daughters who still live at home. His caring glances at each young woman exude warmth, even when he's sighing with exasperation at many of their actions, including use of "Spanglish" at the dinner table. "English or Spanish—one or the other," he admonishes them. Everything about Elizondo says "gentleman" in this gem of a movie. Concern for his family, for his restaurant partner, even for the children in his neighborhood comes through clear as a bell. I began to think of this creative chef as a real person—one I wanted as a friend.

In fact, I wish I knew his three daughters, too. As played by Elizabeth Peña (*Lone Star*), the oldest one seemed the most interesting to me. I'm amazed at the way she combined repressed sexuality, religious zealotry, and comic reactions into one fascinating character. Peña's surprised, then eager, expressions upon receiving a series of mysterious love poems are priceless. For her terrific work here, Peña goes on my short list of the year's best supporting performers.

Portraying the other two daughters, Jacqueline Obradors (*Deuce Bigelow, Male Gigolo*) and Tamara Mello (*She's All That*) also drew me into their struggles for independence from a beloved, but old-fashioned, father. The glamorous Obradors yearns to be a chef, not the high-powered business executive of her father's dreams. Mello, a teenage dynamo, would like to see the world before going off to college. Watching all three siblings start breaking plates in the kitchen, I knew they were ready to make some changes. Little did I suspect their father's life would change too, and more drastically. After meeting gold-digger Raquel Welch, the mother of his daughters' lovely friend (Constance Marie from *Selena*), Elizondo's character re-evaluates his plans for the future and surprises everyone with his decision.

In a highly unsympathetic role, Welch (*Kansas City Bomber*) dares to make fun of her sexy image. Now a senior citizen, she still looks great, especially dancing with Elizondo. I was afraid Welch might go too far over the top in a couple of instances, but she stopped just short of that, even in one outrageous fainting scene.

For me, funnyman Paul Rodriguez (*Born in East L.A.*) appears too infrequently in films, so I was pleased to see him cast as one of the daughter's boyfriends in *Tortilla Soup*. I still chuckle thinking about his first meeting with Elizondo. Trying to entice the perfectionist chef to a baseball game, he says, "We could share corn dogs and sodas." Relief shines on Rodriguez's face when Elizondo replies, "You take care of the tickets and I'll take care of the food."

Because I missed seeing *Eat Drink Man Woman*, the 1994 Chinese version of this film, I'm not sure how *Tortilla Soup* measures up to it. Still, I can't imagine the original being any better than this wonderful American adaptation.

(Released by Samuel Goldwyn Films and rated "PG-13" for sexual content.)

DRAMA:

A. I. ARTIFICIAL INTELLIGENCE

ANNOUNCER: Welcome back to Fantasy Network for today's discussion of Steven Spielberg's new film, *A.I.: Artificial Intelligence*. Roger Ebert couldn't be with us as originally scheduled. But we are fortunate to have in his place HAL, the computer from *2001: A Space Odyssey*. Joining HAL, as promised, is the legendary Pinocchio. Please welcome them and our host, film critic B. J. Tucker from ReelTalk Incorporated.

TUCKER: It's a pleasure to finally meet both of you, HAL and Pinocchio. I'm eager to hear your reactions concerning this unusual film. Pinocchio, isn't *A.I.* just an updating of your famous fairy tale?

PINOCCHIO: Not at all.

TUCKER: Omigosh. What's happening to your nose?

PINOCCHIO: No, not again! Well, okay. I guess you're right. I admit there are similarities between that robot David and me. He also wanted to be a real boy. But he didn't have to worry about his nose growing whenever he lied. And he didn't have Jiminy Cricket to help him.

TUCKER: But the lover robot played so well by handsome Jude Law served the same purpose. Don't you agree, HAL?

HAL: Affirmative. That computes. Joe the Gigolo tried to find the Blue Fairy for David and became his friend. Affirmative also for Pinocchio's other comment. He is correct in stating David didn't worry about lying. Robots cannot perform that human activity.

TUCKER: Still, David's love for his mother seems quite human, especially when actor Haley Joel Osment looks adoringly at Frances O'Connor in their scenes together. Why couldn't she love him back just as he was?

HAL: Machines can be programmed to love humans in *A.I.*, but humans love only each other.

TUCKER: So the robots in *A.I.* appear more human than their creators? An intriguing thought—one that smacks more of Stanley Kubrick than Steven Spielberg. Do you think Kubrick would be pleased by Spielberg's treatment of his story?

HAL: Negative for some parts of it. When I worked with Kubrick on *A Space Odyssey*, he input facts regarding his disapproval of extreme sentimentality. Affirmative for first third of movie. The future of robotics and the responsibility of humans for their creations stand out as Kubrick elements.

TUCKER: I'm glad you mentioned those serious themes, HAL. But I wonder how the movie will go over with younger viewers. Pinocchio, because of your expertise on what appeals to children, I'd like to hear your opinion on whether or not *A.I.* qualifies as a family film, like Spielberg's *E.T.*

PINOCCHIO: You know, a similar question came up regarding Walt Disney's movie about me many years ago. Some people thought youngsters might be terrified when I got turned into a donkey or swallowed by a whale, but most of them knew it was make believe because we were all cartoon characters. However, in this case, *A.I.*'s Haley Joel Osment looks so real and convincing when sad things are happening to him! And those special effects, especially showing robots in various stages of destruction, could fool anyone. Some kiddies might find *A.I.* too disturbing.

TUCKER: But aren't there many things about *A.I.* children would enjoy?

PINOCCHIO: Oh, yes. For example, when David tries to eat spinach and begins to break down, most kids will get a big laugh. And there's a cute teddy bear "Super Toy" who walks and talks. They'll all want one for Christmas! Also, some of the scenes reminded me of The Wizard of Oz, an all-time children's favorite. The more I think about it, the more I'm convinced *A.I.* is the best film Spielberg ever made.

TUCKER: There goes your nose again! Back to you, HAL. What do you compute as the most important message in *A.I.*?

HAL: That being human involves making mistakes, loving sometimes without being loved back, searching for your dream, and accepting your mortality.

TUCKER: An excellent way to end our discussion, HAL. Although *A.I.* may not be Spielberg's finest movie, it's certainly one of his most thought-provoking efforts. Many thanks to you and Pinocchio for joining us today on "Fantasy Network."

(Released by Warner Bros./DreamWorks and rated "PG-13" for some sexual content and violent images.)

CAST AWAY

When an actor appears as the sole character in the major part of a movie and keeps me riveted the entire time, it's quite an accomplishment. That's just what Tom Hanks does in *Cast Away*. This dramatic "man versus nature" adventure shows how a FedEx systems engineer survives being stranded on an island after an airplane crash. In this exceptionally well-filmed movie, Hanks plays Chuck Noland, a time-obsessed, pudgy suburbanite who undergoes tremendous physical and emotional changes as a result of his unique experience.

With that expressive face and his intuitive body language, Hanks (Oscar-winner for *Forrest Gump* and *Philadelphia*) masterfully displays Chuck's intense feelings of anger, fear, pain, and joy. No one can see or hear the frustrated castaway, so he howls when injured and hides when frightened by mysterious sounds.

Exuberant after finally starting a fire, he pounds his chest while shouting at the sky, "See what I have created!"

Finding loneliness as difficult to deal with as the elements, Chuck engages in frequent conversations with a Wilson volleyball—the only part of the film that seems silly at times. He also entertains himself by drawing primitive pictures on the wall of a cave and by gazing longingly at a photograph of his beloved girlfriend (Helen Hunt).

Watching Hanks' gut-wrenching performance caused me to wonder what I might do if faced with such a catastrophe. Would I be able to start a fire without matches, catch fish without a pole, build a shelter or an escape raft? I don't think so. My idea of "roughing it" is spending a weekend at a hotel with room service. But these are just a few of the many tasks Chuck must take care of in his new environment. After seeing *Cast Away,* I have a greater appreciation of everyday items usually taken for granted—including such simple conveniences as ice and flashlights.

In addition to Hanks' superb acting, amazing cinematography by Don Burgess (*What Lies Beneath*) helps lift this movie above the ordinary. During one of the most terrifying airplane disaster sequences on film, I almost felt I was inside the doomed craft as it plunged into those violent waves. In contrast, Burgess' shots of the magnificent ocean view from Chuck's island appear to glow with a kind of peaceful spirituality.

Although avoiding the traditional Hollywood happy ending, director Robert Zemeckis (*Forrest Gump*) and writer William Broyles, Jr. (*Apollo 13*) present a conclusion that celebrates the triumph of hope over despair. Hanks explains, "Chuck realizes the best thing that ever happened to him was almost getting killed in a plane crash and living by himself for four years on an island. If he hadn't gone through that experience—and lost everything—he would never have come to understand what's truly important."

As a reformed Chuck Noland might say, "Just hang in there. Who knows what opportunities will come your way?"

(Released by 20th Century Fox/DreamWorks and rated "PG-13" for intense action sequences and some disturbing images.)

DR. T & THE WOMEN

With friends like filmmaker Robert Altman, women don't need enemies. In an attempt to praise womanhood, Altman's *Dr. T and the Women* does just the opposite. It insults wives, sisters, mothers, mothers-to-be, daughters and women everywhere. Starring Richard Gere as the most saintly gynecologist who ever lived, the movie comes across as a blatant misogynist fantasy. This surprised me completely because a woman, Anne Rapp, wrote the screenplay. (Is there an Uncle Tom-equivalent term for a sister who betrays her gender?)

In the beginning of the film, nothing seems to bother Dr. Sullivan Travis (Gere), a rich and successful Dallas physician who appears to worship women. "Women are sacred and should be treated that way," he tells one of his friends. His ob-gyn practice is booming; he takes hunting trips with his male friends; and his oldest daughter (Kate Hudson) is about to be married. In addition, Dr. T has a beautiful wife (Farrah Fawcett) and a devoted chief nurse (Shelley Long).

Soon everything begins to fall apart for the popular doctor. His patients become more and more demanding. His wife must be institutionalized after taking off all her clothes in a shopping mall. His sister-in-law (Laura Dern), who has moved in with him, can't get through a simple cookie-making activity with her three little girls without hitting the bottle. His youngest daughter (Tara Reid) exhibits signs of paranoia. His other daughter just might be in love with her maid of honor (Liv Tyler). Reacting to all this stress, the longtime faithful Dr. T engages in an affair with a new golf pro (Helen Hunt) who has a hidden agenda of her own.

Regrettably, I found nothing appealing about Dr. T or his women. Gere looks out of place as a man so naïve he thinks all women want is to be taken care of up there on their pedestals or down here on his stirrups. He can't seem to make up his mind whether to play it straight or for laughs. While watching Gere in this movie, I couldn't help wondering what happened to the actor who gave such fine performances in movies like *Primal Fear* and *Sommersby*.

As for the actresses, it's a shame most of them say their lines at the same time in so many scenes. But I guess that's symbolic of how selfish their characters are supposed to be. Only Long (the "Cheers" veteran) projects any sensitivity in her role. As Dr. T's overly helpful chief nurse, she perks things up during her limited time on screen. Always greeting her boss with "Hi, handsome," Long's character is almost sympathetic when she assumes mistakenly she has a chance to win him as a life partner. I say "almost" because, as happens throughout the movie, actions are carried to the extreme. This turns what could have been a poignant encounter into another male fantasy situation.

What disturbs me most about *Dr T and the Women* are the caricatures of Dr. T's patients in his waiting room. They are all depicted as loud, gossip-loving, self-absorbed, intolerant, mean-spirited individuals with no resemblance to women in any waiting room I've ever waited in. Okay, Altman (*Nashville, Cookie's Fortune*) was going for comedy here, but I didn't laugh once. Quite frankly, I think this legendary director owes us an apology for such a dreadful film. (Gloria Steinem, where are you when we need you?)

(Released by Artisan Entertainment and rated "R" for graphic nudity and sexuality.)

ERIN BROCKOVICH

Some people don't have to follow those fussy "dress for success" rules. Case in point—Erin Brockovich, as played by Julia Roberts in the movie of the same name. Although hardly the attire expected of someone working in a lawyer's office, our heroine's wardrobe includes see-through blouses, low cut dresses, skin tight mini-skirts, and the highest high-heeled shoes she can find. After all, single mom Brockovich was once Miss Wichita. She thinks this is how an ex-beauty queen should dress.

It's obvious Brockovich never took a course in "How To Win Friends and Influence People" either. She is confrontational and sometimes even foul-mouthed. But her drive, guts, and determination help win the largest settlement ever paid in a direct-action lawsuit in U. S. history.

Roberts (*Runaway Bride*) portrays Brockovich with even more than her usual screen charisma. She brings incredible energy and enthusiasm to this demanding role (she's in practically every scene), making it one of her best performances to date. Co-stars Albert Finney (*Simpatico*) and Aaron Eckhart (*In the Company of Men*) do themselves proud too.

Finney's interpretation of lawyer Ed Masry, Brockovich's longing-for-retirement boss, emerges as a highlight of this riveting film. In my opinion, Finney can look more amazed by surprises than any other actor today, and his character gets plenty of these from the unconventional Brockovich. When he asks how she plans to obtain important files from a male clerk, she leans over seductively and replies, "They're called boobs, Ed!" Exact opposites, Brockovich and her boss clash about fashion as well as more important issues while working together to help their clients.

Eckhart finally gets a chance to play a sympathetic character here. He's a big bear of a biker who lives next door to Brockovich and takes care of her kids while she's off on important crusades. Projecting warmth and tenderness in his scenes with the children, Eckhart comes across as the answer to a single mother's prayers.

Like John Travolta's *A Civil Action*, this outstanding drama deals with efforts to make a big corporation pay for illnesses caused by contamination of the environment. But it does an even better job of showing the many challenges faced by a single woman who must work outside the home while raising small children.

Expertly directed by Steven Soderbergh (*The Limey*), Erin Brockovich is based on a true story. And it was written with heart by Susannah Grant, a screenwriter whose track record of fine movies about women is quite impressive. Grant's previous credits include the very popular *Ever After* and Disney's acclaimed *Pocahontas*.

In spite of its early release this year, I'm hoping *Erin Brockovich* will not be forgotten during the next round of Oscar nominations. (Ed note: It wasn't!)

(Released by Universal/Columbia Pictures and rated "R" for strong language.)

THE FAMILY MAN

When Jimmy Stewart's suicidal character meets Clarence the Angel in *It's A Wonderful Life*, he gets a chance to see what would happen to his loved ones if he hadn't been born. Turning that fantasy upside down, *The Family Man* presents Nicolas Cage as a high-powered Wall Street bachelor who thinks he "has it all" until a street punk named Cash gives him a glimpse of a very different kind of life. Unfortunately, what works in the Stewart movie falls short in *The Family Man*. After all, who can feel much sympathy for a man who is successful in his chosen profession and seems perfectly happy with the decisions he's made?

Not that there's anything wrong with Cage's performance here. Whether prancing around in a sleek high-rise apartment or bragging about deals in a plush New York office suite, Cage creates a character oozing with sophistication and style in the film's early scenes. Later, he projects genuine confusion and increasing tenderness as the investment whiz becomes another version of himself.

After playing such quirky rolls as a klutzy kidnapper (*Raising Arizona*), a depressed ambulance driver (*Bringing Out the Dead*), and a reluctant car thief (*Gone in 60 Seconds*), this is a nice change of pace for Oscar-winner Cage (*Leaving Las Vegas*). However, *The Family Man* requires his character to change too quickly from a power-driven executive with no personal attachments to a happily married tire salesman with two young children. Okay, I know this is a fantasy, but I usually need some grounding in reality before suspending disbelief while watching a movie.

Waking up on Christmas morning, Jack Cambell (Cage) is shocked to be in bed with Kate (Tea Leoni), his girlfriend of 13 years ago. He's also frightened by the sound of a baby crying in the next room and a six-year-old girl (the darling Mackenzie Vega) calling him "Daddy" while jumping on the bed. The rest of the movie focuses on Jack's reactions to this strange new environment. And Cage makes the most of this chance to showcase his versatility as an actor. I was especially amused by his playful interactions with Vega. Thinking Jack is an alien sent to replace her real father, the youngster tells him stoically, "Welcome to

Earth." Pretending to go along with her theory, our frustrated "big city man" gains a helpful guide to life in the suburbs.

In addition to Cage's fine acting, co-star Leoni's energetic interpretation of Kate is a plus in *The Family Man*. This is her best performance since playing the hilarious social worker in *Flirting with Disaster*. From the minute she orders her husband to bring "Strong coffee!" to the last sequence where she gives crisp directions to a moving crew, Leoni's Kate is like a force of nature. Dynamic, funny, and photogenic, the talented actress holds her own with Cage in scene after scene. And, fortunately, a great on-screen chemistry between these two makes it easy to believe Kate and Nick still love each other and belong together.

Nevertheless, because similar "what if" situations were filmed so well in *Me Myself I* and *Sliding Doors*, I expected more depth from *The Family Man*. Instead, I was disappointed with its overly sentimental tone and rather questionable message. Are married men with children actually more deserving of happiness than single guys? According to this movie, yes. I think that's a much too cynical attitude in a film released during the Christmas season (or probably at any other time). Hey, even Charles Dickens' stingy bachelor Scrooge ended up understanding and appreciating the Yuletide spirit.

(Released by Universal Pictures and rated "PG-13" for sensuality and some language.)

FINDING FORRESTER

Strange things are happening—and I'm not referring to W's election. A bigger surprise is the current interest in films about writers. During the past twelve months, *Almost Famous, Wonder Boys,* and *Joe Gould's Secret*—each depicting the frustrations of the writing profession—have made it to the big screen. In the upcoming *Chinese Coffee*, Al Pacino and Jerry Orbach play wannabe writers arguing about their literary skills. The most inspirational addition to this impressive list is *Finding Forrester*, starring the legendary Sean Connery. Although difficult to imagine writing as a dramatic activity, Connery makes it seem so in the challenging role of a reclusive novelist mentoring a gifted African-American student.

Watching Connery in any movie is a real treat for me. His deep voice with its lingering Scottish accent, his ageless good looks, and his overwhelming charisma make the characters he plays seem larger than life. Was there ever a more dashing James Bond? Or a more sophisticated thief than the one he portrayed in *Entrapment*? Or a more compelling FBI helper than that wise Irish-American cop in *The Untouchables* (his Oscar-winning performance)? I think not, and Connery's latest turn as William Forrester ranks right up there with those other fine performances.

The real test of a good actor is the ability to make viewers forget about his stardom while watching a particular film or play. As Forrester, Connery inhabits his role so completely I actually felt cooped up in that Bronx apartment with him, and I wasn't a bit happy about it. Who wants to spend time with a cranky recluse, especially one who wears his socks inside out, constantly stares out the window onto a neighborhood basketball court below, and takes pleasure in frightening everyone by his mysterious behavior?

Fortunately, things change for this eccentric novelist when Jamal (Rob Brown), a teenage scholar-athlete, enters his life. Breaking and entering Forrester's apartment on a dare, Jamal accidentally leaves his backpack there. Forrester, who wrote a Pulitzer Prize-winning novel 50 years ago but nothing since, returns Jamal's property after making notes in the lad's journal. Because Jamal has ambitions to be an author, he persuades Forrester to mentor him. But who's mentoring whom? Through interactions with Jamal, Forrester finally gains enough courage to re-enter the world.

From this simple story by radio broadcaster Mike Rich comes a wealth of valuable messages about education, integrity, and friendship. Sharing a love of the written word, Forrester and Jamal overcome barriers of age and race to help each other become better human beings and reach their goals. As one character in the film explains, "Family isn't always what you're born with. Sometimes it's the people you find, and sometimes it's the people who find you."

Brown makes a fine acting debut here by projecting a brash-ness tempered with sensitivity that's just right for the role of Jamal. In scenes where the brilliant student confronts a pompous instructor (F. Murray Abraham) who accuses him of plagiarism, Brown reminded me of an intense young actor from days of yore—his name was Sidney Poitier. And Abraham (*Amadeus*) gave me chills again as a jealous villain. I think he has the best haughty sneer in all filmdom.

Director Gus Van Sant (*Good Will Hunting*) made only one mistake with *Finding Forrester*. He allowed his film to run too long at two hours and sixteen minutes. Scenes showing Anna Paquin (*X-Men*) as Jamal's sympathetic classmate add little to the plot and could have been omitted. Still, this is a minor criticism. It should not keep Connery fans from *Finding Forrester*.

(Released by Columbia Pictures and rated "PG-13" for brief strong language and some sexual references.)

PEARL HARBOR

Attack their eyes! Bash their eardrums! Assault their logic! Are these commands from Japanese officials planning a sneak attack on Pearl Harbor in 1941? Nope. Just Hollywood filmmak-ers discussing their plans to attack movie audiences sixty years later with a big budget depiction of that historic event. And suc-ceed they do. After suffering through the cinematic version of *Pearl Harbor* for over three hours, my eyesight, hearing, and rea-soning power may never be the same again. Jerky camera move-ments, overpowering sound effects, and implausible romantic relationships combine to make this ambitious war epic an artistic disaster.

Focusing on a soapy love story involving two pilots (Ben Affleck, Josh Hartnett) and a nurse (Kate Beckinsale) stationed at Pearl Harbor before the bombing, the film contains so many clichés that I stopped taking notes early on during the screening. For example, there's the old "I'm giving him my heart" line which Beckinsale (*Cold Comfort Farm*) says to Affleck (*Bounce*) when talking to him about the shyer, more sensitive Hartnett (*Here on Earth*).

Beckinsale, minus her delightful British accent, needs very little encouragement to fall for both patriotic fly boys at one time or another. Affleck and Hartnett, best buddies from childhood, later become bitter enemies because of their feelings for the lovely angel of mercy. Regrettably, it's not easy to accept Affleck's excessive anger, especially since his character is out of the picture (can't give away more of the plot here) before anything happens between Beckinsale and Hartnett.

As a matter of fact, Affleck's entire performance disappointed me. Although completely convincing as Matt Damon's unselfish companion in *Good Will Hunting* and as a memorable motivational speaker in *Boiler Room*, he appears painfully uncomfortable as a dashing war hero. Could it be the script again? Even in the midst of that relentless sneak attack, Affleck has to say such silly things as "Get me into an airplane!"—as if he can single-handedly stop the Japanese war machine.

I can't help wondering if Randall Wallace really wrote this mediocre screenplay. After all, he's the same man who received an Oscar nomination for *Braveheart*. So what happened here? During an interview in connection with *The Man in the Iron Mask* (his directing debut), Wallace told me he chooses projects that emphasize courage, morality, and heart. "Moviemaking costs too much time, money, and emotional involvement for one not to aim as high as one can," he explained. While *Pearl Harbor* pays tribute to the courage of World War II heroes like Colonel James Doolittle (Alec Baldwin) and Seaman Third Class "Dorie" Miller (Cuba Gooding Jr.), the first black man to receive the Navy Cross for valor, it lacks the heart and soul of Wallace's previous works.

As someone who actually remembers Pearl Harbor (I was in grade school when the attack occurred), I expected so much more. The film doesn't take me back to the things I recall most. Everyone in our family feared the Japanese would come into our town too and kill us all. Why not include some shots of people like us huddled around the radio listening to news about the attack—terrified and dazed? I certainly wasn't prepared to see U.S. nurses, except for Beckinsale's character, portrayed as a bunch of airheads most of the time, nor to watch an overly-mannered Jon Voight (*Anaconda*) become a caricature of President

Franklin D. Roosevelt. Thankfully, at least the Japanese military leaders emerge as human beings instead of the demons we were taught to hate in those days. (Don't forget, Japanese moviegoers are an important part of Hollywood's international market today.)

No doubt my admiration for director Michael Bay's fast-paced visual style (in *Armageddon* and *The Rock*) also contributed to my *Pearl Harbor* letdown. Although Bay's 45-minute sequence showing continuous bombing, strafing, torpedoing, and exploding of the U.S. Pacific fleet packs a devastating wallop of sight and sound, the rest of the movie fails to ignite similar excitement. Still, all is not lost. Viewing *Pearl Harbor* has increased my appreciation of other war movies. *Saving Private Ryan, Tora! Tora! Tora!*—yes, even *Enemy at the Gates*—seem like classics to me now.

(Released by Touchstone Pictures and rated "PG-13" for sustained intense war sequences, images of wounded, brief sensuality, and some language.)

THE PLEDGE

In *The Pledge*, Jack Nicholson plumbs the depths of the human psyche to deliver one of his strongest performances. Playing a homicide detective who refuses to let go of a case even after retirement, this veteran actor projects such genuine emotional suffering I had to remind myself it was only a role in a movie. Too bad the rest of the film fails to match Nicholson's fine work. An obsessive journey into madness may be a compelling theme, but it's not something I want to watch on the big screen—unless the director moves the story along with a pace capturing my attention throughout, like Roman Polanski did with *Repulsion*.

Regrettably, as directed by Sean Penn, *The Pledge* features little of the visual excitement included in *The Crossing Guard*, his previous directorial outing (which also starred Nicholson). Pretentious camera shots—such as superimposing birds in flight over faces and showing close-ups of ticking clocks—receive more attention than plot in this character-driven drama. Only one scene reveals the artistry Penn is capable of as a filmmaker. When Jerry Black (Nicholson) tells a mother and father their young daughter has been murdered, not a word is heard. Instead, the entire screen is filled with turkey chicks surrounding three people in a stunning tableau of sadness.

Based on the novel by Friedrich Duerrenmatt, Penn's latest offering oozes depression and hopelessness as it follows a retired detective in his efforts to solve the murder of an eight-year-old girl. To the victim's mother (Patricia Clarkson), Black swears "on his salvation" that he will bring the evil one to justice. When a mentally challenged Indian (Benicio Del Toro, who seems to be everywhere lately) is cajoled into confessing he killed the youngster, everyone else considers the case closed. But the tenacious Black continues to investigate on his own. Brooding about the murder and others similar to it, he even sets a dangerous trap— one that could ruin any chance of a new life for him with two people he has come to care a great deal about—a single mother (Robin Wright Penn) and her daughter (Pauline Roberts). When Nicholson reads Thumbelina to Roberts at bedtime, his soft voice expresses convincing tenderness towards the little girl, and this makes his character's later behavior seem quite unreasonable.

"I like the idea of the story being about fate, not so much about logic," Penn admits. Here lies the film's major problem. There's not much logic in many of Black's actions or in what he neglects to do. He finds important clues, then doesn't follow-up on them. He talks with the mother of a likely suspect but never interviews her son. After discovering objects similar to those drawn by the murdered child on display in a shop, he just ignores them. Clearly, this man is no Sherlock Holmes—or Columbo, for that matter.

Still, whether muttering to himself or showing concern for a young child, three-time Oscar-winner Nicholson (*One Flew over the Cuckoo's Nest, Terms of Endearment, As Good As It Gets*) is the main reason to see this movie. He does get able support, however, from other cast members. Aaron Eckhart (*Erin Brockovich*) stirs things up as an ambitious detective who calls Black "a clown and a drunk." Helen Mirren (*Teaching Mrs. Tingle*) and Vanessa Redgrave (*Girl, Interrupted*) appear as magnificent as ever in important cameos. Mirren is an inquisitive psychiatrist, and Redgrave, a bereaved grandmother. But Sam Shepard (*All the*

Pretty Horses) seems wasted in his one or two scenes as an "everyman" type of boss.

More a retirement crisis study than a murder mystery, *The Pledge* shows what can happen when a misguided person crosses the line in order to give purpose and meaning to his life. I just have one question for its filmmakers. Which is more intriguing—a murder mystery or a retirement crisis? Case closed.

(Released by Warner Bros. and rated "R" for strong violence and language.)

REMEMBER THE TITANS

Football is not just a game. It's the way to solve one of America's most serious problems—racism. At least that's what filmmakers responsible for *Remember the Titans* expect viewers to believe. One character extols this simplistic theme by declaring that the Titans, a 1971 integrated high school team in Alexandria, Virginia, "taught this city how to trust the soul of a man instead of the look of a man."

Although well-intentioned and generally entertaining, *Remember the Titans* left me feeling uncomfortable about the inaccuracies it presented, especially since it's based on a true story. School integration in Alexandria had been underway for a number of years prior to 1971, but this is not mentioned in the film. In addition, scenes depicting acceptance of a gay athlete and jokes about the mothers of African American players smack more of the 90s instead of the 70s. In fact, they fly in the face of attitudes back then.

Still, I feel guilty writing anything negative about this movie. It contains no drug abuse, no explicit sex, and the only violence takes place on the football field. It shows how bigotry damages both races. It preaches the value of friendship without regard to color. And it features another high-intensity performance by Oscar-winner Denzel Washington (*Glory*) matched by Will Patton's (*Gone in 60 Seconds*) soft-spoken, steely-eyed portrayal of a head coach ousted by affirmative action.

As Herman Boone, Washington plays a coach brought to Alexandria after the integration of an all-black school with an all-white school. In a town where football is king, his job as Head Coach of the T. C. Williams High Titans is to put together the best team possible. His biggest challenge? Winning over Coach Yoast (Patton), the man originally scheduled for the job—and one who has greater seniority as well as a popular following. "We had to give them something," a school board member tells the disappointed Yoast.

Washington and Patton share some compelling scenes as their characters size up each other and finally become friends. Because of their different coaching techniques, they find it almost impossible to work together at first. Boone's tough, taskmaster approach rankles Yoast. "This is a high school team, not the Marines," he complains. Boone gets angry at Yoast for patronizing the African American players. "You're not helping them; you're crippling them for life," he insists. Fortunately, their concern for the team helps overcome their differences.

In order to mold a winning team out of a group of high school students who hate and fear each other, Boone forces each member to room with a teammate of a different race during the training camp period. Is it possible such success can be achieved in a couple of weeks? This is a Walt Disney film, so the answer is a resounding "Yes!" At the end of the training activities, Boone even tells his players (who look much too old for high school), "You are already winners because you didn't kill each other."

Meanwhile, things remain the same back in Alexandria and at T.C. Williams High School. Demonstrations against integration continue, white parents want the former coach reinstated, and Yoast's nine-year-old tomboy daughter (a very funny Hayden Panettiere), refuses to dress dolls with Boone's more feminine daughter (Krystin Leigh Jones). It takes an entire winning season for the Titans to bring harmony to their school and community.

After seeing *Remember the Titans*, it's hard to imagine how school integration was achieved anywhere without a championship football team.

(Released by Walt Disney Pictures and rated "PG" for thematic elements and some language.)

THE SCORE

Coming on the heels of so many movies featuring talking animals, video-game adaptations, and overwhelming special effects, *The Score* renews my faith in the ability of great actors to make magic on the big screen. Marlon Brando, Robert DeNiro, and Edward Norton needed nothing but their facial expressions, body language, and expressive voices to pull me into their plans for stealing a priceless antique. A slight turn of the head, a simple raised eyebrow, a well-timed sigh, an unexpected vocal inflection—little nuances like these reeled me in and held me captive throughout this intense crime drama.

I do, however, feel a bit ashamed for wanting the criminals to succeed. (I confess to having a soft spot in my heart for movie bad guys, going all the way back to Jimmy Cagney and Edward G. Robinson.) Even during the opening credits, my sympathy for Nick (DeNiro, Oscar-winner for *Raging Bull*) kicked in. Discovered in the act of robbing a safe, he improvises a getaway and returns to the haven of his jazz club in Montreal. Staring into the camera as he rests in his snazzy apartment above the club, this world class safe cracker looks about as unhappy as a man can be. Clearly, he wants out. But, in the tradition of most heist movies, there's one last score that will enable him and his girlfriend (Angela Bassett, Oscar-nominee for *What's Love Got To Do With It?*) to live happily ever after.

While I have trouble understanding why someone becomes a thief, I confess to being tempted once. Visiting the Hollywood Wax Museum a few years ago, I spotted Judy Garland's ruby slippers from *The Wizard of Oz* gleaming at me from a glass display case. After leaving the tour, I couldn't stop thinking about those legendary shoes. I wanted them for my very own! A colleague of mine felt the same way. But we didn't resort to stealing. Instead, we began writing a script about a group of children who outsmart Museum officials by substituting a fake pair for the real slippers, and then have a change of heart.

I'm sure Jack, the character played by Edward Norton in *The Score*, had no such sentimental attachment to the jeweled royal scepter he discovered in Montreal's Customs House. For him, the money's the thing—as well as the challenge of working with a master thief like Nick. Not surprisingly, Norton impressed me again with a quasi-dual role similar to his Oscar-nominated performance in *Primal Fear*. Razor-sharp Jack becomes Brian, a mentally-challenged janitor employed in the well-protected Customs House. (Is there another actor who can change completely from one character to another in the blink of an eye quite as effectively as Norton?) Ambitious, and angry because he perceives a lack of respect from Nick, Jack puts his partner through an unnecessary waiting pattern that made my blood run cold. The sadistic look on Norton's face in this suspenseful scene gave me the kind of chills I experienced while watching Hannibal Lecter's famous dinner party. And Norton had no help from bloodshed or gore.

Playing Max, a fence who brings Nick and Jack together, Brando adds more than his gigantic bulk to this key supporting role. The minute he appeared on screen in his wrinkled white suit and announced impishly, "Back from Bermuda," he had my undivided attention. During his limited time on camera, I was reminded why he won Oscars for *On the Waterfront* and *The Godfather*. Brando is one of the few actors I can actually see thinking while he's emoting. Although not in enough scenes here, a little Brando is better than no Brando at all.

The Score falls short of being a great movie. By focusing on clashes among criminals and a thief's desire to go straight, it covers all too familiar territory (*Gone in 60 Seconds, 3000 Miles to Graceland, The Mexican*, and so forth). Its helpful tips for wannabe safe crackers also disturbed me. Still, I can't remember when I've seen a film with better performances. It made me hungry for more movies in which brilliant actors rule the silver screen.

(Released by Paramount Pictures and rated "R" for language.)

3000 MILES TO GRACELAND

One key to the enjoyment of *3000 Miles to Graceland* is acceptance of Kurt Russell and Kevin Costner as Elvis Presley impersonators. That's not hard to do in Russell's case. He's done Elvis before—and brilliantly. For his 1979 television portrayal of the King in *This Is Elvis*, Russell earned an Emmy nomination (and he should have won). Although Costner's Elvis takes a greater leap of the imagination, both actors deliver exciting performances as ex-cons who rob a Las Vegas casino during a convention of Elvis impersonators.

Neither man plays an admirable character, but Russell's Michael at least displays a bit of humanity. Appalled at the violent streak shown by Murphy (Costner) during their bloody getaway, Michael is careful not to kill anyone. He also develops empathy for a young kleptomaniac (David Kaye) and his sexy grifter mom (Courtney Cox, at her feisty best).

Because Russell is Hollywood's most underrated actor (check out *Breakdown* if you don't believe me), his multi-layered depiction of a criminal with a conscience didn't surprise me. By looking skeptical at everyone and everything around him, Russell projects the essence of Michael's outlook on life. Later, his vulnerability shines through in poignant scenes with Cox and Kaye, especially when these three become almost like a family.

Playing a vicious killer, Costner takes on a daring role for a star usually seen as the hero (*Dances with Wolves*) or romantic lead (*Tin Cup*). As a matter of fact, he was originally scheduled to be Michael instead of Murphy. But Costner persuaded director Demien Lichtenstein to make the switch. "I had never played a sociopath with no conscience at all, so that was the character I was interested in," he declares. Obviously enjoying this new experience, Costner's Murphy emerges as a human scorpion eager to poison anyone who stands in his way. Although totally watchable in this dynamic role, Costner sometimes appears more like a cartoon villain than a real person. Taking it down a few notches might have resulted in a more convincing performance.

Working with three other ex-cons, Michael and Murphy disguise themselves as Elvis impersonators in order to pull off a major casino heist. Billed as the "Elvi 5," the group also includes characters played by Christian Slater (*The Contender*), David Arquette (*Scream*), and Bokeem Woodbine (*Dead Presidents*).

Unbeknownst to the rest of his gang, Murphy plans to end up with the entire $3.2 million score.

To begin the fiery robbery sequence, all five men swagger into the Riviera wearing sideburns, dark glasses, and gaudy Elvis costumes. When things go wrong, the Elvi 5 escape with guns blazing, shooting everyone and everything in sight. As the crime takes place, cinematographer David Franco (*The Whole Nine Yards*) cleverly combines shots of the robbers in action with a Las Vegas production number featuring an actual Elvis impersonator and gorgeous show girls. (Am I the only one who wanted to see more of the musical number than the robbery? I don't think so, thank you very much.)

Most of the movie's humor comes from Murphy's resentment at not being recognized as Presley's illegitimate son. He goes nuts when anyone jokes about the King, and his sideburns are the real thing. I also found Michael's relationship with the youngster played by Kaye quite amusing. This precocious lad outsmarts the surprised criminal at every turn, stealing his heart as well as his wallet.

Supporting cast members Kevin Pollack (*End of Days*), Thomas Haden Church (*George of the Jungle*), Howie Long (*Broken Arrow*), and Jon Lovitz (*City Slickers II*) are satisfactory in the roles of two lawmen, a helicopter pilot, and a money-launderer respectively. But it is Russell who makes this violent thriller worth seeing. IMPORTANT NOTE: Be sure to stay for the closing credits. Otherwise you'll miss the best part of the film—Russell doing his great Elvis moves.

(Released by Warner Bros. and rated "R" for strong violence, sexuality, and language.)

TRAFFIC

Like the frenzied war against drugs it attempts to depict, *Traffic* is one big mess. The film's disjointed plot line, jerky camera movements, and unreasonable use of color variations made it almost unbearable for me to watch on the big screen. I wanted to leave after about twenty minutes. Of course, that's not something a critic should do, so I stayed to the very end—enduring almost two hours and thirty minutes of pure torture.

Directed by Steven Soderbergh (who earned a Best Director Academy Award for *Traffic*) and filmed in docudrama style, this jumbled movie loosely links three main stories related to the drug war. Story number one revolves around Javier Rodriguez (Benicio Del Toro, winner of a Best Supporting Actor Oscar for this sensitive performance), an honest Mexican policeman who must deal with corrupt colleagues on his side of the border.

Representing artistic license carried to a ridiculous extreme, the heroic Javier is shown performing his work in a grainy, yellowish environment—except during short visits to a more brightly photographed San Diego. How insulting to Mexico!

In the second story, a pregnant La Jolla housewife (Catherine Zeta-Jones) panics when her husband (Steven Bauer), a wealthy drug dealer, is arrested. "Nobody will help us," she complains to him during a jail visit. After unsuccessfully seeking assistance from a sleazy lawyer (Dennis Quaid), she hires an assassin to kill the principal witness against her spouse.

The third story focuses on Robert Wakefield (Michael Douglas), a conservative judge appointed by the President to lead the U.S. war against drugs. But when Wakefield discovers his own daughter (Erika Christensen) is an addict, he begins to doubt his effectiveness as a drug czar. "How can one fight a war when the enemy is your own family?" he asks.

That question is one of the important issues raised in *Traffic*. Another is the practicality of waging a war against drug kingpins who have more money to spend than the governments trying to stop them. A cynical drug dealer (Miguel Ferrer) draws attention to this fact by accusing his DEA captors (Don Cheadle and Luis Guzman) of being "like the Japanese soldiers left behind who kept fighting because they didn't know World War II was over."

Although not recommending legalization of drugs, *Traffic* shines a spotlight on the hopelessness of current policies. Despite all our government's efforts, illegal drug use continues. Still, there's nothing new here. Anyone who watches television programs like *NYPD Blue* and *Law and Order* has seen numerous portrayals of the discouraging drug scene.

Taking home an Oscar for his efforts, Stephen Gaghan adapted *Traffic* from a British television miniseries. Because that format allows time to develop various characters and provide in-depth background information, it seems a more appropriate one for such complicated and controversial subject matter.

(Released by USA Pictures and rated "R" for pervasive drug content, strong language, violence, and sexuality.)

WONDER BOYS

What could be worse for an author than writer's block? Perhaps writing too much and not being able to end the work in progress. At least that's the situation depicted in *Wonder Boys*, a character-driven film from Curtis Hanson, the acclaimed director of *L. A. Confidential*. In this sometimes misguided film, Michael Douglas stars as Grady Tripp, a college professor whose first novel won the prestigious Pen Award.

That was several years ago, and Tripp has published nothing since. Why not? Maybe because he's been smoking pot, having an affair with the chancellor (Frances McDormand), and trying to motivate budding writers. He keeps telling editor Robert Downey Jr. he's almost finished with his second book, a gigantic tome of more than one thousand pages. But Tripp is the Energizer Bunny of prose—he just goes on writing and writing and writing.

During one fateful weekend, the professor takes a talented, but disturbed, student (Tobey Maguire) under his wing. As a result of this act of kindness, events unfold that force both Tripp and his student to make drastic changes in their lives. A blind dog, a transvestite, a sexy classmate (Katie Holmes), a pompous author (Rip Torn), and Marilyn Monroe memorabilia—all play a part in the ensuing mayhem.

Cast members deliver first-rate performances in *Wonder Boys*. Douglas (*The Game*) may look a little too rumpled and seedy, but he certainly gets everyone's attention in this very different type of role. Maguire (*The Cider House Rules*) shows terrific star potential. With his hypnotic voice and wide-eyed innocence, he arouses the audience's empathy no matter how bad his behavior.

Unfortunately, a questionable moral tone permeates this uneven movie. The college professor engages in illegal activities; the student lies incessantly; adultery is treated matter-of-factly, etc. There's lots going on, but much of it is more serious than funny. Billed as a comedy/drama, *Wonder Boys* is about as amusing as a driver's license exam.

Still, there are moments of brilliance here—particularly Maguire's dour recitation of suicides by movie stars and his expression of delight while viewing a Judy Garland musical on television. McDormand's understated portrayal of the college chancellor is also a gem. It's her best work since winning the Oscar for *Fargo*. Douglas, of course, always brings something special to his roles. Regardless of the movie's faults, fans will not want to miss Douglas' unique over-50-coming-of-age performance in *Wonder Boys*.

(Released by Paramount Pictures and rated "R" for strong language, drug content, and sex-related material.)

HORROR:

AMERICAN PSYCHO

Stylish, satirical, and soulless, *American Psycho* goes inside the mind of a 1980's serial killer who looks more like a matinee idol than a murderer. It also questions if Patrick Bateman, the film's title character, is any more demented than the society in which he lives.

Symbolizing the materialism and self-centeredness of the eighties, Bateman (Christian Bale) cares about things, not people. Exotic body lotions, expensive suits, hi-tech equipment, and fancy business cards mean more to him than his fiancée (Reese Witherspoon), his mistress (Samantha Mathis), or his co-workers. As part of a cookie-cutter group of Wall Street brokers, he is often mistaken for one of his firm's many other vice presidents. Whether reacting to a dehumanized environment or simply following his own psychotic impulses, Bateman spends his leisure time in torturing and killing numerous victims. When he tells anyone about these killing sprees, each person is too self-absorbed to listen. He informs one woman that he is involved in "murders and executions," but she hears it as "mergers and acquisitions." While narrating his story, he states calmly, "There is no real me; there is an idea of myself, some kind of abstraction."

Although playing an unbalanced character, Bale has no problem balancing horror with dark humor in this remarkable performance. His monologues about pop music, delivered so authoritatively in the midst of terrifying and raunchy activities, both shock and amuse. The hunky Welsh-born actor even manages a comic flair while wielding a chain saw! (His current role is a far cry from that sympathetic youngster in *Empire of the Sun*.) Based on Bret Easton Ellis' controversial novel, the film version of *American Psycho* emphasizes black comedy over gore, but it's still a very frightening movie. The senseless killing of a homeless man, the brutal axe murder of a colleague, and the bloody slaughter of a debutante are among its most disturbing scenes. *American Psycho* is the first movie since *Natural Born Killers* to give me nightmares.

"My mask of sanity is about to slip," Bateman observes as it becomes more and more difficult to keep his two lives separate. At this point in the film, my own sanity seemed in danger too. Why? Because the dreaded "maybe this is a dream or a hallucination" ploy rears its ugly head, causing me to doubt the movie's entire premise. And, just when Bateman has convinced me he's all bad, he lets one of his victims go. His humble secretary (Chloe Sevigny), who worships him, is the lucky lady.

Most of the screen time in *American Psycho* belongs to Bale, so the other cast members have little to do. In addition to those already mentioned, Jared Leto appears as one of Bateman's fellow brokers (who is not as lucky as his secretary), Willem Dafoe as a detective investigating a missing person case, Cara Seymour as an unhappy hooker, and Guinevere Turner (one of the screenwriters) as a doomed debutante.

Director Mary Harron also co-wrote the script for this cinematic adaptation of Ellis' book. Even the opening credits are visually creative, as witness the dessert sauce, dripping on screen like blood from a wound. Unfortunately, because this fascinating film includes no relief from depravity, no glimmer of hope, it appears to lack sensitivity and soul. Patrick Bateman himself concludes, "There is no catharsis—no punishment. I gain no degree of knowledge of myself." Nevertheless, *American Psycho* emerges as a powerful indictment of the Me Generation and its lingering value system.

(Released by Lions Gate Films and rated "R" for strong violence, sexuality, drug use and language.)

BLESS THE CHILD

In *Bless the Child*, one of Satan's henchmen takes a six-year-old girl to a rooftop, shows her the bright lights of the big city, and declares, "All this could be yours if you join me!" Is that the kind of thing any child desires? Of course not, but this movie is filled with such nonsense.

Finding it difficult to keep track of the film's many illogical situations and plot holes, I tried to concentrate on its main characters. The starring role is played by Kim Basinger, Academy Award winner for *L .A. Confidential*, who may need more than a blessing to boost her career after appearing in this absurd movie. She portrays Maggie O'Connor, a New York City nurse raising an autistic niece named Cody. Although lovely to look at (no one in films today has a more beautiful peaches and cream complexion), Basinger wears an overly-concerned, cranky expression throughout most of the film. Still, her character has every reason to worry about the little girl she loves.

Played with nervous energy by newcomer Holliston Coleman, Cody beats her head against walls, spins objects obsessively, makes candles light without touching them, and is kidnapped by Eric Stark (Rufus Sewell), the head of a satanic cult. In a bizarre coincidence, Stark just happens to be married to Maggie's sister (Angela Bettis), the woman who abandoned Cody as a baby.

Stark is convinced this special child was born with superhuman powers that the forces of evil have waited centuries to control. When he attempts to convert Cody to the dark side, a ferocious battle between demons and angels ensues. Sewell, who gave fine performances in *Dark City* and *Cold Comfort Farm*, goes over-the-top in this role. By glaring at everyone and rolling his eyes whenever his character is upset, he makes Stark appear more cartoonish than cruel.

The film's special effects are disappointing too. Only one scene impressed and frightened me. It depicts a bedroom full of red-eyed rats crawling on the floor and furniture as Cody screams for help. And those other supposedly horrible demons? Most of them resemble the flying monkeys from *The Wizard of Oz*— except they're not as scary.

Wasted in small supporting roles are Jimmy Smits (*Mi Familia*) as an investigator of occult crimes, Christina Ricci (*Sleepy Hollow*) as a frightened former Stark follower, and Ian Holm (*The Madness of King George*) as a dealer in religious artifacts and information. Playing the nanny from Hell, Dimitra Arlys (*Eleni*) delivers the film's most convincing performance. Even while doing simple tasks like brushing Cody's hair, she projects a sinister elegance that reminded me of the mysterious housekeeper in *Rebecca* (as portrayed by Dame Judith Anderson).

Successful movies about children with supernatural powers include *The Omen, The Exorcist*, and the recent box office smash, *Sixth Sense*. Director Chuck Russell (*The Mask*) probably found similar intriguing elements in Cathy Cash Spellman's book upon which *Bless the Child* is based. Granted, the universal theme of Good versus Evil is emphasized. And, a precious child in jeopardy creates the usual atmosphere of terror. But this film version didn't work for me. No matter how far-fetched the concept, a good supernatural thriller needs realistic characters and suspenseful scenes that make your nerve ends tingle. Instead, *Bless the Child* merely evoked my sympathy for the misguided filmmakers and actors involved. I felt blessed when it was finally over.

(Released by Paramount Pictures and rated "R" for violence, drug content, and brief language.)

BOOK OF SHADOWS: BLAIR WITCH 2

"It's not even worth talking about," I overheard one disgruntled moviegoer complain after seeing *Book of Shadows: Blair Witch 2*. He was right, but I decided to review it anyway, mostly because of all the fuss surrounding the original horror movie—

which turned out to be scary only to those who believed three film students actually vanished in the woods while making a documentary about the Blair Witch legend. Unfortunately, I found nothing in this sequel that would scare anyone.

Still, the first part of the film seems promising enough. In realistic documentary style, it depicts how Burkettsville, Maryland, the site of *The Blair Witch Project*, has become a frenzied tourist attraction. Various citizens give their opinions about what is happening to their community. During one interview, a woman complains, "I can't even walk to the mailbox without full make-up. People are videotaping us all the time."

Cautioning visitors to "Get out of the woods—there is no blankety blank witch," Sheriff Cravens (Lanny Flaherty) tries to keep some semblance of order. He is especially concerned about Jeff (Jeffrey Donovan), a former mental patient conducting tours of the Blair Witch's purported haunts. At this point, the movie switches from a documentary approach and goes downhill fast.

Lured through Jeff's internet web site (gasp!), four young people join him for his first tour. Erica (Erica Leerhsen) practices Wicca and wants to learn more about the Blair Witch mythology. Grad students Tristen (Tristen Skyler) and Stephen (Stephen Baker) are writing a book about the Blair Witch. The fourth member, Kim (Kim Director), a Morticia Addams lookalike, spooks the others with her psychic abilities. While I can't fault these young actors for their performances, their lengthy sophomoric discussions caused me to doze off more than once.

Something mysterious happens to this group during their sleepover in the woods. They can't account for missing hours when tourists from another group are murdered. They start hallucinating weird things—the most annoying being flashbacks and flashforwards that meant nothing to me. They become violent and turn on each other. Has the Blair Witch put a curse on them? Is Jeff acting out another psychotic episode? Is one of them really the Blair Witch? Can someone else who has seen the movie answer these questions for me? There's no hurry. I'm not all that curious.

One thing I do know for certain. Artisan Entertainment really knows how to market a film on the internet. Check out the *Book of Shadows* web site (www.blairwitch.com) to see what I mean. It's much scarier than the movie.

(Released by Artisan Entertainment and rated "R" for violence, language, sexuality, nudity, and drug use.)

THE CELL

In *The Cell*'s spectacular opening scene, a woman in a flowing white garment gallops her sleek black horse over gigantic dunes of dark pink sand. She is Catherine Deane, a psychologist inside the mind of a young coma patient. But this dreamlike landscape pales in significance to the nightmarish world of serial killer Carl Stargher, the man she agrees to treat next.

Deane (Jennifer Lopez) has mastered a new therapy technique which enables her to experience what is happening in another person's unconscious mind. When Stargher (Vincent D'Onofrio) loses consciousness after a seizure, the innovative therapist must help FBI Agent Peter Novak (Vince Vaughn) find out where his latest victim is hidden before it's too late. The only way to do so is by taking a dangerous trip inside the madman's head.

Breaking new ground in terms of visual excitement, this sci-fi thriller overflows with incredibly wild images. (Some even caused me to worry about the sanity of its filmmakers.) When Deane enters Stargher's imagination, she sees what he sees—a grotesque museum of horrors. Bleached bodies turned into gruesome dolls, a horse is cut into sections while standing in an art gallery, a huge dog shaking off water into a blood-filled bathtub, and heartbreaking child abuse scenes are among the disturbing sights she must confront.

In the meantime, another woman tries desperately to escape from the claustrophobic water torture cell where Stargher brings all his victims. Sequences showing this time-triggered deathtrap add considerably to the film's chilling suspense. In order to help Deane discover where this terrifying cell is located, Novak decides to travel into Stargher's mind also.

Plot and dialogue play second fiddle to *The Cell*'s amazing visuals. Acting seems incidental here, too. Lopez looks as beautiful as ever, especially when she becomes a glamorous nun doll in one of her own fantasies. Still, her talent commanded the screen more dramatically in *Selena*. (If there was any justice in the show biz world, that sensational performance should have earned her an Oscar.) In *The Cell*, Lopez's best scenes show her interacting tenderly with children, even with Stargher as a child. Vaughn (*Psycho*) just looks concerned most of the time, but his sense of urgency helped bring me back to the real world in between those surrealistic mind-probing adventures.

In the movie's most challenging role, D'Onofrio (*Feeling Minnesota*) uses more body language than words to create a monster serial killer. Besides playing Stargher, he assumes the man's strange alter egos. "Stargher has five different images of himself," D'Onofrio explains. "It's a schizophrenia that makes up his different desires and neuroses. The challenge for me as an actor was to make each side of Stargher unique and yet connected to the whole." Stargher may seem beyond redemption, but D'Onofrio endows this character with an animal magnetism that kept me engaged during his frightening scenes.

Outstanding cinematography, special effects, costume design, set decoration, make-up, and background music contribute to the quality of this unique film. Helmed by first-time director Tarsem Singh (noted for his imaginative commercials and music videos), *The Cell* is not just another serial killer flick. Despite its horrific theme and graphic violence, it's a stunning work of art.

(Released by New Line Cinema and rated "R" for bizarre violence, sexual images, nudity, and language.)

FINAL DESTINATION

Nothing pleases a critic more than seeing a movie that is much better than expected. *Final Destination*, a teen horror flick, falls into this category. The terrifying opening scenes alone make this frightening film worth the price of admission. Strong performances by a wonderful group of young actors keep it from being just another gruesome scarefest.

Because of my extreme fear of flying, I found the movie quite disturbing to watch in parts. Although there have been many plane crashes in films before, this is the first one that made me feel I was sitting in the cabin when it happened.

The story centers on six people who get off a plane when one of them (Devon Sawa) has a vision of the craft exploding on take-off. This astonishing event causes them to question everything related to it. Did they cheat death? Was it really their time to die? If so, is there any way to keep death from coming after them to even the score?

Sawa (*Idle Hands*) projects just the right amount of frustration as Alex Browning, a high school student with the gift of clairvoyance. Because of Sawa's frenetic, nervous approach to this challenging role, I became concerned for his character right away. I desperately wanted everything to work out for him.

The awestruck people Alex saves alternate between blaming him and thanking him. That group includes his two skeptical friends (Seann William Scott and Chad E. Donella), a young woman (Ali Larter) who believes in Alex's visions, a bully (Kerr Smith), his girlfriend (Amanda Detmer), and a teacher (Kristen Cloke). Each cast member managed to hold my attention in some rather farfetched scenes, but Larter (*Varsity Blues*), in particular, stands out. She can look forlorn, afraid, and sexy with the best of them.

Filmmakers Glen Morgan (producer/screenwriter) and James Wong (director/screenwriter) come highly qualified for the thriller genre. Their work on television's *The X-Files* earned them several Emmy nominations and a Golden Globe Award in 1996. They now serve as executive producers on *The Others* for DreamWorks Television and NBC. Working from a story by New Line Cinema marketing assistant Jeffrey Reddick, this talented team aimed to do for planes and air travel what *Jaws* did for sharks and swimming. It worked for me.

In addition to all its bone-chilling action, *Final Destination* reminds us of our own mortality and of how important life is. How many other horror flicks can make this claim?

(Released by New Line Cinema and rated "R" for strong language, terror, and violence.)

HANNIBAL

More seductive than Dracula and as slippery as Jack the Ripper, Dr. Hannibal Lecter returns to horrify and fascinate viewers again in *Hannibal*. With his calm voice and steely eyes, Sir Anthony Hopkins projects the same creepy elegance that earned him an Oscar as Lecter in *Silence of the Lambs* ten years ago. It's hard to imagine anyone else portraying the world's most famous cannibal.

For me, it's also difficult to accept an actress other than Jodie Foster in the role of FBI Agent Clarice Starling. Regrettably, Julianne Moore (*Magnolia*), who plays Clarice in this uneven sequel, lacks Foster's shy manner and soft accent. She also fails to establish the dynamic connection with Hopkins that Foster achieved.

As a cinematic work of art, Hannibal dazzled me with its sensational cinematography and lush location shots of Florence, Italy. But it also features gruesome scenes that go too far over the top, even for a horror film. *Silence of the Lambs* emphasized intellect and plot. In contrast, Hannibal revels in gore. Wild boars feasting on humans and a guest's brains served as the main course at a dinner party are not for squeamish viewers like me.

Based on the best seller by Thomas Harris, the movie begins ten years after Dr. Lecter escaped from a maximum-security hospital for the criminally insane. Going by the name Dr. Fell, he is enjoying the good life in Florence as a man of culture and refinement-attending the opera, giving lectures on art, playing the piano, etc. Apparently, Lecter has retired from his old cannibalistic habits. Still, he can't forget an important person from his past, the FBI agent who interviewed him with such civility and sense of purpose before his escape.

After learning that Clarice is in trouble, Lecter heads back to America to help her, even though he realizes she wants to capture him. He knows Clarice is being used by her boss (Ray Liotta) and by a vengeful millionaire (Gary Oldman), one of Hannibal's disfigured victims, to lead them to him. Nevertheless, the psychotic psychiatrist thinks he can outwit them all. "It's time for me to come out of retirement," he declares.

For his coming-out party, Lecter brutally kills an Italian detective (Giancarlo Giannini) who is planning to turn him in for the reward. Although the cat and mouse game between these two goes on too long, at least it takes place amid such splendors of Florence as the famed Santa Croce courtyard, the Palazzo Vecchio, and the Pazzi Chapel. In fact, the film's most beautiful sequence takes place in the Pazzi Chapel. During an original opera presented there, actors wearing exotic costumes depict the death of Dante on a silk-draped stage while lighted candles flicker in the aisles, giving everything a dreamy glow. Director Ridley Scott and cinematographer John Mathieson, who also worked together on *Gladiator*, are experts at creating impressive "you-are-there" scenes, and this is one of their best.

Because he's trying to save Clarice, Lecter becomes a sort of hero-villain in *Hannibal*. Men motivated by revenge and greed represent the greater evil. Liotta (*Goodfellas*) exudes sexist arrogance as Clarice's supervisor who can't forgive her for jilting him, and Oldman (*The Contender*) evokes plenty of chills as a grotesque freak with diabolical plans for Lecter's painful death.

Ultimately, *Hannibal* reveals Lecter and Clarice as kindred spirits. Despite their different philosophies and morality, they are both outsiders who persist in achieving their goals. And they are inside each other's heads. Although the movie's ending is not the same as Harris' novel, it paves the way for another sequel. Why am I not surprised?

(Released by Metro-Goldwyn-Mayer/Universal Pictures and rated "R" for strong, gruesome violence, some nudity and language.)

HOLLOW MAN

Because *Hollow Man*—a big budget, high-tech, special effects movie—contains an annoying detail goof, it was difficult for me to suspend disbelief while watching it. Imagine, if you will, an intelligent scientist making a mask to cover an invisible man's entire head, then cutting holes for eyes and mouth, but not for nostrils! Filmmakers didn't catch this mistake soon enough, so Kevin Bacon's character walks around without a way to breathe through his nose for most of the movie. No wonder he loses his sanity.

Maybe I'm being too picky, but I also had trouble accepting the peeping tom aspects of this sci-fi suspense thriller. Sebastian (Bacon), a scientific genius who discovers how to make animals invisible, decides to be the first human to experience the process. But does he use the gift of invisibility for any constructive purpose? Not at all. Instead, he spies on his former girl friend (Elisabeth Shue) and on other women in various states of undress. Eventually losing all sense of morality, Sebastian becomes a murdering monster. "It is amazing what you can do when you don't have to look at yourself in the mirror anymore," he declares.

Fortunately, *Hollow Man*'s incredible special effects keep it from being a total waste of time. One extraordinary scene shows a huge invisible gorilla being brought back to the visual world. First, bright red liquid seems to flow through veins in thin air, then other layers of the body gradually appear until the animal is completely restored. Also, Sebastian's various stages of visibility are remarkably well-done. When he leaves a swimming pool, water droplets cling briefly to his ephemeral shape as his form slowly disappears. And, after the final restoration fails, Sebastian appears as a mass of internal organs so gory it makes your skin crawl.

In addition to the film's cutting edge special effects, Oscar-nominee Shue (*Leaving Las Vegas*) makes watching it worthwhile. As Dr. Linda McKay, Sebastian's fellow-scientist and ex-lover, Shue projects both strength and vulnerability. When Linda tells Sebastian that the mystery man she's now seeing is "Everything you are not," Shue's voice is firm and definite. But after Sebastian retorts, "He must be dull then," Shue's puzzled look makes us wonder about Linda's true feelings. This glamorous actress has come a long way since *Adventures in Babysitting*. She gives one of her best performances to date as a woman who must defeat and destroy the man she once loved.

Although no match for Shue in this film, Bacon demonstrates once again his ability to portray evil personified. However, because his face is either covered or unseen during much of the movie, he's not as effective as in *The River Wild*. Still, at the beginning of *Hollow Man,* his arrogant facial expressions and cocky walk help create a character on the verge of megalomania.

Josh Brolin (*Flirting with Disaster*), playing the third member of the film's love triangle, comes across as a welcome contrast to Sebastian's insanity. His character doesn't swagger when he walks or brag when he talks. He's just a hard-working member of the team assigned to research invisibility. Even his physical appearance is more solid than Sebastian's wiry frame (when visible).

Philosophically, *Hollow Man* raises some intriguing questions. If there's no danger of being caught, will most individuals engage in illegal and immoral activities? Is there a universal moral code that motivates people to be good and just? Should geniuses be exempt from laws that others must follow? How far should scientists go in experimenting with human behavior?

Director Paul Verhoeven (*Basic Instinct*) calls *Hollow Man* "a precise study in evil." Because he grew up in Europe during World War II, this Dutch-born moviemaker must have a keen understanding of how a charismatic leader can become evil incarnate.

(Released by Columbia Pictures and rated "R" for strong violence, language and some sexuality/nudity.)

SCARY MOVIE

Once upon a time, making fun of teen horror flicks seemed a good idea for a film comedy. Now, after the *Scream* trilogy and its many imitations, that particular theme doesn't work so well. *Scary Movie,* the latest attempt at teen scarefare, delivers plenty of raunchy dialogue and objectionable sight gags, but it falls short in terms of humor and frightening moments. Hitting new lows in depiction of gross-out behavior, this misguided parody is painful to sit through.

Mean-spirited treatment of race, sexual organs, gays, abstinence, teachers, parents, policemen, senior citizens, and the mentally handicapped pops up all over the place in *Scary Movie.* A young girl gets massive police assistance by sending an emergency message stating, "White woman in trouble;" a boyfriend insists refusal of sex is grounds for murder; a teacher smokes in class while flirting outrageously with her students; a parent compliments his daughter for helping with his illegal drug dealings; and so forth. (Other incidents are too gross to describe in mixed company.)

Still, there are glimmers of comic brilliance here by Keenen Ivory Wayans (*I'm Gonna Get You Sucka!*), the man who directed and co-wrote this generally disappointing effort. One such flash peeks through in a clever scene showing a compulsive movie-talker (Regina Hall from *The Best Man*) getting her hilarious comeuppance. When the entire audience rose up to silence her so *Shakespeare in Love* could be watched in peace, I wanted to cheer. Why didn't Wayans feature more entertaining sequences like this? But hey, it doesn't take much creativity or planning to emphasize juvenile potty humor, such as a grown man defecating in his pants. It's the easy way out—and a sure-fire formula for box office success these days.

No need to say much about the plot. It's the usual one involving teenagers and an unknown psychopath who knows they killed someone, then got rid of the body. Most of the actors do their best in ridiculous, cartoonish roles. Gorgeous Carmen Electra (*Good Burger*) starts things out right as the film's first unlucky victim. Making her movie debut as a Neve Campbell-like heroine, Anna Faris displays a considerable flair for comedy. By playing it straight, she manages to be quite amusing in a few scenes, especially during her *Matrix*-y fight with the Scream-masked villain. Shannon Elizabeth follows her success as the sexy foreign exchange student in *American Pie* with another "glamour gal" performance, but this time she literally goes to pieces. (Well, what do you expect? This is a slasher film.)

Jon Abrahams (*Outside Providence*) plays Faris' sex-starved boyfriend with an appropriate tongue-in-cheek manner. (One of his scenes gives new meaning to the term "tongue-tied.") As the high school's toughest football player, Lochlyn Munro (*Dead Man on Campus*) wins the film's Mr. Testosterone Award, in spite of his character's slight sexual deformity. Shawn Wayans and Marlon Wayans (both from *In Living Color*), who served as co-writers with brother Keenen, also appear in the movie. Shawn is a hunky football player who denies his true sexual preference, while Marlon does his quirky version of a pothead who "sees dead people." In two glaring examples of miscasting, Cheri Oteri (*Saturday Night Live*) and Dave Sheridan (MTV's *Buzzkill*) chew the scenery shamelessly as an ambitious TV newswoman and a bumbling sheriff's deputy.

Running throughout the film are pointless barbs at previous movies including *The Blair Witch Project* , *The Sixth Sense, The Matrix, Scream,* and *I Know What You Did Last Summer*. When one character identified *Kazaam* as her favorite "horror film," it gave me a warm, nostalgic feeling. I couldn't help wishing I were watching that obscure little children's fantasy instead. As I recall, it's a lot funnier and more frightening than *Scary Movie*.

(Released by Dimension Films and rated "R" for strong, crude humor, language, drug use, sexual situations, and violence.)

VALENTINE

Attention, all teenage girls! Never refuse to dance with a boy on Valentine's Day. Who knows what terrifying things can happen thirteen years later? That nerdy boy might grow up to be a psychotic killer with a memory like an elephant. Exploiting this horrific theme, *Valentine* emerges as another predictable slasher film, but it held my interest throughout because of its exciting visual style.

Rejection leads to obsession and revenge in this thriller about four single women (played by Denise Richards, Marley Shelton, Jessica Capshaw, and Jessica Cauffiel) who realize their lives are in danger after receiving strange valentines. Inside each colorful card is a threatening message, such as "Roses are red/Violets are blue/They'll need dental records/To identify you."

At first, because the cards are signed only with the initials "J.M," the friends can't figure out who sent them. Later, they recall a "Jeremy Melton" from junior high, the boy they all rejected at a Valentine's Day dance so long ago. When an investigating detective (Fulvio Cecere) tells them Jeremy could have undergone plastic surgery and changed his name, they become suspicious of all the men in their lives, even the detective.

Who are the major suspects? That list includes: Campbell (Daniel Cosgrove), a mysterious stranger sponging off poor little rich girl Dorothy (Capshaw); Adam (David Boreanaz), Kate's (Shelton) on-again-off-again boyfriend; Max (Johnny Whitworth), an artist Lily (Cauffiel) has become enthralled with; and Brian (Woody Jeffires), one of Paige's (Richards) many conquests. Although the killer wears a Cherub mask, each one of the guys in question appears as the guilty party at one time or another. And that, of course, adds to film's suspense. Still, it's not too difficult to solve this mystery long before the end of the movie.

None of the acting here rates rave notices, but this isn't *Macbeth*, right? But no one is bad enough to pan either. Unleashing a saucy come-hither look, Richards seems more comfortable as a flirt than the nuclear physicist she portrayed in *The World Is Not Enough*. Among the male cast members, Boreanaz (from television's *Angel*) shows the most promise. Projecting vulnerability as an alcoholic struggling to shake his addition, Boreanaz gives a convincing performance—one that leads me to believe better things are in store for this young actor.

Director Jamie Blanks (*Urban Legend*) staged some nasty death scenes for this horror flick. A gory hot tub disaster, a savage bow-and-arrow attack, and a bloody impaling on jagged glass are among the gruesome highlights. "It just goes with the territory," Blanks says. "In real life, I'm opposed to violence but this is a movie—a very scary movie."

To me, the best thing about *Valentine*, based on Tom Savage's novel of the same name, is its fascinating visual style. The movie unfolds against such vivid backgrounds as a gorgeous family mansion, funky nightclubs, trendy galleries, and elegant restaurants. One of the most impressive sequences takes place at an avant-garde video art show where gigantic lovers' images surround the victims as the masked killer stalks his prey. Explaining why the movie sets its most frightening moments against a background of charm, wealth, and beauty, production designer Steven Geaghan (*The Outer Limits*) declares, "Death seems more shocking somehow when it visits such luxurious surroundings."

Although it's too soon to tell, *Valentine* could end up being my favorite guilty movie pleasure of 2001.

(Released by Warner Bros. and rated "R" for strong horror violence, sexuality, and language.)

MUSICAL:

CENTER STAGE

Bloody feet, aching muscles, strict diets, and rigorous physical workouts may seem more appropriate for Olympic athletes than dancers. But viewers lucky enough to see *Center Stage* will learn how much these sacrifices apply to wannabe ballet stars, too. Filled with sensational dancing by talented newcomers, this musical drama pleases the eye while emphasizing such admirable principles as courage, dedication, and self-awareness.

The story follows a group of students vying for spots in an exclusive professional dance company. One of these students, a striking blonde named Jody (Amanda Schull), has trouble with her "turn-out" and is told she may not make the cut. Another student, Charlie (Sasha Radetsky), falls in love with Jody. The group also includes: Eva (Zoe Saldana), who has a bad attitude learned on the streets of Boston; Maureen (Susan May Pratt), an overachiever keeping her weight down by purging; Erik (Shakiem Evans), a gay man who lends support wherever he can; and Sergei (Ilia Kulik), a young Russian who sometimes prefers Salsa dancing to traditional ballet.

When a famous ballet star/choreographer (Ethan Steifel) makes a play for Jody, the usual love triangle develops. That's enough about the film's soapy plot. Dancing is the most important thing in *Center Stage*. And it's great!

I'm glad I didn't pass up this opportunity to watch Steifel, considered by many to be the most advanced male dancer in the world, in a dazzling performance of the George Balanchine-choreographed *Stars and Stripes* ballet. He's also unforgettable in an exciting jazz class sequence. Steifel, a principal dancer with American Ballet Theatre, seems to defy the laws of gravity—and with no help from computer enhanced special effects. Radetsky, another member of the American Ballet Theatre troupe, gives Steifel serious competition. It's difficult to decide which of these fine artists to watch during the closing Rock Ballet number. Kulik (yes, the champion ice skater!) and Saldana also shine in a romantic ballet set to music from Rachmaninoff's second piano concerto.

The film's vibrant dancers leave most of the acting to Peter Gallagher (*American Beauty*) and two-time Tony Award winner Donna Murphy. Playing the egotistical head of a prestigious ballet company, Gallagher is totally convincing. Murphy's strong portrayal of a strict dance instructor shows why she is such an acclaimed stage actress. Hopefully, viewers will see more of her on screen in the future.

Director Nicholas Hytner (*The Madness of King George*) obviously used his knowledge of Broadway musicals while working on this film. Winner of a Tony as Best Director for *Carousel*, he also directed the popular *Miss Saigon*. In addition, choreographers Susan Stroman and Christopher Wheeldon make an impressive team. Stroman previously won a Tony for her *Show Boat* choreography, and Wheeler has choreographed several ballets for the New York City Ballet.

Although *Center Stage* may not be in the same class as those fabulous MGM musicals like *An American in Paris* and *Singin' in the Rain*, it's definitely an entertaining look at the joys and challenges of the world of dance.

(Released by Columbia Pictures and rated "PG-13" for language and some sensuality.)

MOULIN ROUGE

Watching those old MGM musicals, I felt sure something special was in store for me every time Mickey Rooney said to Judy Garland, "Let's put on a show!" Never mind the strikingly similar plots, dialogue, and characters in *Babes in Arms, Babes on Broadway, Girl Crazy*, and so on. That didn't faze me. I couldn't wait for the singing and dancing to begin. Other glorious musicals like *Singin' in the Rain, Easter Parade,* and *The Pirate* also enchanted me while I was growing up. But why has it been decades since a film had that kind of impact on me? Did movies change all that much? Or have I become too cynical as an adult? After seeing *Moulin Rouge*, I have my answer. Grown-up me can still be thrilled by a well-filmed musical.

Nevertheless, I must admit *Moulin Rouge* is unlike any musical I've seen before. Instead of presenting the usual joyful story, filmmaker Baz Luhrmann (*Strictly Ballroom*) successfully combines romance, comedy, and a La Boheme-like tragedy as he showcases two doomed lovers who meet at the Moulin Rouge, a decadent Paris night club made famous by painter Toulouse Lautrec (John Leguizamo), during the late 1800s.

Ewan McGregor (*The Phantom Menace*) and Nicole Kidman (*Eyes Wide Shut*) give the best performances of their careers as this ill-fated romantic duo. McGregor plays Christian, a poor writer, with such innocent charm it's easy to see why the courtesan Satine (Kidman), Moulin Rouge's star attraction, falls for him. Equally effective, Kidman absolutely sizzles on screen with her come-hither looks and sexy theatrical costumes by Catherine Martin (*William Shakespeare's Romeo and Juliet*). She reminded me of sirens Marlene Dietrich, Marilyn Monroe, and Rita Hayworth all rolled into one, especially when singing "Diamonds Are a Girl's Best Friend." Besides displaying her seductive charms, Kidman made me sympathize with Satine, a woman hiding an illness in order to maintain her vibrant public persona.

Although neither McGregor nor Kidman are professional singers, their voices sound just fine. McGregor won me over with his absolutely stunning rendition of Elton John's "Your Song." (How did he manage to smile so captivatingly at Kidman while singing to her at the same time? I guess that's called acting.) Happily, both stars put genuine emotion into the lyrics of each tune. In one terrific scene, they seemed to be having as much fun singing a medley of love songs as I had watching and listening to them. In fact, I had to force myself not to hum along as the couple performed a combination of such pop favorites as "All You Need Is Love," "I Was Made for Lovin' You," "One More Night," "Silly Love Songs," "Up Where We Belong," and "I Will Always Love You."

McGregor and Kidman don't do enough dancing, but making up for that is a comical, rousing version of "Like a Virgin" by Jim Broadbent (*Topsy-Turvy*) and Richard Roxburgh (*Mission Impossible II*) who are backed up by a group of energetic dancing waiters. Broadbent, as Moulin Rouge impresario Zidler, puts a table cloth over his head to imitate Satine, hoping to placate the evil Duke of Worcester (Roxburgh) when the lovely courtesan fails to show up for a tryst. I couldn't help laughing out loud as Zidler lied to the Duke by telling him that Satine said he made her feel like she was "being touched for the first time." Excelling as the snobbish backer of Zidler's "Spectacular, Spectacular" show who plans to close down everything if he can't have Satine, Roxburgh sneers and frowns with the best—or the worst—movie bad guys.

Because this story takes place mostly inside the Moulin Rouge, of course there's a lively, provocative Can-Can number. But in one of the movie's few weak spots, it's filmed with too much speed and excessive cut-away shots. There's also a tango (to "Roxanne") which works much better, even though the camera still pans to other scenes during this intense, dramatic routine.

Sheer cinematic artistry comes through loud and clear in *Moulin Rouge*. It's an outrageously creative film. From the opening of a plush red curtain at the beginning of the movie to its closing at the end, I was bowled over by the film's imaginative production design (including a "gentlemen's club" inside a structure built like an elephant, for gosh sakes). *Moulin Rouge*'s touching romance also had a profound emotional effect on me. Corny as it seems, I believe in the film's "Nature Boy" theme. "The greatest thing you'll ever learn is just to love and be loved in return."

C'est magnifique.

(Released by 20th Century Fox and rated "PG-13" for sexual content.)

O BROTHER, WHERE ART THOU?

"That's mighty fine pickin' and a singin'," exclaims one of the characters in *O Brother, Where Are Thou?* Although referring to the Soggy Bottom Boys and their lively rendition of a popular hymn, his comment is appropriate for all the wonderful musical numbers in this outrageous comedy. Set in Mississippi during the Great Depression, the movie follows the wacky adventures of three chain gang escapees who unknowingly become singing sensations. George Clooney, John Turturro, and Tim Blake Nelson simply couldn't be better as clueless friends on a journey to find over one million dollars of buried treasure.

Despite outstanding performances by these key actors, music is the real star of the film. Joel and Ethan Coen, who directed and wrote the movie respectively, both love country "folk music." Working with record producer T-Bone Burnett, they decided to highlight this American art form in *O Brother*. "It began to take over the script as Ethan and I went on—until the film became almost a musical," Joel admits. "The film is a valentine to this music."

As an ardent fan of movie musicals, I was enthralled with the expert interweaving of music, comedy, and drama in *O Brother*. Based loosely on Homer's "Odyssey," the convicts meet characters resembling those in the ancient poem. For example, the hypnotic singing of three seductive women (Sirens?) keeps the men distracted for awhile. And a blissful religious group (Lotus Eaters?) humming "Down to the River to Pray" draws two of the convicts into joining their baptism ritual. The men also confront a Cyclops of sorts, played by a very mean John Goodman (*The Big Lebowski*).

In a masterful comic performance, Clooney (*Three Kings*) portrays the fast-talking Ulysses Everett McGill—a vain charmer convicted for practicing law without a license. With his mustache, over-pomaded hair, and Depression duds, he looks like a homeless Clark Gable. But when he sings, watch out! Those big brown eyes dance right along with the rest of his body. Clooney is absolutely terrific when lip-synching to Dan Tyminski's "I Am a Man of Constant Sorrow."

Both Turturro (*Cradle Will Rock*) and Blake (*The Thin Red Line*) get their share of laughs, too. Turturro makes every hillbilly movement count while cavorting to "In the Jailhouse Now." Blake, not as amusing as the others in the musical numbers, is very funny when he believes Turturro's character has been changed into a frog. "Them sirens loved him up and turned him into a horny toad," he cries (and almost convinced me).

Politics and the KKK are lampooned unmercifully in *O Brother*. Featuring choreography Mel Brooks would be proud of, a Klan rally appears more ridiculous than scary—until lynching plans are revealed. Charles Durning (*The Last Producer*) gives his usual fine performance as a governor running for re-election against the Reform Party. Responding to his son's question about why they can't "have some of that Reform stuff," Durning looks absolutely dumbfounded. "Because we're the incumbents!" he shouts. Very light on his feet in spite of his size, Durning also cuts quite a figure when he joins the Soggy Bottom Boys and blues man Chris Thomas King in their final number, "You Are My Sunshine."

Surprisingly, one cast member disappointed me. Portraying Ulysses' ex-wife Penny, Holly Hunter lacks the spark she displayed previously in films like *Raising Arizona* and *Living Out Loud*. Granted, a woman left with several children to care for during her husband's incarceration wouldn't sparkle much in real life either.

For those wondering about the title *O Brother, Where Art Thou?*, it comes from *Sullivan's Travels*, a 1942 film directed by the late Preston Sturges and starring Joel McCrea and Veronica Lake. It's the name of a proposed film about the troubles of the downtrodden poor. Admired for his screwball comedies, Sturges probably would appreciate this homage from two of today's premier filmmakers.

Still, the Coen brothers don't always hit the right notes with their offbeat movies. *The Hudsucker Proxy* and *Barton Fink* left me cold. But when at their best, these two can't be beat—witness *Fargo* and *Raising Arizona*. With *O Brother*, the Coens have reached near perfection again, and that's something to sing about.

(Released by Touchstone/Universal and rated "PG-13" for some language and violence. This review also appeared in the Colorado Senior Beacon.)

ROCK STAR

In my wildest dreams, I never imagined I could write the following sentence—except under duress—but here goes. Mark Wahlberg deserves an Oscar nomination this year. His electrifying performance in *Rock Star* took me completely by surprise. As an ardent fan who becomes lead singer of the heavy metal band he idolizes, this former model and hip-hop artist oozes energy and charm. I actually feel like taking back all the negative things I've written about him in past reviews, including my complaint about his failure to project any feeling for the fisherman he portrayed in *The Perfect Storm*. I admire this new Marky Mark.

Do I know anything about rock groups? Not really, but like the character Jennifer Aniston plays in this fast-paced movie, I recognize talent when I see it. Aniston (from television's *Friends*) shines as Wahlberg's longtime girlfriend/agent—a woman who believes in her lover's ability to become a big star. No wonder this loyal manager wants her client to write his own music instead of doing an imitation of Bobby Beers, the popular front man for Steel Dragon. Watching Aniston stick by Wahlberg's character after he wows fans as "Izzy," the new Bobby Beers, was painful for me, especially during a raunchy sex and drugs orgy scene. Despite all those flippant remarks her character tosses off to everyone at the party, Aniston's soulful eyes reveal a wounded psyche trying to deal with too much excess. It's a brilliant piece of work.

In one of my favorite scenes, Wahlberg and Aniston sing together as members of a church choir. At the end of the hymn, Wahlberg belts out a "Hallelujah" to end all hallelujahs. Aniston looks at him adoringly, and even the choirmaster is amused. I was, too.

It's hard for me to believe Wahlberg performed his musical numbers so well here. "I had never really listened to rock or metal," the young actor admits. "My background as a musician was pretty different than what is portrayed here, and I thought it would be a challenge. Just walking around in those tight pants and being comfortable enough on stage to move the way these guys did—that was a challenge right there."

According to producer Toby Jaffe, Wahlberg immersed himself in the character. "His dedication was amazing—he would typically work a twelve-to-fourteen hour day, after having arrived on set hours early to rehearse stage choreography or work on guitar and vocals," he explains.

Fortunately, Wahlberg's intense rehearsing paid off handsomely. Long hair flying and loud voice snarling, he dances and prances across the stage like someone born to be a heavy metal rock star of the 80s. He mesmerized me, right along with those screaming fans and sexy groupies depicted in the film.

I applaud director Stephen Hereck's (*Bill and Ted's Excellent Adventure*) decision to cast real-life musicians (such as guitar virtuoso Zakk Wylde, formerly of Ozzy Osbourne's band and now lead guitarist for Black Label Society) as members of the Steel Dragon band. "In the various movies about rock and roll I've seen over the years, invariably there are actors portraying musicians," he says. "There always seems to be a certain edge and validity missing from their performances." Not so in Hereck's film.

Comparisons seem inevitable between *Rock Star* and *Almost Famous*, Cameron Crowe's semi-autobiographical movie about a young journalist's experience on tour with a rock band. Although both movies deliver serious messages, they are very different films—each compelling in its own way. *Almost Famous* focuses on the problems of being an objective critic, while *Rock Star* shows how living a dream can become a nightmare.

(Released by Warner Bros. and rated "R" for language, sexuality, and drug content.)

ROMANCE:

CAPTAIN CORELLI'S MANDOLIN

When two people from opposing sides of a war fall in love, they face extraordinary obstacles, no matter the time or place. In *Captain Corelli's Mandolin*, Nicolas Cage and Penelope Cruz co-star as lovers caught in the crossfire between Greek patriots and Italian soldiers on the island of Cephallonia during WWII. Although I found Cage completely endearing as the musical

Italian captain, it was hard to believe his character could develop such strong feelings for the pouty, unpleasant woman played by Cruz.

In the interest of full disclosure, my objectivity where Cruz (*All the Pretty Horses*) is concerned deserves scrutiny. I've yet to see her give a convincing performance. Her whiney voice irritates me, and I marvel that it has only two inflections—soft and loud. Even Cruz's so-called physical charms escape me. She looks like a little drowned rat during most of her scenes here. One exception—she glows in a tango dance sequence. Smiling and dynamic as she teases the crowd with her seductive footwork, Cruz took me completely by surprise. Maybe this popular Spanish actress has been miscast in American films and should be taking roles in other types of flicks. (Wonder how she would be as Carmen Miranda in a splashy biopic musical?)

With the beauty of a well-filmed travelogue, *Captain Corelli's Mandolin* makes the most of its gorgeous settings. Although the story takes place primarily in the capital city of Argostoli, it wasn't possible to film there because an earthquake destroyed the town in 1953. Instead, filmmakers settled on Sami, a smaller village with a deep water port and nearby lush scenery. Cinematographer John Toll (Oscar-winner for *Braveheart*) thought the island's beauty might be a problem, so he worked on creating visuals that were not "overly sentimental or glossy." The stunning look of this film took my breath away and overcame its shortcomings for me.

Still, besides Cruz's annoying performance, a couple of other problems stand out. The last part of the film drags a bit. Director John Madden (Oscar-nominee for *Shakespeare in Love*) could have tightened up the ending sequences. I didn't appreciate the lengthy letter-writing narrative by Cruz's physician father, played brilliantly up to that point by John Hurt (Oscar-nominee for *The Elephant Man*). It seemed to break the dramatic flow needed for closure. And I wanted to see more of the great Greek actress, Irene Papas (*Zorba, the Greek*), who portrayed the mother of a freedom fighter (the mesmerizing Christian Bale from *American Psycho*) engaged to Cruz's character. She's as impressive and fiery as ever, especially when smoldering at Cruz while peeling potatoes during a very tense moment between the two women.

I haven't read Louis de Bernieres' novel about Captain Corelli, so I don't know which dialogue comes from screenwriter Shawn Slovo (*A World Apart*) or from the original author. Whoever is responsible for so many memorable lines earns my admiration. For example, "Falling in love is like a temporary madness, but love itself is what's left over after the temporary madness has burned away," Cruz's father tells her. He also advises one of his patients, "If you love your wife, then when she has a chill, put a shawl around her shoulders, and when you come back from the fields bring her a flower every day." And an Italian soldier chastises a German captain with "Sometimes it's better to lose than have so much blood on your hands."

Although Cage's Italian accent is somewhat off-putting at first, he settles into the role of a soldier trapped in a war he doesn't believe in with conviction and sensitivity. I loved watching him play the mandolin. He seemed to feel the music in his soul. "I have no musical ability to speak of, no training," Cage (Oscar-winner for *Leaving Las Vegas*) admits. He claims his approach was to attack and conquer the skill by constant practice. He certainly succeeded. Cage's mandolin numbers almost brought me to tears, they were so lovely and romantic. Aha! Now I realize what should have been done with this film. It cries out to be a musical.

(Released by Universal Pictures and rated "R" for violence, sexuality, and language.)

CHOCOLAT

Chocolate is as good as life gets. I even have dreams about it. But sometimes they're nightmares. The worst one involves a hold-up man pointing a gun at me and demanding "Your chocolate or your life!" When I don't respond, he asks, "Well?" And I reply (like Jack Benny), "I'm thinking it over." No doubt about it, the delicious dark stuff is dangerous for chocoholics like me. Watching *Chocolat*, a charming romantic fantasy about how a woman and her chocolate confections change an entire French village, just added to my addiction problem. But it was well worth it!

"This is your favorite," Vianne Rocher (Juliette Binoche) tells each of her customers as she gives them samples of her yummy treats. Intuitive and free-spirited, she dares to open a chocolaterie at the beginning of Lent in a town grown cold from the tradition of repression. Accompanied by her pre-teen daughter (Victoria Thivisol), Vianne has a history of traveling throughout the French countryside, bringing the magic of chocolate and the wisdom of tolerance wherever she goes.

But the town she chooses in 1959 proves quite a challenge. A tyrannical mayor, played with uptight intensity by Alfred Molina (from TV's *Ladies Man*), tries to turn all the residents against her. He prides himself on having an ancestor who chased the Huguenots out of the village. "You and your truffles present a far lesser challenge," the pompous official tells Vianne. "If you expect me to just shrivel up and blow away, you will be very dis-appointed," Vianne replies indignantly.

Instead of leaving, she irritates the mayor even more by tak-ing up with Roux (Johnny Depp), a handsome Irish river drifter. In addition, she harbors a victim of spousal abuse (Lena Olin) and tries to unite a cranky landlady (Judi Dench) with her estranged daughter (Carrie-Anne Moss) and grandson (Aurelien Parent-Koenig).

Portrayed by the luminescent Binoche, Vianne emerges as a sexy earth mother who wants everyone to be happy. While not as challenging as her Oscar-winning nurse in *The English Patient*, this lighter role suits the lovely actress and has earned her anoth-er Academy Award nomination. With her cheerful smile and col-orful wardrobe (she wears red and pink as a contrast to the gray-ness of her surroundings), Binoche's Vianne contributes warmth and color to the film.

All other cast members deliver admirable performances as well. Depp, who modeled his intriguing character after ex-Pogues singer Shane MacGowan, is not in the movie as much as I was expecting. That disappointed me, especially since he looks and sounds so terrific. His musical brogue delighted me, and I even liked his pony tail hairdo. Maybe Irish river drifters were never a real problem in France, but who cares? A little dramatic license can do no harm in a fairy tale like this. And Depp's exciting chemistry with Binoche deserves mentioning. They sizzle together on screen. At the film's London premiere, Binoche described Depp as "My perfect chocolate—he's dark, sumptuous, and tasty."

Dench, an Oscar-winner for *Shakespeare in Love*, manages to evoke sympathy in spite of her character's unpleasant personality. Sharing a tender scene with young Parent-Koenig, she looks genuinely amazed at the portrait he has drawn of her. "You've made me look younger," she whispers in a voice full of love. It's easy to see why Dench received another Academy Award nomination for her work here.

Based on a novel by Joanne Harris and directed by Lasse Hallstrom, who helmed such acclaimed films as *Cider House Rules* and *What's Eating Gilbert Grape?* (which also starred Johnny Depp), *Chocolat* earned an Academy Award nomination for Best Film of 2000. However, because of its stereotypical depiction of a particular religious group, I omitted it from my own "Best Movies" list. Nevertheless, I found most of *Chocolat* quite appetizing. Now where's that Snickers bar?

(Released by Miramax and rated "PG-13" for a scene of sensuality and some violence.)

THE MEXICAN

Symbolic of the theme that love is worth fighting for, a priceless gun assumes paramount importance in *The Mexican*, an unusual action romance starring Julia Roberts and Brad Pitt. Looking more like a jewel box than an instrument of death, this beautiful handcrafted pistol was originally created to impress a Mexican nobleman engaged to the gunsmith's daughter. But tragedy resulted, leading to the belief that the gun was cursed. In spite of the legend—or because of it, certain people want to possess this valuable weapon called "The Mexican."

Both Roberts and Pitt are very funny as bickering lovers who separate when Pitt's character goes to Mexico for the legendary gun. It's supposed to be the last job he undertakes for his mob boss. Although Jerry (Pitt), a reluctant bagman, feared for his life if he refused this assignment, Samantha (Roberts) can't forgive him for leaving, especially after promising he would go to Las Vegas with her.

"I have no option," Jerry explains. "I, I, I," mocks Samantha, reminding him about their therapy sessions. "I wonder what the group would say about that," she shouts while throwing his belongings at him.

After Jerry leaves for Mexico, Samantha heads off to Las Vegas on her own. But she's not alone for long. To make sure Jerry will return the gun, his employer (Bob Balaban) hires a hit man to take Samantha as a hostage. Enter James Gandolfini from *The Sopranos*. Although the role of a hired gun may not be a stretch for this popular television star, he certainly livens things up as a tough guy with just as many relationship problems as Samantha.

When Sam and her protective kidnapper bond in discussions about failed romances, I was surprised and moved by the depth of their interactions. But come to think of it, why? Gandolfini has an Emmy Award, a Golden Globe Award, and a Screen Actors Guild Award for *The Sopranos*, and Roberts seldom disappoints in scenes like this. Listening intently, she raises her lovely eyebrows at just the right moment, then unleashes that million-dollar smile of hers, and all's right with the world. Granted, this performance doesn't rank up there with her Oscar-worthy work in *Erin Brockovich*, but it'll do for now.

Meanwhile, back in Mexico, if it weren't for bad luck, Jerry would have no luck at all. Although managing to locate the gun, he can't hold onto it. His car is stolen, a ragged old dog follows him everywhere, people make fun of his ridiculous attempts to speak Spanish, and he loses his passport. Pitt displays impressive comedic talent as this well-meaning dork, a character far removed from his aggressive *Fight Club* persona. I particularly enjoyed Jerry's love/hate relationship with the mysterious canine who seems to adopt him. Pitt also convinced me of Jerry's childlike nature, especially when he becomes so excited about driving a rented "El Camino."

I wish the rest of *The Mexican* deserved as much praise as its stars. Regrettably, a big name actor disturbs the movie's flow with his surprise cameo appearance. And sometimes the plot is too confusing. My husband and I are still arguing over who hired whom, what really happened when the gun was first crafted, where a flying wedding ring came from at the end of the film, and so on. This movie is over two hours long, so director Gore Verbinski (*Mouse Hunt*) and screenwriter J.H. Wyman (*Pale Saints*) had plenty of time to clarify such matters. Still, I applaud *The Mexican* for its excellent offbeat performances by Roberts, Pitt, Gandolfini, and the mangiest dog in films today.

(Released by DreamWorks and rated "R" for violence and language.)

SOMEONE LIKE YOU

Some people go to unreasonable lengths to rationalize their romantic failures. Isn't that why astrology and fortune-tellers are so popular? In *Someone Like You*, lovely Ashley Judd plays one of these misguided individuals. Frequently dumped, her character develops a ridiculous idea called "The New Cow Theory" as a way of explaining why men leave women. I know what you're thinking. Men dumping the charming Judd? That does take quite a suspension of disbelief, but the delightful actress makes this quirky role work for her.

Ably assisted by Hugh Jackman as her womanizing roommate and Greg Kinnear as her latest ex, Judd turns in her best performance since *Simon Birch*. Her portrayal of Jane Goodale, a talent booker for a popular television talk show, reveals the Double Jeopardy star's previously unknown flair for comedy. Judd is surprisingly funny, especially when dictating a bio for the nonexistent scientist/author Jane pretends to be. "Dr. Marie Charles (her pseudonym) is a co-founder of the Institute for Pathological Narcissism," our heroine begins—with an impish grin that tells us we're in for a fun ride.

Displaying the same powerful charisma that won him rave reviews as Wolverine in *X-Men*, Jackman simply ignites the screen in all his scenes. I predict great things for this handsome Australian actor. Playing Eddie, a man hurt once who tries to stop his emotional pain with casual sex (Jane refers to him as "The

Poster Bull"), Jackman projects macho magic tempered with a streak of sensitivity. Any woman who can resist him, particularly in a scene showing Eddie just holding Jane all night to comfort her, should resign from Romantics Anonymous. Waking first, he gently smells her hair, looks longingly at her for a brief moment, then pretends to be asleep—thus creating one of the year's most tender film moments.

Oscar-nominee Kinnear (for *As Good As It Gets*) completes the love triangle as Ray, an executive producer who breaks Jane's heart. While he's excellent in this type of role, Kinnear needs to branch out and do something more challenging for a change—something more like his egocentric superhero in *Mystery Men*. (He was the only one worth watching in that bomb.) Still, Kinnear's Ray emerges as a perfect contrast to Jackman's Eddie. Ray's problem with over-commitment and his inability to go the distance seem believable because of Kinnear's expert interpretation of this character. With his clean-cut good looks and intense facial expressions, Ray can't help attracting women, and Kinnear makes it easy to understand Ray's appeal to the opposite sex.

Among the supporting cast, Marisa Tomei (Oscar-winner for *My Cousin Vinny*) and Ellen Barkin (*Drop Dead Gorgeous*) do themselves proud as Jane's wisecracking best friend and ambitious boss respectively. Tomei delivers one of the movie's most biting lines when she consoles Jane by reminding her "Time wounds all heels." And Barkin exudes nervous energy in the role of a high-powered talk-show host.

Someone Like You benefits from a witty script by Elizabeth Chandler (*The Little Princess*) who adapted it from Laura Zigler's novel *Animal Husbandry*. Its only flaw is a rushed ending that requires the leading lady to renounce her theory without sufficient explanation. Deftly directed by Tony Goldwyn (*A Walk on the Moon*), this romantic comedy concludes with a message similar to the one in *When Harry Met Sally*, a 1989 classic that emphasized the importance of being good friends before becoming lovers. Twelve years later, that's still sound advice.

(Released by 20th Century Fox and rated "PG-13" for sexual content including dialogue and for some language.)

THE TAO OF STEVE

Over thirty years ago, Michael Caine achieved stardom playing the endearing and exasperating Alfie, a cockney ladykiller who finally realizes the emptiness of his life. In *The Tao of Steve*, Donal Logue takes on a similar role as Dex—an overweight, womanizing kindergarten teacher living in Santa Fe, New Mexico. Although a veteran of over forty films, Logue has appeared previously in a supporting capacity only (most notably in *Runaway Bride* as the priest who was one of Julia Roberts' spurned suitors). This is his first starring performance, and he makes the most of it. Like Caine before him, he brings a seriously misguided character to life with humor and heart.

By twisting the ideas of some great philosophers, Dex believes he has developed a foolproof theory of dating. Quoting Heidegger, he tells one of his followers, "We retreat from that which pursues us." According to guru Dex, that means never appear eager. From Lao-tzu, he incorporates the important principle of ridding oneself of desire. Like Alfie, Dex avoids emotional attachment to one woman. "Be desireless, be excellent, and be gone," he advises his disciples. Alfie says much the same thing when he remarks to the audience, "If you're not attached to anything, you can't lose it."

For Dex and his friends, becoming "Steve," as in Steve McQueen, is the ultimate goal. Dex puts it this way, "Steve isn't just a name. It's a way of living. James Bond is a Steve. Spider Man is a Steve." In this philosophy, the opposite of Steve is Barney Fife—a state of existence too horrible to contemplate.

During his college career, Dex was a big man on campus. Now, he's just big. But despite gaining more weight than wisdom, Dex still has no trouble dating plenty of women. His "Tao of Steve" seems to work well for him until he meets the lovely and talented Syd (Greer Goodman) at their ten-year college reunion. Puzzled at first because he doesn't remember her, Dex can't help falling under the spell of this charming woman who rides motorcycles and designs sets for the Santa Fe Opera. His volatile relationship with Syd soon exposes the shallowness of Stevedom.

Logue and newcomer Goodman project a quirky romantic chemistry as Dex and Syd. They are especially amusing when forced to share a tent during a miserable camping trip. "So help me, if you touch me, I have a knife," she threatens. He thinks she means it and looks much too frightened to be a "Steve." In another humorous scene, Goodman shows Syd's tender side while watching Dex play poker (using crayons instead of money) with his kindergarten students. From the expression on Syd's face, it's clear she's captivated by Dex's behavior with the kiddies. And we are, too. Like Alfie again, Dex is at his most humane around children. His appealing playfulness keeps them interested, but he also treats each child with respect and concern.

Both director Jenniphr Goodman and her sister Greer (Syd) make impressive feature film debuts with *The Tao of Steve*. In addition to their directing and acting chores, they served as co-writers with Duncan North, the real-life inspiration for Dex's character. (One wonders how much North himself has been influenced by *Alfie*.) Their collaboration paid off with a very different type of romantic comedy—one as enlightening about relationships between the sexes as it is entertaining.

The Tao of Steve ends on a much brighter note than *Alfie*. Although beginning to understand "what the heart hungers for is what makes something beautiful," Alfie remains a lonely man. Happily, things work out better for Dex and Syd. Together, they discover the truth behind an old Indian proverb that states, "Where love reigns, the impossible may be attained."

(Released by Sony Pictures Classics and rated "R" for language and some drug use.)

THE WEDDING PLANNER

"If there's anyone who knows any reason why this movie shouldn't be made, speak now or forever hold your peace." Too bad that issue wasn't raised before *The Wedding Planner* went into production. But, hey, I'm sure filmmakers thought everything would be okay. After all, they persuaded the sensational Jennifer Lopez, fresh from her success in *The Cell*, to accept a starring role. And romantic comedies about weddings usually do well at the box office. Remember *My Best Friend's Wedding* and *Runaway Bride*? Unfortunately, even though Lopez is almost as watchable as Julia Roberts, Matthew McConaughey can't match Hugh Grant or Richard Gere as a leading man. To make matters worse, on-screen chemistry between the film's two stars is sadly lacking.

Still, things get off to a very good start. Lopez exudes confidence as A-list San Francisco wedding planner Mary Fiore. Looking and acting oh-so sophisticated in her chic business suit, our heroine knows just what to do at a posh wedding when little details need attention—such as the FOB (father of the bride) starting to fall apart or the bride having second thoughts. Finding the bride's father crying on a staircase, Mary uses the "first aid" arsenal she hides around her waist to spruce him up, then scoots him on his way. Consoling the unsure bride, Mary says, "You are exquisite. You are timeless. No wonder the groom told me 'I can't believe she picked me.' Your marriage will last forever."

And so this wedding, like the others she has coordinated, turns out to be a big success. While watching Mary supervise the ceremony from a balcony, one young girl whispers to her friend, "There's the wedding planner. She must lead a very romantic life."

Nothing could be farther from the truth. Mary invests all her energy in her career, hoping to become a full partner in the business she loves. Then, by accident, she meets the man of her dreams, pediatrician Steve Edison (McConaughey), and falls hard for him. "You smell like sweet plums and grilled cheese sandwiches," she moans as he rescues her after a dislodged dumpster almost runs her down on a busy San Francisco street. But there's a big disappointment in store for Mary. Why? Because Steve turns out to be the groom of her next wedding assignment.

From here on out, *The Wedding Planner* goes downhill faster than that runaway dumpster. Although Lopez maintains her charisma throughout the film, McConaughey seems as out of place as Will Rogers playing Rhett Butler. He's painfully awkward in two dance sequences with Lopez, even though his character claims he's had many ballroom dancing lessons. He forces his smiles, looks goofy when trying to appear romantic, and projects insincerity in a serious confrontation scene with the woman he's supposed to marry (Bridgett Wilson-Sampras). McConaughey should stick to action films like *U-571* and leave the romantic comedy roles to others. (I can't help thinking how much better this movie would be with someone like David Duchovny as Lopez's co-star.)

Other casting errors produce similar problems here. Justin Chambers (*Liberty Heights*) shamelessly chews the scenery as a persistent suitor from Sicily—a part that should have been given to an older actor. Judy Greer (*What Planet Are You From?*) hams it up as a scatter-brained wedding planner assistant—a role requiring someone with impeccable comic timing (Joan Cusack perhaps?) to make it work. Trying his best to come across as an overprotective father, veteran actor Alex Rocco doesn't pull it off for me. I couldn't forget he's the guy who was executed by getting shot in the eye in *The Godfather*.

One of today's top movie choreographers, Adam Shankman, makes his feature-length directorial debut with *The Wedding Planner*. His dance numbers added sparkle to such films as *She's All That* and *Blast from the Past*. It's a mystery to me why he goofed up with two big dance scenes in his own film—other than because of McConaughey's clumsiness, of course. One routine, a forced tango, features Lopez and McConaughey conducting a ridiculous argument during the entire number. The only saving grace is Lopez in her sexy red dress. In the other case, Shankman shows couples dancing in the park in front of a movie musical. But he chose the forgettable *Two Tickets to Broadway* for the background film. As I watched Lopez and McConaughey waltz to the singing of Janet Leigh and Tony Martin, oh, how I longed for a glimpse of truly great musical stars like Gene Kelly and Judy Garland!

(Released by Columbia Pictures and rated "PG-13" for language and some sexual humor.)

WHAT WOMEN WANT

It just might take a miracle to turn a "man's man" into a "woman's man." Still, in *What Women Want*, Mel Gibson works a miracle of his own by changing from action hero to romantic comedy lead without skipping a beat. Playing a chauvinistic advertising executive who becomes more sensitive to women, Gibson delivers an engaging performance filled with energy and enthusiasm. Sure, he may look goofy sometimes, especially struggling into a pair of panty hose and putting on make-up, but that just adds to his charm. And leading lady Helen Hunt matches Gibson with a brilliant turn as his beautiful, intelligent boss.

Nick Marshall (Gibson) thinks he's God's gift to women. His mother, a Las Vegas showgirl, raised him around a bevy of glamour girls, so he feels comfortable with gorgeous women. His two assistants (Delta Burke and Valerie Perrine) cater to his every whim. His ex-wife (Lauren Holly) even invites him to her wedding. Enjoying the bachelor life, Nick reluctantly agrees to take care of his teenage daughter (Ashley Johnson) until her mother returns from her honeymoon. Uneasy in the parental role (his daughter calls him "Uncle Dad"), Nick begins one of the relationships that will alter his life by making him more understanding of the opposite sex.

His other key relationship involves Darcy McGuire (Hunt), a talented woman hired for the job Nick thought he would get. Although stunned by her beauty and competence, he tries to sabotage her by stealing her ideas. This suddenly becomes easy for him because, as the result of a freak accident, he actually hears women's inner thoughts. Of course, falling in love with Darcy was not in his plan, but she's so great he just can't resist. How many men could? Playing a role completely opposite to the alcoholic single mother in *Pay It Forward*, the amazing Hunt (Oscar winner for *As Good As It Gets*) endows her character with elegance, sensitivity, and strength. Hunt's Darcy emerges as a wonderful role model for today's women.

Nick's gift also allows him to discover what women really think about him—that he's a jerk. His off-color jokes and patronizing manner irritate most of his female co-workers. Fortunately, he finds out what women want is to be listened to and taken seriously. (I think that goes for men too!) Naturally, this insight boosts his career, but at Darcy's expense.

Director Nancy Meyers certainly knows her stuff where romantic comedies are concerned. She also directed the amusing update of *Disney's The Parent Trap* and co-wrote *Private Benjamin, Father of the Bride,* and *Baby Boom.* Hunt compliments Meyers by saying, "The great thing about Nancy is that she's absolutely in love with the Tracy/Hepburn movies, so there's a classic feel to our movie. That means it's smart and well thought out. And the relationships between every character in the movie are funny and real, too."

In addition to Gibson and Hunt, cast members Alan Alda (*M.A.S.H.*) and Marisa Tomei (*My Cousin Vinny*) excel in their roles. Alda, who has aged quite gracefully, is convincing as an impulsive ad agency head, and Tomei exhibits her unique comic flair as a sexy, but uncertain, coffee shop waitress.

A witty screenplay by Josh Goldsmith and Cathy Yuspa, who write for television's popular *King of Queens,* also contributes to the success of this entertaining movie. For example, when Gibson's character complains to his psychiatrist about hearing women's innermost thoughts, she (a subdued Bette Midler) tells him, "If men are from Mars and women are from Venus, he who speaks Venutian can rule the world!"

Deftly combining comedy and romance, *What Woman Wants* emphasizes the importance of communication between the sexes. It's refreshing to see Gibson in this type of movie. Not only does he appear to be having a great time, he also displays a surprising talent for dancing. One delightful scene features the Oscar-winning director (for *Braveheart*) in a solo number reminiscent of Gene Kelly or Fred Astaire. Here is a new Mel Gibson, and I like it!

(Released by Paramount Pictures and rated "PG-13" for sexual content and language.)

THRILLER:

ALONG CAME A SPIDER

Is it too much to ask for reasonable explanations of human behavior in a psychological thriller? After watching *Along Came a Spider* from beginning to end, I'm still not sure how the villain became obsessed with police psychologist Alex Cross or why he lured the noted doctor into his web. Morgan Freeman, with his soft velvet voice and penetrating dark eyes, delivers another spellbinding performance as Cross, but that's not enough to make up for such appalling lack of attention to motivation.

Even Freeman, who played the same detective in *Kiss the Girls*, has trouble with some of the film's unbelievable dialogue. When Gary Soneji (Michael Wincott), a psychotic kidnapper, asks for a diagnosis of his condition, Cross replies, "You're suffering from an overwhelming desire to burn in Hell."

Puhleez! Shouldn't that answer display a more scientific flair—especially from a distinguished psychologist? Judging by the unhappy look on Freeman's face, he wondered the same thing. To be fair, Cross is in mourning over the death of a partner killed while trying to help him catch a serial killer. Blaming himself, he's not quite ready for another case when the sinister Soneji contacts him about a high profile kidnapping.

Unable to resist this challenge, Cross bonds quickly with Secret Service agent Jezzie Flannigan (Monica Potter), who seems to be hurting, too. She tells him about her guilty feelings over not being able to prevent Soneji's abduction of Megan Rose (Mika Boorem), a U. S. congressman's (Michael Moriarity) daughter. Recognizing the potential for another "crime of the century" like the Lindbergh baby case, Cross and Flannigan join forces to find Megan, capture Soneji, and prevent further child kidnappings. Unfortunately, adding to the film's unreality factor, Potter (*Head Over Heels*) appears more like an FBI Barbie doll than a bona fide government agent in this key role. (Where are you, Helen Hunt, when we need you?)

About halfway through the film, the already confusing plot changes course to focus on others involved in the crime. Emphasizing surprise and a murky relationship, it neglects to offer satisfactory reasons for either. By this time, I felt like I was having an existential dream instead of viewing a movie. No such luck. The film's overpowering music kept stopping me from taking a much-needed catnap.

But seriously, folks, it's not likely I would sleep through any scenes featuring the wonderful Freeman. A thinking actor, he endows his characters with a quiet dignity (yes, his hit man in *Nurse Betty* had that same quality), and I always want to know more about them. Freeman projects both outer calmness and inner turmoil as Cross, the reluctant mind hunter. He made me wish this film was worthy of him.

Director Lee Tamahori does manage to achieve two highly suspenseful sequences in *Along Came a Spider*, but neither matches the quality of his work in *The Edge*, the most frightening movie of 1997. Spider's exciting opening scene shows a car teetering on a bridge. Before it plunges into the rapids below, Cross reaches out to save his partner, who is trapped in the doomed vehicle. Both detectives express panic without saying a word. In one fatal moment, their terrified eyes tell it all. In the second instance, Boorem (the young actress playing Megan) projects intense fear as she tries to escape from a killer in an old barn. A child in jeopardy always gets to me, but Boorem, with her tiny huddled body and nervous facial expressions, does some exceptional acting here. I could hardly breathe until she was safe.

Along Came a Spider, based on James Patterson's best seller, proves how important it is to highlight motivation in films about deviant behavior. Using religious admonitions in place of psychological theories just doesn't work. Even the great Dr. Alex Cross can't get away with it.

(Released by Paramount Pictures and rated "R" for language and violence.)

ANTITRUST

A young computer genius brings down a multi-billion dollar modern corporation in the cyber-thriller *Antitrust*. But that's not what Milo Hoffmann intends when signing on as a computer programmer for NURV (Never Underestimate Radical Vision). In fact, he's quite pleased at being recruited by Gary Winston, his professional hero. He thinks it's a privilege to work with the brilliant, charismatic businessman. However, Milo soon discovers evil secrets behind Winston's plans for launching the world's first satellite-delivered global communications system—and he is the only one who can stop his former idol. Despite the film's sometimes confusing techno-babble and its overemphasis on computer graphics, co-stars Ryan Phillippe and Tim Robbins play off each other as Milo and Winston with just the right amount of tension and admiration. They helped make this suspenseful movie work for me.

Phillippe (*The Way of the Gun*) displays a winning combination of vulnerability and strength as a modern-day David fighting against the forces of greed in today's high-stakes computer industry. He looks truly amazed when introduced to the Egg, his new place of work. And why not? It's designed with the joys of geek life in mind. There's a sense of fun and visual stimulation that was missing from his lowly garage workspace. Phillippe also projects genuine enjoyment in scenes showing Winston giving Milo extra attention while working at his computer. The up-and-coming actor is equally adept at expressing fear when his situation becomes a nightmare.

In the role of Winston, Robbins (*Arlington Road*) has a rollicking good time. His eyes light up during motivational speeches to employees; his voice rises with excitement while commanding everyone to "Be creative; be luminescent!" But when things don't go Winston's way, Robbins seems to relish turning him into a frightening egomaniac who inspires terror instead of trust.

Playing the women in Milo's life, Claire Forlani (*Boys and Girls*) and Rachael Leigh Cook (*She's All That*) bring intelligence as well as physical appeal to their performances. Forlani portrays Milo's artist girlfriend, and Cook is a gifted colleague at NURV. One of them helps Milo and the other betrays him, but don't expect me to mention which is which and spoil it for you.

I will reveal, however, that the production design in *Antitrust* ranks among the best I've seen recently. Winston's fabulous mansion is especially impressive. Who could guess its vast exterior design was done entirely with computer-generated graphics? And I can't wait to own a huge flat screen (like the one inside Winston's den) that senses who happens to be walking by and immediately displays art by their favorite artists! The selection of the stunning Chan Center, a building used for performing arts at the University of British Columbia campus, as NURV's main office location was an excellent decision. Sleek and oval-shaped, it provides an appropriate futuristic setting for the film's timely story.

Although aimed at entertaining audiences rather than educating them, *Antitrust* explores two reality-based issues by focusing on private control of information versus open access and the limits of individual power (shades of Microsoft and Bill Gates!). Even "digital convergence," the incredible technology sought after by Winston, is not as far-fetched as one might think. Many diverse communications systems—computer, cable, telephone, etc.—are linked already.

In my opinion, director Peter Howitt and screenwriter Howard Franklin make a great team. Howitt already demonstrated his flair for combining the real and unreal in *Sliding Doors*, while Franklin showed a talent for building suspense in *Someone To Watch Over Me* and *The Name of the Rose*. Working together on *Antitrust*, they have created a gripping movie with considerable relevance in today's high-tech world.

(Released by Metro-Goldwyn-Mayer and rated "PG-13" for violence and profanity.)

THE GLASS HOUSE

Nothing is as it seems in *The Glass House*, a classy suspense thriller starring Leelee Sobieski. Playing a rebellious teenager who, after losing her parents in a car accident, must live with a suspicious married couple in their coldly elegant mansion, Sobieski outshines such veteran performers as Diane Lane, Stellan Skarsgard, and Bruce Dern. I'm amazed at the depth of this statuesque teen's performance as a sister trying to save herself and her ten-year-old brother from people she believes will harm them both.

Sobieski (*Here on Earth*) reminds me of a young Ingrid Bergman here. Like the late Swedish actress, her clean-cut beauty projects more soul than sex. And her voice has the same haunting resonance. While watching Sobieski in *The Glass House*, I couldn't help thinking about Bergman in *Gaslight*—despite the difference in time and setting. In this later film, Sobieski's character begins to have doubts about her perceptions of reality, just as Bergman's troubled bride questions her own sanity. And both actresses carry me right along with them through the shadowy maze of their fear.

The Glass House may not be about ghosts or the supernatural, but it's much more frightening. Evil comes in the form of ordinary people with greedy agendas. Skarsgard (*Good Will Hunting*) and Lane (*Hardball*) portray the Glasses, best friends of Sobieski's ill-fated parents. They are named as the children's guardians in the will. Consequently, the Glasses have access to a large trust fund left for the siblings, according to the parents' lawyer, played enigmatically by Dern (*All the Pretty Horses*). Lane and Skarsgard did a super job of keeping me guessing about their true motivations during the first part of the film. They seemed so caring and concerned, especially Skarsgard, who delivered such a touching funeral speech. Besides, how could anyone living in such a luxurious house and working so hard at respectable careers (she's a doctor; he's a business executive) want to hurt their departed friends' children?

Still, I found something odd about that house even before things started falling apart inside its massive interior. No, it's not one of those spooky haunted castles. Nothing like that. In fact, a few eerie spirits floating around might have made it less scary. Constructed of concrete, glass, and steel, the huge residence is perched on a promontory and surrounded by mountains, with a view of the Pacific Ocean. Director Daniel Sackheim, making his feature film debut with *The Glass House*, describes the place as a sort of beautiful, pristine prison. "I think one of the things I was trying to create in this house was this notion of being able to see through everything, and yet not see anything at the same time," he explains.

To me, this strange house is as much a character in the movie as the humans. And, although magnificent to view, it's definitely not child-friendly—which might explain why the Glasses set aside only one bedroom for the sister and brother (Trevor Howard from *Jurassic Park III*) to share. "It's only temporary," the kids are told.

After recently sitting through *Jeepers Creepers*, a film with countless scenes of annoying bickering between a sister and brother, I was pleased to see this type of relationship downplayed in *The Glass House*. Sure, Sobieski's character complains to her brother, "You've been bought off," and shows anger at his acceptance of the Glasses because of all the electronic toys he's been given, but there's none of the obnoxious give-and-take that ruined *Jeepers Creepers* for me. (I almost took the monster's side in that one!)

Combining a coming-of-age story with an updated Gothic theme, *The Glass House* emphasizes how important it is to trust yourself and take responsibility for your own safety. Although a little too heavy on revenge, it shows the strength and courage of one young woman when faced with a deadly crisis. As a fan of good suspense thrillers, I enjoyed it from beginning to end.

(Released by Columbia Pictures and rated "PG-13" for sinister thematic elements, violence, drug content, and language.)

THE IN CROWD

Groucho Marx once declared, "I refuse to join any club that would have me as a member." In *The In Crowd*, Adrien Williams (Lori Heuring) would be better off adopting that philosophy. She's a former psychiatric patient whose doctor (Daniel Hugh Kelly) finds her a job at a posh country club. While working there, she meets a group of beautiful, rich young people who notice her right away—mostly because of her resemblance to the sister of their leader Brittany Foster (Susan Ward). Brittany goes out of her way to befriend Adrien. She gives her a sexy dress and invites her to various activities. Finding it hard to resist all this attention, Adrien gives in. But Brittany, who is not what she seems, soon involves her in murder, mayhem, and madness.

Unfortunately, I didn't care much about Adrien's plight. Why not? Because she mistreats one of her fellow inmates in the film's early scenes, violates her hospital probation by drinking and partying, and is stupid enough to meet with a killer on a dark night at a deserted golf course. In addition, bad acting by Heuring (*The*

Newton Boys) put me off. She seems to rely on just two emotional expressions—surly and surlier.

Lack of a sympathetic main character is only one of the film's many faults. Silly dialogue like "I'm so thirsty I could drink a glass of water" caused me to cringe at its banality. However, one particular line actually made some sense. When alcoholic Bobby (Nathan Bexton) greets Adrien with "Welcome to the world of the rich and tasteless," I couldn't help thinking he was referring to the movie itself. Tastelessness is the order of the day for members of the in crowd. They talk about sexual exploits around a beach campfire, make fun of staff workers who wait on them, and do nothing when one of their group wagers sex with his girlfriend in a game of pool, and then loses.

Casting look-alike actors adds to the annoyance factor of this dreadful film. During some scenes, it's hard to tell if Adrian and Brittany are interacting with Matt (Matthew Settle), the tennis pro who causes their rivalry, or with Tom (Ethan Erickson), another one of Brittany's minions. The movie's many darkly-photographed sequences contribute to this confusion. It's film noir carried to the extreme.

And where is that villain we love to hate—a role so important to the success of most suspense thrillers? As the sinister Brittany, Ward (from television's *Sunset Beach*) projects none of the evil necessary to make this character believable. With her baby-doll voice, big smile, gorgeous figure, and constant use of lip gloss, she's more like Barbie come to life than a menacing murderer. Even her seduction scene with lesbian Kelly (Laurie Fortier), Brittany's former best friend who is jealous of Adrien, generates chuckles, not shocks.

Director Mary Lambert (*Pet Sematary*) wanted *The In Crowd* to be "a psychological thriller filled with great looking people." Concentrating on the looks department (babes and studs galore cavorting in skimpy bathing suits), she came up short as far as thrills are concerned. And more bad luck! *The In Crowd* opened the same week as *What Lies Beneath*, an infinitely superior suspense film.

(A Morgan Creek Production released by Warner Bros. and rated "PG-13" for sexuality, violence, partial nudity, and some strong language.)

ORIGINAL SIN

Overblown and implausible it may be, but *Original Sin* wins my vote as one of the year's most watchable movies. Filled with romance, suspense, mystery, and colorful locations, this thriller intrigued me from beginning to end. Most of the credit for my interest goes to Antonio Banderas and Angelina Jolie. They sizzle on screen as a man obsessed and the femme fatale he desires.

It's only fair to admit these two stars are among my favorite contemporary actors, so I'm not entirely objective. I also enjoy thrillers immensely—to the point of watching Hitchcock's *Vertigo* every chance I get. Hey, I even liked *What Lies Beneath.* So the *Original Sin* co-star/genre trifecta worked for me, whereas most other critics are giving the film negative reviews. Still, I have to agree with criticisms about those nude sex scenes. (Have spouses Melanie and Billy Bob seen what Antonio and Angelina were up to?) Leaving a little to the imagination always makes things more interesting to me. Beautiful as they are, I would rather see Banderas (*Spy Kids*) and Jolie (*Tomb Raider*) bare more of their souls than their bodies in a movie like this.

But, ah, their performances in other scenes! That's what blew me away. Playing a wealthy Cuban businessman in the 1900s, Banderas exudes class and breeding in the early part of the film. He comes across as a man very much in control of his life, a man who thinks love is not for him. "Love should be left to those who believe in it," he tells a friend before going to meet his future bride, a woman he knows only by her letters and photograph. As a result of deception and betrayal by this mysterious woman he marries, Banderas' character is a different man entirely by the end of the film. (Because of the way our hero believes whatever his wife says, my husband thinks the title should be changed to *Gullible's Travels.*) This role requires tremendous changes in temperament and physical appearance—all accomplished quite convincingly by the versatile actor. His eyes are especially expressive here—moving from surprise and tenderness to a murderous intensity.

As the woman who seduces and deceives Banderas, Jolie seems perfectly cast. She manages to make her character appear sensual and dangerous, even while pretending to be sweet and proper. What is her true identity? Is she a murderer? Does she love the man she married, or is she in love with someone else? Jolie's suspicious glances and enigmatic comments (like "You can't walk away from love") caused me to be very curious about the person she played. Granted, filmmakers did go a bit overboard by showing huge, unflattering close-ups of her famous lips, but that's not Jolie's fault.

Competing for acting kudos in *Original Sin*, Thomas Jane (*Under Suspicion*) plays a detective who also kept me guessing about his true identity. I can't decide who he reminded me of the most—William Holden or Richard Widmark, but he has such a chameleon-like quality that's not surprising. I'd like to see him in an update of *Sunset Boulevard*.

Standing in for Cuba, Mexico provided elegant location shots for *Original Sin*. Cinematographer Rodriego Prieto (*Amores Perros*) captured the sultriness of the landscape and included some haunting visuals I won't soon forget. Two examples: a colorful Caribbean carnival spills from the street into a hotel lobby and onto my list of celebrations I'd like to attend, and a beautiful white horse thunders across the lush countryside, imprinting the image of steed and rider in my memory.

Writer/director Michael Cristofer (*Gia*), who adapted *Original Sin* from Cornell Woolrich's novel *Waltz into Darkness*, must know something about comic relief. Although primarily a thriller, this movie includes humor at the most unpredictable moments, and some of it is intentional. I was particularly amused by scenes involving a rejected suitor and a young priest's confrontation with temptation. Nevertheless, the messages in *Original Sin* are deadly serious. Nobody is all good or all bad; each of us has a dark side; and behind every femme fatale is a gullible man.

(Released by MGM and rated "R" for strong sexual content and some violence.)

THE OTHERS

After her stunning musical performance in *Moulin Rouge*, Nicole Kidman returns to the big screen playing the worried mother of two light-sensitive children in *The Others*. Unlike most films about the supernatural, this psychological thriller creates suspense through character development and atmosphere, not by relying on creepy special effects. I, for one, appreciated the movie's unusual plot, fine acting, and eerie moodiness. With its spooky house, strange noises, and foggy scenes, *The Others* reminded me of *The Uninvited*, one of my favorite films of the Forties, starring Ray Milland and Gail Russell.

However, I believe *The Others* may be even more frightening. Whenever children are in danger, my heart goes out to them right away. In this movie, Kidman's son (James Bentley) and daughter (Alakina Mann) have to be sheltered from light by drawing the curtains in the daytime. They also must be locked in rooms to keep them from being exposed if someone comes in accidentally—or if they decide to go out on their own.

These two youngsters are pathetic little creatures who depend on their mother for everything, including academic and religious lessons. Setting weird things in motion, the daughter scares her little brother by telling him she sees another boy as well as other people in the house. Viewing this as an act of rebellion, Kidman seems to come unglued. She also starts hearing unexplained noises. At that point, I'm beginning to be afraid, too. Very afraid. Kidman's convincing looks of terror are contagious, especially when she's uncovering a roomful of white-sheeted objects in a frantic attempt to expose those pesky intruders.

Convinced she can't handle the huge house and her children alone, the mother hires three servants to replace the ones that disappeared mysteriously. Fionnula Flanagan (*Waking Ned Devine*), leader of the trio, calms everyone down at first, then gets too uppity for Kidman. I found the enigmatic housekeeper played by Flanagan to be the most intriguing character in the movie. This talented Irish actress held me spellbound during all her scenes. She appeared so comforting at times—but changed her expression to a suspicious frown when no one was looking. I couldn't help fearing what she was up to. (I also predict a Best Supporting Actress Oscar nomination for Flannagan.)

Writer/director Alejandro Amenabar (*Open Your Eyes*) successfully exploits all kinds of fear in this chilling film. "My childhood was beset by fears—fear of the dark, fear of half-open doors, fear of closets, and generally speaking, fear of anything that could conceal someone or something," he recalls. With *The Others*, Amenabar hoped to make a film "full of long, dark corridors, a tribute to those beings, never unmasked, that stalked the hallways of my boyhood nightmares."

When a movie is this good, I feel sad it's not perfect. *The Others* needed more clarification of the shell-shocked husband's war-weary condition. During a visit home from WWII action, Christopher Eccleston (*Gone in 60 Seconds*) displayed a befuddlement that matched my own. And Kidman's frequent whispering annoyed me. I couldn't understand what she was saying in too many scenes. Also, the reality-bending ending seemed rather abrupt. But it certainly surprised me and left me as frightened as ever. (Now don't ask. You know I can't even give out a hint.)

Upon arriving home from the movie, I immediately checked under the bed and in all the closets. Whew! No sign of the Others in our house yet—or so they would like me to believe.

(Released by Dimension Films and rated "PG-13" for thematic elements and frightening moments.)

UNBREAKABLE

When a movie generates as much discussion as *Unbreakable*, it's obvious viewers have seen something special on the big screen. Starring Bruce Willis and Samuel L. Jackson, this suspense thriller offers much food for thought. Although Willis underplays his role as an unhappy security guard, and Jackson comes on a bit too strong as an obsessed gallery owner, these two fine actors are just as compelling to watch together as they were in *Die Hard with a Vengeance*.

Giving away too much about the plot could spoil this unusual film for anyone who hasn't seen it, so I'll focus on other aspects of *Unbreakable*. As everyone knows by now, this is filmmaker M.

Night Shyamalan's first movie since *The Sixth Sense*, one of the most successful films of 1999. However, while offering the same somber tone and emphasis on hard-to-explain events, *Unbreakable* deals with more complicated ideas and issues, particularly the concept of human potential.

Shyamalan began asking himself questions about his own destiny at age seventeen. He came from a family of twelve doctors, including his mother and father, and received scholarships to several medical schools. But his passion for filmmaking caused him to wonder "What am I supposed to be doing with my life?" Shyamalan claims the theme for *Unbreakable*, which he wrote as well as directed, stems from this personal dilemma.

In an impressive and original bit of storytelling, Shyamalan has created two characters who illustrate the importance of finding out "what you are supposed to do." David Dunn (Willis) emerges from a train accident that kills all the other passengers, but there's not a scratch on him. In fact, Dunn can't remember ever having a day of illness or injury. Elijah Price (Jackson) was born with osteogensis imperfecta, a condition describing bones so brittle they break under very little pressure. Although opposites, these men need each other. The most intriguing part of the film involves surprising twists and turns in their relationship, leading to an amazing conclusion.

Philadelphia, complete with its rich historical architecture and beautiful suburban landscapes, provides a perfect backdrop for *Unbreakable*. Cinematographer Eduardo Serra (*Wings of the Dove*) uses dark silhouette images of the city to emphasize the kind of real and surreal atmosphere needed for this story, and his filming of an accident on a public stairway made me cringe and groan as if it were actually happening to me.

Supporting cast members Robin Wright Penn (*Message in a Bottle*), and Spencer Treat Clark (*Arlington Road*) make the roles of Dunn's estranged wife and adoring son come to life, despite one ridiculous family incident involving the boy and a gun. Charlayne Woodard (*The Crucible*) appears convincing as Elijah's mother, a woman who believes in her son and helps him overcome his handicap. Her method? I can only reveal it involves comic books about super heroes. (Hope I haven't said too much here!)

According to the Hollywood rumor mill, *Unbreakable* is Shyamalan's first movie in a planned trilogy involving the same incredible characters. If true, this is good news indeed.

(Released by Touchstone Pictures and rated "PG-13" for mature themes, some disturbing violent content, and a sexual reference.)

THE WATCHER

Because of its jerky camera movements and high-speed photography, I found *The Watcher* impossible to sit through without closing my eyes a good part of the time. The bloody nature of this psychological thriller didn't bother me as much as its MTV video format, which is fine for television but annoying on the big screen. The movie stars James Spader as an FBI agent in hiding and Keanu Reeves as a serial killer on the loose in Chicago. Although both actors give satisfactory performances, they carry the burden of a lackluster script and confusing flashbacks. Also, it's difficult to understand why filmmakers didn't switch Spader and Reeves during the casting process, thereby allowing each actor to play a role better suited to him.

When we first meet Joel Campbell (Spader), he looks so pathetic it's easy to feel sorry for him. His apartment is a mess. The only food in his refrigerator is an orange, and he seems to be living on pain pills. He keeps having flashbacks about a beautiful woman burning to death. (If you miss the first one, don't worry. That same ghastly memory is shown over and over again ad nauseam.) Spader (*2 Days in the Valley*) may be more convincing in smarmier roles, but he gained my sympathy immediately as an investigator traumatized by his failure to catch a psychotic killer in Los Angeles. With his disturbed facial expression and squinting eyes, he projects the excruciating pain of migraine headaches quite realistically. As a fellow sufferer, I can vouch for that.

Campbell, guilt-ridden over his lack of success, has moved to Chicago to find a less stressful life. Unfortunately, the elusive killer follows him. David Allen Griffin (Reeves) starts sending

Campbell photos of women he plans to kill, giving him a certain amount of time to find the victims in order to save them.

Surprisingly, Reeves (*The Replacements*) plays against type effectively during most of his scenes, exuding a seductive evil in this villainous role. Even his usually soothing voice takes on a devilish tone as he smiles while assuring one of his prey, "This will be fun!" But what was the talented actor thinking by appearing in combination dance/martial arts shots throughout the film? They make no sense to anyone—except maybe first-time director Joe Charbanic (who also helms videos for Reeves' Dogstar band).

Actually, not much else makes sense here either. The story lacks any background of motivation for its main characters. Sure, Campbell likes to capture killers and Griffin enjoys killing. But what draws them together in such a symbiotic relationship? Why does Griffin use a piano wire to strangle women? Why does he abduct his own psychiatrist (Marisa Tomei) and tie her up in a warehouse full of lighted candles—other than because this makes another good music video scene?

This disappointing film is the least compelling of the recent movies about serial killers. *The Cell* and *American Psycho* feature greater suspense and better production values. Despite their graphic violence, both films are more watchable than *The Watcher.*

(Released by Universal Pictures and rated "R" for violence and language.)

WHAT LIES BENEATH

With no ghostbusters to call, Claire Spencer (Michelle Pfeiffer) must solve a poltergeist case on her own in *What Lies Beneath*. When doors keep opening mysteriously and pictures start falling from shelves with no apparent rhyme or reason, she begins to suspect her house is haunted. Hubbie Norman (Harrison Ford), a professor and research scientist, is frequently away from home, and her daughter from a former marriage (Katherine Towne) just went off to college. That leaves Claire alone most of the time in a remodeled old house located beside a foreboding Vermont lake—the perfect setting for this exquisite suspense thriller.

Still recovering psychologically from a year-old car accident, Claire also worries about a missing neighbor. She thinks the woman's husband murdered her. When these suspicions prove groundless, Claire's credibility plummets, especially in the eyes of her own spouse. Like the little boy who cried wolf too many times, she finds it impossible to persuade anyone there is a ghost slowly taking charge of her life. Who and why are the two questions Claire tries to answer at the beginning of her investigation. Later, she must also determine how her husband might be involved in the disappearance of a beautiful young woman.

Telling any more about the plot of this riveting film could spoil it for you. Sooooo—just believe me when I say Pfeiffer (*The Story of Us*) has never been better. I forgot completely about her Hollywood stardom. She actually became Claire to me and drew me helplessly into her frightening world. When she peered over the neighbor's fence to find out what was happening, her curiosity seemed so palpable it became urgent for me to know too. As she crept barefoot down hallways looking for the source of weird sights and sounds, I skulked along with her. During her terrifying bathtub ordeal, I could almost feel Claire's paralyzing fear of drowning. Pfeiffer's expressive eyes in that well-filmed scene pierced right through the celluloid and into my soul.

Playing an ambitious, patronizing husband, Ford takes on a role quite different from his Indiana Jones, Han Solo, and Jack Ryan portrayals. At his most convincing during the beginning of the film, he makes a terrific romantic partner for Pfeiffer. "You are so brilliant!" she teases him while making love. "Yep," he agrees facetiously, then adds, "Say that again—and speak up." Because of Ford's charisma and mature good looks, it's easy to see why Claire fell in love with such a charming man. Still, this is Pfeiffer's movie. Her performance outshines everyone else's, even the ghost's (Amber Valletta).

In classic suspense movies like *Vertigo* and *Psycho*, the legendary Alfred Hitchcock concentrated on psychological rather than supernatural dynamics. And yet, I can't help thinking he would appreciate Robert Zemeckis' (*Forrest Gump*) inspired direction of *What Lies Beneath*. I imagine him applauding the way Zemeckis combined long camera shots and realistic special effects in filming Clark Gregg's intriguing screenplay. Would he complain about the use of heavy-handed background music to boost key scenes? Probably not. After all, it only makes things more intense.

WARNING: Remember how some people gave up showering after watching *Psycho*? *What Lies Beneath* might cause others to feel the same way about taking baths. That's too bad, for those sponge-offs can be pretty scary themselves—especially on these cold winter mornings.

(Released by DreamWorks and rated "PG-13" for violence, terror, sensuality, and brief language.)

CREDITS

As the leading man in this autobiography, my husband, Larry Tucker, deserves kudos for putting up with me in spite of my addiction and for making me laugh every day. Co-stars Kelly Tucker and Sue Litton, our son and daughter, also get rave reviews. They never let me down. And I'm proud to say both of them have great taste in movies. In a major supporting role, my sister, Ruella Anderson, has always been there when I needed her.

By listening patiently to my opinions about film, many other family members, colleagues, and friends have earned my applause and appreciation.

For encouraging me to write *Confessions of a Movie Addict*, Diana Saenger and Sandy Scoville share the coveted Best Motivator Award. Honorable mention goes to Liz Larrabee and Leslie Tucker for their valuable suggestions after reading my first draft. Summer Mullins wins the important Excellence in Editing Citation.

Finally, thumbs up to Thomas Edison and the Lumiere brothers. Without their inventive genius, I would probably be obsessed now with shadow puppets and old vaudeville routines. Viva la cinéma!

Betty Jo Tucker

INDICES

INTERVIEWS:

MOVIE REVIEWS:

PHOTOGRAPHS: